Fathers,
Sons
& Baseball

Fathers, Sons & Baseball

Our National Pastime and the Ties That Bond

WAYNE STEWART

THE LYONS PRESS
Guilford, Connecticut
An imprint of The Globe Pequot Press

The Lyons Press is an imprint of The Globe Pequot Press.

10 9 8 7 6 5 4 3 2 1

ISBN 1-58574-504-9

The Library of Congress Cataloging-in-Publication Data is available on file.

Dedication

Who else? Whom could I possibly dedicate this book to other than my father, Owen (O.J.) Stewart, and my two sons (pretty good ballplayers themselves), Sean and Scott. They just happen to be my two favorite infielders of all time.

Contents

Acknowledgments

So many of the players I interviewed for this book went way beyond what was necessary. Fathers of players were very accommodating as well. For example, Dr. Olerud, father of John, gave an hour-and-a-half interview despite being the head of the department of dermatology at the University of Washington. Likewise, although I asked Ed Spiezio, father of Scott, for about twenty minutes of his time, we spoke for nearly two and a half hours over several sessions. Tom Grieve also spoke with me for more than an hour, even though I would have been content with less. Jaret Wright's mother, Vicki, made it a point to help set up an interview with her husband. All these people were so kind, it made this project a great deal easier and more enjoyable for me.

Plus, a very special thanks to my editor, Mark Weinstein. Originally, I planned to do a book on Kenny Griffey—that's what we all called him when I went to high school with him—and his son. Mark pointed out that the Griffey market had been tapped out, but what about a book on baseball and how it helps fathers and sons bond? Great idea. He pushed for the idea to become a book, and it worked.

Then there were the public-relations workers who also went out of their way to set up interviews. A few of those men who stood out include Jason Perry of the Milwaukee Brewers, Larry Babcock of the Anaheim Angels, Jim Young with the Oakland A's, and, from the Cleveland Indians, the always-helpful Susie Giuliano and Bart Swain.

Last but not least, I'd like to acknowledge the reporters and editors at publications like *USA Today/Baseball Weekly, Sporting News, Baseball America, Sports Illustrated,* and the Cleveland *Plain Dealer* for granting me permission to quote from their works and to cull information from their stellar reports.

Introduction

A few years ago interleague play brought Ken Griffey Sr. and the Cincinnati Reds to Cleveland. I decided to get media credentials to cover the game and drop by for a chance to shoot the breeze with my former Donora High School classmate.

I strolled through the concourse by the visitors' clubhouse at Jacobs Field and there, walking in the opposite direction, was Kenny (what we called him in school, as opposed to his real name, George, or the name by which he became known to baseball fans, Ken). I said hello, he paused for a split second, and said, "Wayne?" I was surprised that after thirty years he still recognized me. We shared some high-school and hometown memories, and he asked about some of our fellow grads; all in all, it was a pleasant chat.

When I got home, it hit me: I could do a book on the Griffeys from a unique point of view. Two classmates go on to a career dealing with baseball (even though his was much more illustrious than mine). I could tell stories from his youth and follow his career through to the present.

In theory that was a good idea, and I peddled it to The Lyons Press. I got a call from my editor, Mark Weinstein, who informed me that he thought the Griffey market was a bit too narrow, if not already exhausted. Instead, he suggested, how about a book on fathers and sons and how baseball helps them bond? It was, I agreed, a great idea. So, indirectly, a short conversation with an ex-classmate spawned this book, and it's been a joy to write it.

One of the first stories that came to my mind concerning fathers and sons and sports was a basketball, not a baseball, story. Still, the theme of the story applies to the love of a father and a son. It's a tale about the NCAA's Al McGuire, a coach who once won the national title at Marquette University (interestingly, with an old neighbor of mine and one of the acquaintances Kenny spoke to me about, Ulice Payne, on the squad). There came a time when McGuire had to choose between two players for his final cut. One player would survive; the other was through. It so happened that one of the boys was his son, and he was, in fact, the one who made the team.

The other player reportedly went up to McGuire and said, "Coach, we were pretty even. I think I was actually a little better. Why'd you pick him?" McGuire conceded that everything the player had said was true. Then he added, "But I love my son, I don't love you."

Many major-league ballplayers have, at least to some degree, an awareness of being "macho." After all, the very nature of the game is very manly, mano a mano. Brushbacks, beanballs, and brawls are very real elements of the game. Despite that, it's amazing how many players interviewed for this book tossed around the word *love* in connection with their fathers as easily and readily as they'd lob casual, pregame warm-up throws. And, remember, they were opening up and showing their emotions concerning their dads to a total stranger. That in itself tells a lot about fathers and sons and the intensity of the bonding that goes on between them.

In April of 2001 Livan Hernandez, who had defected from Cuba to play baseball in the United States, revealed that he was pitching under great duress. His father, Arnaldo, was dying of cancer back home in Cuba and Livan could not return to see him. "I'm suffering," he said tersely.

Slugger Cecil Fielder, a monster of a man, had no qualms about speaking candidly of his devotion to his father. He said that he feels children have to be taught to live the right way in life. "The discipline begins at home," he said. "My father was my role model." So many of the fathers in this book taught their sons how to live, how to be good men, not just how to play baseball—although they all believe baseball was an enormously strong bonding agent.

Sure, a father can bond by, say, fishing with his boy, but there remains something very special, almost atavistic, about a game of catch. I seem to remember a short story based on that very premise. Players universally speak of the intensity of the power of baseball in helping a boy bond with his dad. And *that* deserves a close look. This book shows dozens of men who made it to the highest level of baseball achievement, and reveals how the sport has touched their lives.

The estimated number of father-son combinations with both players having reached the major leagues is slightly above the neighborhood of 150.

During the time this book was being written, thirty-three players who were part of a father-son tandem were active in the majors, and the trend is growing. In one recent draft, no fewer than five sons of big leaguers went in the first 151 selections, with four of them going by the sixty-first pick. They were Jason Fingers, son of Hall of Fame reliever Rollie; David Parrish, son of standout catcher Lance; Aaron Herr, whose father was Tommy; Lance Niekro, the son of knuckleball specialist Joe; and Kyle Gross, whose father was infielder Wayne.

Larry Ekin's book *Baseball Fathers, Baseball Sons* states that in 1903 Jack Doscher made his first appearance in a big-league game. Since his father, Herm, had been in the National Association during the 1872 season, they earned the distinction of becoming the first father and son to both make it to the major leagues.

Sometimes a grandfather and a grandson both make it to the bigs, too, as was the case for Shano Collins (1910–1925) and his grandson Bob Gallagher (1972–1975). A slightly more famous case, though, was that of Lloyd Spencer (1913) and his slick-fielding grandson, first baseman Jim Spencer, who played in the majors for fifteen seasons.

While the emphasis of both this book and Larry Elkin's book remains the relationship between fathers and their sons, one thing should also be pointed out. Many of the fathers and sons in this book showed an earnest desire to talk about, praise, and credit the females in their lives: their mothers, sisters, and daughters. The Spiezios, to name one family, were grateful for all the help Scott's mom supplied. They were also proud of Scott's sisters, two fine tennis players.

Then there was David Segui, who said, "It was my mom who taught us [his two brothers and him]. You talk to guys whose fathers played in the bigs and it's always the mom who was there and playing ball. Robbie and Sandy Alomar said it. Ken Griffey Jr. did, too. Everybody says the same thing. She's your hitting instructor, hitting you fungoes, throwing batting practice—all that stuff. They don't get any credit for it. My dad is the first one to say it."

In 1978, when Eddie Mathews was inducted into the Hall of Fame, he said to the Cooperstown crowd, "I'm just a beat-up old third baseman. I'm just a small part of a wonderful game that is a tremendous part of America today. My mother used to pitch to me, and my father would shag balls. If I hit one up the middle, close to my mother, I'd have some extra chores to do. My mother was instrumental in making me a pull hitter."

Then there was the e-mail message Vicki Wright sent me. She wanted to inform me that her husband would help out with my book project. She also wrote: "It's funny that you should be doing a book about fathers and sons. I've been kicking around the idea of doing a book on mothers with sons who have become professional athletes. Having a husband and a son who have been professional athletes, I have seen and heard a lot where the mother was so influential in her son becoming who he was. I've always wanted to hear the mother's side of the story. But since we live in a man's world I think the mother is often overlooked, particularly in sports." She did concede, though, that "when you see football players look right at the camera they say, 'I love you, Mom.' They never say, 'I love you, Dad.' "

Alas, the theme of the book prohibits much discussion of the fine women associated with the men herein. By the same token, many men gave credit to their brothers and to their families in general. Our apologies that we couldn't dwell on them, either.

When a writer interviews a large number of people for a book, he is bound to run into some less than stellar respondents. However, in compiling data for this book, it was incredible how amiable and cooperative the fathers and sons were. An inordinate number of the fathers were also highly successful people, even when their playing days were far behind them. Ed Spiezio, for example, runs a furniture store in the Chicago area; Tom Kennedy, who played ball but didn't make it to the majors, has become a huge success as a high-school baseball coach; Tom Grieve was yet another class act, and is highly successful as well. It was hardly surprising to see that the sons of men such as these were successes, too, by every definition of the word.

Ed Spiezio even granted me a second interview after a lengthy first one resulted in every writer's nightmare: much of the recorded interview was too garbled to use. I had heard the horror stories of writers or announcers finishing an interview only to look down at their tape recorder and realize that their batteries were dead or they had forgotten to press RECORD. I had also heard stories about men like Stan Musial who, upon learning that his interview was ruined, said, "No problem, let's do it again."

In my case, Ed displayed class and generosity, graciously repeating the information I had lost by granting yet another interview that ran over an hour. Again, the adage "like father, like son" holding true, it's easy to see why his son Scott is so well liked and respected.

In discussing his childhood, Paul Konerko made a point about his father that, by extension, pertained to almost all baseball dads. Konerko said that one thing he truly appreciated was the fact that "when you're growing up, obviously your dads are always taking you to and from games and hitting you ground balls. Pretty much until you get to high school your dad is pretty instrumental. After that, other coaches usually take over from there on up." He wasn't one to forget all those early hours his father had spent driving cars and driving balls into the ground and up in the air for him to snag with his tiny mitt.

Interestingly, too, many of the fathers interviewed said they'd be pleased with and proud of their sons no matter what they did for a living, even if they wound up having a less than glamorous job. Yet, even as they speak, the impression lingers that they are, in fact, delighted that their sons are playing the game they played, thrust into the national spotlight, capturing the interest of a multitude of fans. Their pride is palpable.

As a rule, players have a deep respect for their families. When rookie shortstop Jack Wilson made the Pittsburgh Pirates' opening-day roster in 2001, he wanted his parents to be able to see him play in the team's home opener, but he couldn't afford to fly them in from their home in Thousand Oaks, California. When veterans Brian Giles and Jason Kendall, whose father played in the majors, learned of this, they both chipped in and took care of the cost of the trip.

There's no doubt that players think of their folks a great deal. Stories of players buying satellite dishes or season passes for their dads are common. Long-distance phone bills to fathers are often astronomical. When Detroit Tigers outfielder Bobby Higginson signed a $35.4 million contract extension in April of 2001, he immediately thought of his father. He said, "My dad used to give me $5 allowance when I was a kid. Now I'll give *him* an allowance."

During the third game of the 2000 World Series, New York Mets reliever John Franco, a seventeen-year veteran, turned in a key performance during his first Series ever. The possessor of the second-highest save total in history picked up a victory over the rival Yankees.

Franco grew up in Brooklyn listening to his father, Jim, tell him stories of famous New York subway World Series. Although his dad died before John ever got a chance to pitch in New York, John dedicated his Series win to him. In fact, John, who now pitches batting practice to his son before games, even wears an orange Department of Sanitation T-shirt under his jersey every game in honor of his dad—as a sort of gift to his father, who worked there.

Charles Nagy has a different type of gift for his dad. He's collected baseball cards for his father for some time. He said, "My father has gotten a lot of cards since I've been playing. Guys [players] get cards from companies all the time, so I give those to my dad."

Charles's wife, Jackie, said, "Once he had the opportunity [as a big lea-guer], he rarely asks another player for an autographed item. But he's not going to miss out on a Cal Ripken—there are certain players that he won't let slip by." He tends to ask players that he "knows his mom or dad is in awe of or would love to have some memorabilia from. He doesn't hesitate." While he doesn't like to intrude, he will still go out of his way to please his parents.

"His mom really wanted a Scott Erickson autograph, and Chuck was like, 'Oh, God, I got to go tell Scotty that my mom thinks he's cute.' " But off he went to plead for that autograph. Nagy said to his folks, "O.K., you're hum-bling me up, but, all right."

Players also constantly think about their own children. Andre Dawson, for example, said in a mid-1990s interview that when he was a child he had baseball cards stored in shoeboxes. "Somewhere along the line they got lost and I didn't really start collecting again until a couple of years ago, and I only did that for my son," he said. Many a player has done the same, and has un-abashedly approached fellow players with an autograph request, even at the risk of being a pest, because, of course, they're doing it out of love.

When his son was just 5 months old, Jay Buhner said he was already collecting autographs. He had a collection of baseballs autographed by Hall of Famers. "I'm most proud of the Joe DiMaggio and Mickey Mantle balls be-cause they were signed for me," he said. However, he added, "I'm doing it [col-lecting] for my kids."

Ken Griffey Jr. said he is a collector, too, but in his case he has col-lected stories about himself from magazines and newspapers. That pastime is not, however, an ego trip as it's his parents, not his own glory, that's on his mind. "If I happen to come across a story about myself, I read it," he said. "If it's good or there's a picture, I send it [back home]."

When Jeff Torborg was hired in June of 2001 to replace Felipe Alou as the manager of the Montreal Expos, one of Torborg's first acts was to name his son the team's batting-practice pitcher. His son Dale, a 6'8", 285-pounder, was out of work, so Dad was looking after him. Dale had been a pro wrestler (known as Demon) but lost his job when the WCW was bought out by the WWF. He also hired another son, Greg, to handle the team's computer work. Greg is an attorney by trade, but he enjoys his work with the Expos and is able to run the computer analysis from his New York office. Torborg's third son, Doug, is the only one who's not associated with the game.

The August 1, 2001, issue of the Cleveland *Plain Dealer* contained a blurb about Indians player Wil Cordero. It seems that during a game he wore a

T-shirt "with a picture of his two children, Wilanny and Wilfredo Jr. on it. Below the picture was the message 'We love Daddy.' "

All-Star pitcher David Wells has a different type of reminder of his son, and he takes it with him wherever he goes. It's a tattoo with the likeness of his then-infant son on his arm. If he keeps getting new tattoos each year as his child gets older, much like parents buying annual school photos, Wells's body will soon become a living scrapbook—until the day he runs out of space on his ample body.

In May of 2001, Tony Gwynn discovered that the job of head coach at San Diego State would be open in June of 2002, so he announced that he was interested in the position. "I'm the perfect guy for that job," he said. Three strong reasons to support his contention: he played at that college; his son, Anthony, was currently on the team; and the ballpark is named Tony Gwynn Stadium.

Some players even give consideration to a son they don't even have. In 2001, Jim Thome passed Albert Belle as the all-time leading home-run hitter in a Cleveland Indians uniform. While he had given away the ball that had tied him with Belle to his manager as a thank-you, when he was presented with the historic home-run ball he said he'd keep that one. Said Thome, "If I ever have a boy, I will give it to him to take to school for show-and-tell."

The subject of players' sons even comes up during reporters' interviews. In May of 2001, a writer asked Cleveland Indians catcher Eddie Taubensee if he wanted his three young sons to be baseball players when they grew up. Taubensee joked, "I'd like them to be doctors so they can fix my body when I retire."

Baseball has a hold on fathers and sons. In May of 2001, when an 82-year-old Ted Williams was in a San Diego hospital, his son John Henry said Ted still wanted to watch baseball. Boston's general manager at the time, Dan Duquette, obliged by sending Red Sox tapes to the Hall of Famer in order to keep him occupied.

Around the same time, Philadelphia Phillies third-base coach John Vukovich underwent brain surgery to remove a benign tumor. The next day his son, Vince, told John that he wanted to stay home with him. John told Vince, who was an outfielder for the University of Delaware squad, to forget it. He told him to go to his scheduled game versus Rider. Vince did as he was told and ended up collecting three hits while driving home five runs—a great way to dedicate a game to a recovering father.

When Todd Hundley went to the Chicago Cubs for the 2001 season and became their catcher, he was literally following in his father's footsteps.

Randy Hundley was a fine catcher for the Cubs from 1966 to 1973 and again from 1976 to 1977. When it came time for Todd to choose his Chicago jersey number, he wanted the numeral he had worn before, 9, to honor his father, who had also worn it. Unfortunately, that number was already taken by outfielder Damon Buford. Buford, himself the son of a former big leaguer, Don, had selected that number because Don had worn it when he roamed the outfield.

No problem. Hundley went with 99, obviously the highest number ever worn in baseball (tied with Turk Wendell and three digits higher than the jersey number of pitcher Bill Voiselle, who hailed from a town named 96). It is not uncommon for sons to wear the same number as their fathers. In fact, when the Cubs released Damon Buford in May of 2001, Hundley claimed his father's old number.

Dads also love to spend time with their sons at the park. When the Milwaukee Brewers' new Miller Park opened in April of 2001, one of the features they kept from their old ballpark was the slide their mascot, Bernie Brewer, went down to celebrate a home run by a Milwaukee player. On April 14, when the Giants made their first trip to the new facility, J. T. Snow and San Francisco's broadcaster Duane Kuiper sneaked Kuiper's son Cole out to the slide. All three took a test ride—another perk of being a member of (or son of someone associated with) a big-league team.

Baseball families have always been a part of the lore of the game, and fans delight in oddities such as the time Felipe Alou, who would later father a son (Moises) who made it to the majors, played in the same outfield with his two brothers, Jesus and Matty. That took place on September 15, 1963, and was not only an unprecedented baseball event but has never been replicated, either. One can bet that's a story Moises has heard from his father many a time.

There are just so many wonderful baseball tales and oddities involving fathers and sons. The Alous were also involved in another one. When the Braves played their first regular season game in Atlanta, having moved from Milwaukee, the first Braves batter to appear at the plate was Felipe. Several decades later, in the last regular season contest ever played at that venue, the very last man to bat there was Moises. Call it part of baseball's beautiful symmetry.

"I can see a lot of Felipe in his boy, quite a bit," Tito Francona said of Moises. "The stance and the way they swing at the ball." That, too, is part of the beauty of the game, seeing baseball's version of the cycle of life.

Most of the major leaguers interviewed for this book felt that being the son of a ballplayer was a pretty strong asset. However, not all experts agree fully that having been exposed to the big-league life as the son of a player is a big plus. Chicago White Sox slugger Frank Thomas said that when those "kids do grow up in the baseball world like this, it's part of their life and they're groomed a lot earlier, but I think it really doesn't make a difference if you go through the right college programs and high-school programs—they're groomed in the same manner."

He did concede that "the intimidation factor is a little different if you've grown up in here. If they've been in the major-league clubhouse, you know what it's all about, but from the outside looking in, you still think it's a little different when you get here. So they have a small advantage." All squabbling aside, being the son of a big leaguer is a fascinating subject. Still, not all the people in this book are sons of players—the key here is that baseball formed a bond between father and son, something that is so universal it goes beyond those whose relatives played the game professionally.

Fathers,
Sons
& Baseball

Chapter One: My Dad and Me

My own father didn't really care about baseball—not much. But he cared about me—a lot.

Throughout the nearly twenty-five years I spent with him before he passed away in 1976, he devoted a great deal of time, energy, and money (none of which he could easily afford) to support my love of the game. Because my father married late in life, when he was well into his thirties, by the time I was old enough to start lobbing a ball around or to begin taking my first feeble cuts with a Wiffle-ball bat, he was nearly 45 years old. As I began my school years, I eventually came to realize that I had the oldest father in the class.

While I've known this for some time, until I typed the words "nearly 45 years old," it never dawned on me just how difficult it would have been for him to put in his grueling eight-hour (sometimes longer) shift at United States Steel, make his way home, and then manage to work with me on my baseball skills. I can't recall ever playing catch with my dad.

I never really resented that fact, not for a moment, but I can better understand why he didn't toss the ball around now that I'm getting older. Having just recently seen the age of 45 shoot by, I realize that it's no longer easy to squat behind a crudely constructed home plate and catch ball with my sons. For that matter, I can't even handle their fastballs. And as for catching with my younger son, Scott, forget it—I'm actually afraid to catch his unpredictable, darting knuckleball.

1

But I'm getting way ahead of myself. Back to my father. Don't get me wrong about him; he found other ways to relate to me and baseball. My first memory, albeit a hazy one, involving baseball concerns obtaining my very first baseball card. I was about 4 years old, living in an apartment above a penny-candy shop, as we called it. I asked my dad for a penny to buy a single card.

I wended down a long flight of stairs, entered the store, and experienced the joy of purchasing a "bubble gum card." Opening the wrapper was a delight, one that I'd relive hundreds of times over the next forty years or so, through my childhood and on into my own sons' years of collecting. I vaguely remember charging up those steps and proudly displaying the card to my dad; my collection (thanks to both of my parents' hands-off policy) remains intact to this day.

The funny thing is this: I'm not sure how accurate my memories are of the purchasing power of that penny and of my solo journey to cop my first card. I do know that my dad gave me money to buy the card. Beyond that, for example, I'm not positive about my recollection of going to the store alone. Life in a small town in the 1950s was very different from the way it is now, so perhaps I did make my way to the store alone.

I also think the penny card came sans a slab of that wonderful pink, oh-so-sweet gum. After all, at a penny a pop, getting a card was sufficient. Frankly, I'm not even sure if Topps ever really did put out individually wrapped cards. Furthermore, I don't care if I'm wrong about those minor items—it's a great memory.

As a grown-up and a writer, I've had the chance to check on my Topps single-card memory/dream, but never did. In fact, I've written for Beckett Publications and had access to card experts such as the always helpful and highly knowledgeable Pepper Hastings, but, again, I'll cling to my memory rather than research it clinically.

My family never had a great deal of money, and if, say, my dad's union went out on strike, we really had to watch our wallets. Despite that, my folks somehow managed to spoil their only child, keeping me in gloves, balls, bats, and other baseball paraphernalia throughout the twenty-one years that I lived at home. Although my first glove, a battered, dark-leather, three-fingered relic, was a hand-me-down from an uncle, my father bought me my next one.

Having broken in with an ancient glove, I was quite anxious for a new one; I had always felt a bit self-conscious about wearing that archaic piece of leather. It belonged, I felt, on a shelf in a museum, not on my left hand. My dad, realizing this, told me one day that the time had come to purchase my own first "real" glove.

He drove me to a local sporting-goods store and allowed me to pick out the glove. He did this for several reasons. First of all, his knowledge of baseball was limited, although he did enjoy playing the game when he was a boy. Second, allowing me the freedom to select the mitt was just the way he was. My dad was an overly generous man; often, especially when it came to me, he would spend more than he could afford, even if it meant a sacrifice on his part. That glove, that gift of love, is still in my cellar.

Along about this time, my father shared a great baseball story, his favorite tale from when he was a kid. But first, some background. My father grew up on a narrow street called Heslep Avenue in Donora, Pennsylvania. All his life, when the name Donora appeared in a national publication, my dad (and, now, I) would see our hometown described as "smoky and polluted," or some similar phrase. This was due to Donora's infamy concerning an incident that took place on October 26, 1948, and lasted throughout the last week of the month.

Because of the pollution the steel plants pumped into the air, and on account of freakish weather conditions, a deadly smog nestled over our valley for five days, claiming the lives of some elderly citizens (one source says 20 people died) while causing many others to fall sick. Donora was immobilized as an estimated 5,910 people became ill, a figure that represented nearly half the population of the town.

However, many times when the name Donora appeared in print, it was due to the aspect of our town that we residents were so proud of: sports. Although the population of my hometown never, to my knowledge, topped 20,000 (it has often been closer to 10,000—and continues to dwindle), it has produced an inordinate number of pro athletes. "Deacon" Dan Towler, who led the National Football League in rushing in 1952 as a member of the Los Angeles Rams, hailed from Donora, as did three players who became bona fide stars in the majors: Stan Musial, Ken Griffey Sr., and Ken Griffey Jr.

In fact, in addition to those three, Donora was home to several other men who also made it to the major leagues. There was Bob Coulson, Steve Filipowicz, and, according to one source, William A. Stewart (no relation), who played in the pre-1900 days of baseball. So even if three of the six men were hardly famous, for a town the size of "the Home of Champions," that's not too shabby.

I played on the same high-school baseball team as Ken Griffey Sr. His son was born in Donora on the same day, November 21, as the pride of Donora, Hall of Famer Stan "the Man" Musial, who is the central figure in my father's favorite sports story.

My dad was playing in a field that lies behind Heslep Avenue with a bunch of kids his age, around 15 or so at the time. Along came a younger boy, pestering my dad to let him play. Of course, the boy was Musial, eight years younger than my father. Although Musial displayed a love of the game, constantly looking for some playing time, and although he continued to beg my dad's group to allow him to play, they repeatedly chased him away. My father delighted in recounting—and I delighted in hearing—how he had told a future superstar that he wasn't "good enough to play with [us]." From time to time over the years, I'd ask my dad to repeat this story, and it made me smile each and every time he told his tale.

In 1963, Musial announced that he would retire at the end of the season. In those days a player didn't exactly make his "Farewell Tour," as some superstars now do. Still, when Musial played in his final game against the Pittsburgh Pirates in beautiful ivy-clad Forbes Field, Donora, located about 30 miles south of the ballpark, was prepared to bid a fond farewell to its "Man." The townspeople decided, as I recall, to make that day a sort of "Donora Day," with many residents, including personal friends of Musial, in attendance.

I begged my father to take me to this historic event. As usual, I didn't have to beg too hard. We piled into our pale green '54 Ford Fairlane and headed toward Pittsburgh. I don't remember much about the game; I think Musial hit one of the last of his 725 career doubles that day (upon his retirement only Tris Speaker owned more two-base hits). I do remember a small group of Donora fans clustered in the stands, waiting for Musial to join them after he'd had a chance to shower and change.

I asked my father if I, too, could hang around. Maybe I'd get a chance to approach Musial, I reasoned. I had never seen him around town, even though from time to time he'd visit his mother, who lived in a house he had purchased for her. That house, coincidentally, was on the same street that we lived on, but many blocks up a long hill. At any rate, my dad said I could stick around with the Donora contingency but that he was going to go outside the park, kill some time, and wait there for me. He was patient, willing to put off our departure until after I had seen Stan and obtained his autograph.

However, he made it clear that he didn't want to join the herd of people nearby. You see, my father was an unassuming man, and he was the kind of guy who didn't like to impose on others. He told me that because he was older than Musial he never really knew him very well. He certainly wasn't in the same school with Musial at any time, and, though they lived in the same part of town, his only involvement with the (at that time) all-time National League hit leader was that he'd banished him from the makeshift diamond years earlier. No, he told me, he didn't want to bother Musial. But he encouraged me to "go ahead, get his autograph."

I'll never forget how I hovered timidly near Musial, waiting my turn to speak up. He beamed at his old buddies as I, along with the rest of the townsfolk, eavesdropped on his conversations. After a while the St. Louis great took notice of me. I cleared my throat and rattled off a staccato string of short sentences, "I'm from Donora. My dad O. J. Stewart used to know you. Can I have your autograph?"

"Sure," he said. "But bring your dad here first."

I was delighted. I dashed up the steps, breezing by row after row of grandstand seats, sprinted outside the park, and found my dad. I explained the situation and how we just *had* to go back into the park. As much as my dad loved me and as much as he did for me, he occasionally drew the line. Surprisingly, he refused. He felt awkward; he didn't want to be a nuisance. He felt that the people who were gathered around Musial should be close friends only. Not being a huge fan, he didn't—in fact, he *couldn't*—understand what a Musial autograph would mean to me. So, not wanting to be a pest—after all, my father had already done me a favor by standing by patiently even though I knew he was exhausted from his latest shift at the mill—I quietly hopped into the car.

I think I managed to maintain my stoic stance for a day or two. Finally, I could no longer hold my feelings in. I'm not sure, but I may have cried; I know that I whined and complained to my father, but there was nothing he could do now. He was sorry. I remember him telling me that if I had spoken up more forcefully outside Forbes Field he would have relented. Now I felt foolish for not acting more like a spoiled brat that day.

Months passed, and I more or less forgot my lost opportunity. I rationalized that, hey, at least I got to speak with Musial. Not many kids could say that. Then one day my dad gave me a thrill that I'll never forget. He had heard through buddies at work that Musial was due for an off-season visit to his hometown. My dad arranged for us to visit Stan's mother's house and spend a few moments with the Cardinals' legend.

When my dad told me what he had done, I was overwhelmed. I knew what it must have taken for him to do this. He had to have felt that he was imposing, and he loathed the idea of people badgering others. He realized he was asking Mrs. Musial to give up a few minutes of her precious visit with her "Stash," but he also knew that he loved me enough to violate his own code. He was going to make up for the disappointment I had felt outside Forbes Field.

We drove up the steep hill, pulled into Mrs. Musial's driveway, and were soon standing there next to her and her son. Musial spoke easily with my father, convincing me that he did indeed remember him. He then gave me not one but four autographs on pieces of paper about the size and appearance of the name cards high-school seniors collect, then toss into a drawer, soon to be forgotten.

Musial's cards did not suffer that exile. From time to time, I'd look at those cards or proudly show them off to envious friends. I still have those autographs next to a Musial-signed baseball my uncle Bobby Jones got for me, and occasionally I still think back to that wonderful day that my dad went to bat for me.

My dad always generously found the money to allow me to make the trek to Forbes Field several times a year, and I was usually rewarded with great baseball memories. When I was around 8 years old, I insisted that we sit near the visiting dugout, since my favorite team was coming to town. While those seats were more expensive than general-admission tickets, my dad found himself granting me yet another wish—a minor luxury, I guess, because those tickets were certainly beyond the family budget.

He wrote to the Pirates requesting the seats I wanted so that I could get a close-up of my heroes, the Milwaukee Braves, led by my all-time idol, Hank Aaron. The Pirates were used to getting requests, I figured, for tickets near the home dugout, so it was probably easy for them to find a seat in the section I wanted. In my youthful mind, though, I pictured the person who filled out my father's request being baffled. "Now, why would *anyone* want to sit in that section?" he would say, scratching his head. In reality, of course, it was merely another ticket order to be processed.

At any rate, I really appreciated the effort my dad made when I saw Brave after Brave stroll to the plate: Aaron, Eddie Mathews, Joe Adcock. I even liked players such as Stan Lopata, Ray Boone, and Lee Maye, mainly because I owned their colorful baseball cards. Throughout my youth, I perceived myself as an Aaron fan trapped in a Roberto Clemente city with my father as my ally, helping me get the view I wanted.

I then vowed that the next time the Braves came to town, I would get a seat opposite their dugout so that I could gaze in and watch them on their bench. Chalk that up to either my greed—always wanting more—or simply to a desire for variety.

Of course, I'll never forget the first time my father took me to a big-league game. Forbes Field never looked more beautiful or green. My first impression when I walked up the ramp the day my dad took me to a Pirates-Reds game is still etched in my memory: I was indoors, yet I was outdoors. At first, that impression felt like an impossibility to me, a puzzling paradox.

Roughly thirty years later, I read an article by a man who, coincidentally, also took in his first game at Forbes. His feeling and his words were nearly identical to mine. At first I felt cheated. It was as if my emotions and memories were no longer special, unique. I felt almost as if my words had been plagiarized, too. Then it hit me. I had stumbled across a baseball universal. The shared feelings of being engulfed by a baseball field, surrounded by the beautiful green of the grass (and the impressive scoreboard, which loomed over the diamond and the multicolored seats) was, if not atavistic, certainly a marvelous communal feeling.

Another time, I was to see the Dodgers invade pastoral Forbes, but the game was rained out. No problem, said my dad. And even though the make-up game was part of a doubleheader that was scheduled to take place the next night—a school night—I was given permission to attend. This time I saw a most unlikely event: the Pirates swept a twin bill from Sandy Koufax and Don Drysdale!

Kids can be unyielding, almost unmerciful critics. As great as my father was, and despite his having come through for me in the rendezvous with Musial, I still managed a few childish complaints from time to time. Looking back, I recall one such instance, which came right after I didn't make it when I tried out for a berth on a Donora Little League team.

Although I knew I possessed a candy arm (and an erratic one at that), I tried out for a spot in the outfield, trying to emulate my favorite baseball All-Star, Hank "the Hammer." While I was fast and could glide under fly balls, it grieves me to admit that my bat was weaker than my arm. If my arm was made of candy, then I guess my bat was made of Swiss cheese.

Now, rather than accept the fact that I wasn't much of a baseball player, I chose to lay part of the blame on my father. Somehow I determined that it was his fault that I hadn't progressed as far as some of my friends had. After all, he didn't work out with me during my formative baseball years.

So clearly it wasn't my fault that I didn't survive the first cut. In some ways I felt like Marlon Brando's pugilistic character, Terry Malloy, in *On the Waterfront*. I thought I coulda' been a contender, but I was merely a bum.

Again, while it's true that to this day I cannot recall playing catch with my dad, I should have accepted the fact that that was just the way it was. My dad's most physically demanding pastimes were reading and, if you can call them pastimes, repairing items around the house and tinkering with the family car.

Still, he remained supportive in everything I did, and I finally quit blaming him for my failure. It dawned on me that many busy fathers in town didn't groom their sons to be baseball standouts, yet many of those boys made our local teams. Furthermore, though I had played a great deal of sandlot ball, I simply did not impress any of the coaches on the day of the tryouts.

Years after my Little League fiasco, I did make Donora's traveling Colt League team. A friend of mine told me about the upcoming tryouts, and, with encouragement from him and my dad, I did go out for the team. I still remember how proud both my dad and I were when I first donned that pristine white uniform. That, too, is a memory deeply entrenched in my mind's scrapbook.

I also played in my senior year on a mediocre, but Ken Griffey—powered, Donora Dragon team. I still believe that my dad was easily my No. 1 fan. And, let's face it, not many "good glove, no stick" players like myself had a thriving fan club.

During my days at good ol' D.H.S. I became a sportswriter for our newspaper, the *Varsity Dragon*. I wrote about Griffey's exploits in the four sports in which he excelled. When the paper hit the newsstands, I'd take it home and show my dad.

Nearly twenty years after graduating from high school, I sent a manuscript off to *Baseball Digest,* hoping I had maintained some of my journalistic skills. They bought the story, and I was ecstatic. That sale launched my writing career. Soon I was writing about baseball with regularity for newspapers, magazines, and major-league publications, contributing to their yearbooks and programs. I really wish my dad had lived long enough to see my byline on those stories; he passed away almost exactly a half year before that first story went into print.

Although I was saddened by the fact that he never had a chance to read any of my works, I devised a plan to honor his memory. I created the dedication to my first book long before I actually had a definite book concept in mind. I had faith that someday I would write a book on baseball. In reality, it would, in fact, take me another ten years of writing for magazines before I was able to find a publisher who accepted my first viable book proposal. That it took so long didn't matter to me. I was vindicated, as I had felt that I would ultimately prevail, and I did.

So when I wrote my book in 1998 I paid homage to my father and to my family. The dedication to that book, *Baseball Oddities,* reads as follows:

"I dedicate this book to five of the people I love: my father, the late Owen (O.J.) Stewart, who taught me to love words; my mother, Margaret, who taught me to love reading; and my wife, Nancy, and our sons, Sean and Scott."

Baseball, at least to some degree, was a part of my years with my father. Just as I'll always love baseball, so, too, will I always love him and all that he did for me.

Chapter Two: The Boones

The Boones are the first three-generation family in baseball history. Their bloodlines go way back. I once read a source that said the baseball Boones are, in fact, related to the pioneer Daniel Boone. Although Bret Boone said he had "no idea" if that story is true, when I finally spoke to his father, Bob, he confirmed my source, saying, "We're direct relations." That being the case, a baseball fan might ponder, "I wonder if Daniel could've hit a curve?"

Bret said that, like his father and his grandfather, he "was born in the San Diego area [El Cajon, on April 6, 1969], but I grew up as a kid in New Jersey because my dad was with Philly. In high school and college, I was back in Southern California."

Bret Robert Boone graduated from El Dorado High School in Placentia, California, where he played alongside future big leaguer Phil Nevin for one season. Four times he was an all-league selection, and he also earned All-CIF [California Interscholastic Federation] honors. He moved on to the University of Southern California, where he still holds club records for runs, doubles, triples, and runs driven in, and he capped his amateur career by being a member of Team USA in the summer of 1989.

By the 1990 June free-agent draft, he was snatched up in the fifth round by the Seattle Mariners, and by 1994 he was a full-time major leaguer. In that season he wound up tied for the eighth best batting average in the National League as a member of the Cincinnati Reds.

The following year he led the league in fielding percentage, a feat he repeated again in 1996. The next season he tied the all-time record for second basemen by leading the league in fielding for a third consecutive year while setting a new mark for superlative fielding (.996, on just two miscues). His 136 games played were the most ever for a second baseman with two (or fewer) errors. Finally, in 1998 he copped his first Gold Glove Award. In 2001, *Baseball America*'s survey of players listed Bret as the second best defensive second baseman in the American League.

Bret, listed as 5'10", 190 pounds, entered the 2001 season with nine years' experience in the majors and a career batting average of .255. In 1,072 games he had homered 125 times, with a single-season peak of 24 in 1998, which was also his best year for runs driven in, 95.

Then, in 2001, he went berserk, shattering career highs. By the All-Star break he had hit 22 homers (only six American Leaguers had more), with 84 RBI (tying him for league leadership), while hitting a robust .324 (eighth best in the league). He was selected for the All-Star squad, making his second appearance in that event. He not only got his first All-Star start, he batted cleanup on a team that included such vaunted sluggers as Manny Ramirez and Juan Gonzalez. By August 1, he had reached the century mark for ribbies. His previous personal best for home runs in a season was 24, but he had swatted 25 in 2001 by August 4. On that same day, his RBI total of 102 was seven over his previous best.

The Seattle team record for the most home runs hit by a second baseman in a season was 20 by David Bell, also the product of a three-generation baseball family. Boone tied that record in only his team's seventy-fourth game, before the halfway point in the year.

When Bret was named to the 1998 All-Star team, the Boones became the first family with three generations to make an All-Star team. Grandfather Ray made it in 1954 and 1956, while Bret's father, Bob, was an All-Star in 1976, 1978, 1979, and 1983. In all, Bret has played for four clubs: the Mariners, Reds, Braves, and Padres.

Aaron Boone has also done well for himself. A participant in three sports at Villa Park High School in California, he also played his college ball at U.S.C., where he hit .308 over three seasons. The 6'2", 200-pound infielder was tabbed by the Reds in the third round of the June 1994 draft.

Born on March 9, 1973, in La Mesa, California, he teamed up with his father in 2001 to form a manager-player father-son combo. The only other times that a son has played under his father were: Connie Mack with his son

Earle on the Philadelphia Athletics; Yogi and Dale Berra as Yankees; Cal Ripken Sr., with both Cal Jr. and Billy with Baltimore; Hal and Brian McRae when they were Royals; and Felipe and Moises Alou in Montreal.

Aaron, a .280 career hitter in the majors, had succeeded at every step of the minors, often leading his league in one or more fielding categories. In 1995 and 1996 he was on the All-Star team, setting a league record with his 44 doubles in 1996. In 1997 not only was Aaron an All-Star but he was the MVP of the American Association owing to his excellent play at Indianapolis.

By 2000 he'd hit a career high of .285 in the majors while showing a little punch, with 12 homers and 18 doubles. As tough as they come, Aaron suffered a broken nose when he was hit by a Russ Ortiz pitch, but he missed only one game. Another time in 2000, his Reds opposed Bret's Padres; the Reds won, but the Boones glowed as they accounted for 6 hits, 3 home runs, and 7 runs driven in. A year prior to that, when Bret was with the Braves, both Boones hit home runs. That was the first time brothers on opposing teams had homered against each other since 1981, when Hector and Jose Cruz accomplished the feat.

Meanwhile, the youngest brother, Matthew, stands 6'2" and weighs 175 pounds. He was born in 1979, in New Jersey, but also graduated from Villa Park High. The Detroit Tigers made him a third-round pick in June of 1997, and he has shown some early signs of belonging, including a seventeen-game hitting streak in 2000 at Lakeland. In his second pro season he hit .293, ninth in his league, and was on the Gulf Coast League All-Star squad. The next year, 1999, he was the Tigers' Minor League Player of the Month in May, when he cracked out a .358 batting average.

Going back a generation, there's Bob Boone, whose middle name is Raymond, after his father. He graduated from Crawford High School, in San Diego, in 1965 and four years later earned a degree in psychology from Stanford University. He had quite a career, spanning 1972–1990 with the Phillies, Angels, and Royals. In 1995, 1996, and 1997, he managed the Royals. At Kansas City he replaced another man who was the father of a big leaguer, Hal McRae, who had just been fired. (McRae would bounce back as the manager of Tampa Bay in 2001.)

Born in 1947, Bob had coached his son Bret when the Reds hired him as their bench coach in 1994. He moved on to Kansas City but returned to Cincinnati as a coach in 1997. He was named the Reds' manager in the off-season prior to 2001, and became only the sixth father to manage his son.

Bob is a nineteen-year veteran of big-league play who, until Carlton Fisk came along, owned the record for most games caught in the majors. He still holds the record for the most seasons catching 100 or more games, with 15. He won seven Gold Glove Awards, more than any catcher not named Johnny Bench, who copped ten awards, or Ivan Rodriguez, who has nine. In 1991, he led the National League with his .991 fielding percentage for catchers.

He hit .254 with 303 doubles, 105 home runs, and 826 RBI. He had a great eye, striking out less often than he walked—a rarity. He drew 663 walks and fanned 608 times. In postseason play he was dynamic, owning a .310 average in League Championship Series play and a .412 average in the World Series, and appearing in the 1980 Fall Classic as a member of the Phillies.

Finally, tracing the roots back to the Boone paternal grandfather, the next stop is Ray, who was born in 1923. He attended Hoover High School, catching on a team that, just six years earlier, was led by a player named Ted Williams. Often, a young Ray Boone went to the school to watch Williams hit. Ironically, both Boone and Williams retired from the Red Sox on the same day, the final day of the 1960 season—although Williams's announcement managed to garner a little more ink.

Despite winning baseball scholarships to U.C.L.A. and Texas A&M, Ray decided to enlist in the Navy. He then spent thirteen seasons in the majors, appearing in the uniforms of the Indians, Tigers, White Sox, Athletics, Braves, and Red Sox. After his playing days were over, Ray went on to work for the Red Sox organization for thirty-one years, displaying his longevity, before finally retiring in 1993.

His decision to become a scout rather than a coach or a manager was an easy one, because it was predicated on the needs of his family. Scouting allowed him to stay in the San Diego area, with loved ones, while avoiding the extensive traveling that he dreaded.

Ray's career batting average was .275, and he amassed 162 two-base hits with 151 home runs, with a career best of 26, and 737 RBI. From 1953 to 1956 he belted 20 or more home runs each year. Like his son, he drew more walks (608) than his strike-out total (463), an unheard-of statistic nowadays. Twice he topped the 100-RBI plateau, and twice he hit over .300.

He and Bob were opposites when it came to the position they played. Ray began his career as a catcher, then switched to third base, a move he found to be smooth and easy, while Bob started in the infield before shifting behind the plate.

Ray got a chance to appear in a World Series after spending just six games in the majors. That Series was a classic example of "Appreciate it while you're there, because you may not get there again." He had one World Series at bat in the 1948 Classic, a great personal moment, but it was also his last ever in postseason play. He told *Baseball Digest,* "It was a wonderful and exciting time. Beating Boston [Red Sox] in the playoff, and then taking the World Series from the Boston Braves."

Bob Boone recalls that his sons' love of and involvement with baseball goes back seemingly forever. "They all played from the time they could walk, and they got excellent instruction," he said. "We never pushed them in any way, but we couldn't take it away from them."

Likewise, when Bob was growing up, his father never foisted the game on him. "I was just around it," Bob said. "He didn't discourage me by any means, but I was around it—I'd go with him to the ballpark and my kids would go with me to the ballpark. I never had to prod them at all when it came to batting a ball." He said two of his sons, Bret and Aaron, "grew up in Philadel-phia and were allowed on the field, so they came to the park with me all the time." Further, when Bob was a kid he spent "quite a bit of time [at the park] in Detroit mostly" with his father.

Bob said that for his family baseball was something that "was just there"—something they didn't necessarily think about deeply but took part in diligently. "I don't think we're any different from any other family, except the topic for conversation when we're all together is certainly baseball." He added that he has never asked other parents of big leaguers about their experiences. But, he said with a chuckle, "They ask me more than I ask them; we've already lived it."

Bret, the oldest of Bob's sons, served as the main spokesperson for the Boone family. Speaking of his childhood, Bret said that his love of baseball goes back to "ever since I can remember." But while he agrees that baseball helped him bond with his father, he also said, "At the same time, he was away a lot. I mean, this is a life where it's tough—it's tough on the family. You're away a lot, you're traveling a lot.

"I'm going through it right now. During the season I don't see my wife and kids for three months because I'm gone—every ten days I'm gone for ten days, and . . . that's one of the tough parts. But I had a great childhood. I've always been close to my dad, and it continues."

Still, because of Bob's commitment to playing, he never had the chance to coach Bret in his youth. For that matter, he couldn't even attend Bret's first big-league game. Such missed moments are indeed the downside to life in the majors.

Bob can now follow Aaron, of course, but he must rely on the media to help him keep up with Bret's progress. In 2001, when Bob granted his interview for this book, Bret had bulked up through weight lifting, adding about fifteen pounds of muscle during the 2000 off-season. Whatever the reason, Bob was delighted that Bret was scorching hot, putting up numbers that ranked among the best in the game. A proud father, Bob said, "Oh, I see it all. I see a lot of his games on cable." Like the other fathers of players, he's grateful for modern technology.

Bret said that on the rare occasions that his father hasn't been in uniform, baseball has provided the family with the chance and the money to travel to see him play. One splendid moment had to be the time Bret enjoyed a monster day at the plate. He had to be ecstatic that his father had the chance to see him hit three home runs in a game.

Bob knows that Bret's career is more than just one great game; Bret could have added other personal highlights beyond the three homers. "I've seen him do a few things special—that's fun for me," he said. As for being united with his son Aaron on the Reds squad, Bob commented, "It's a very professional relationship, but it's fun for me, in that I get to see him play every game, and that's something I haven't been able to do his whole life."

Now that father and two sons are all in the majors at the same time, Bret said that Bob will call him "all the time" if he sees him on television and has noticed, for example, a hitch in his swing. He says his dad watches him play any time he can, and they stay in touch accordingly.

Bret thinks of Bob as a good coach, a sort of personal coach, and he asserts, "He can help me. He was a big influence from a just-what-he-did standpoint. He was just basically there. If I had any questions, I went to him, but there was never any pressure to play or anything like that."

When it came time to give Bret fatherly advice about life in the majors and the pitfalls to avoid, Bret said his dad tended to lead "more by example—he handled himself like a pro and I think I learned just by watching more than by word of mouth."

It was suggested that Bob's college degree would help him perform his coaching and managing jobs, but that wasn't entirely the case. He felt that his insight into human nature didn't really help him manage players per se. "I don't think there's a direct correlation," he said. "I think my experiences help me.

That's part of my experiences, but it's not like, 'Gee, you went to Stanford and you have a degree in psychology, therefore you're an expert and you can psychoanalyze everybody.'

"I think that's completely a farce, but I think all of my experiences, all of any manager's experiences [help]—you are a compilation of your experiences. Those are what help you in dealing with players. If you are good at it, you'll deal with them well."

The off-season gives the Boones a chance to get together. Bret noted, "I'm in San Diego now [in 2000 with the Padres] and he [Bob] lives in Anaheim, so I get to see him, probably, once a month." As for his grandfather, Ray, Bret said, "I see him quite a bit. He comes to all the games, so I see him a couple times a week when I'm home."

Circumstances changed when Bret became a member of the Mariners in 2001, but the family still spends time together. That appears to be a constant in the life of the Boones.

So how does Bret Boone feel about being a part of a three-generation baseball family? "Well, I'm definitely proud of my family and what we've been able to accomplish," he began, "but it was nothing ever talked about or thought about. I mean, I played baseball, I always did. It was our life. So the three-generation thing was never really an issue; the media made more of an issue than it really was to us. But, looking at it, yeah, I'm very proud to be a part of a family that's done what we've done."

In the middle of Bret's 2001 pyrotechnics, when his bat was sizzling, he spoke to *Sports Illustrated*. Interestingly, he said, "It's not that I'm not proud of my family. I am. But this is better." Admittedly, for a baseball player nothing could be better than enjoying what must be, or at least what seems to be, a career year. At the time of the interview, Bret was tied with Manny Ramirez for first place in the American League for runs driven in—and that's some fast company to be in.

Bret's hitting was so torrid that by August 4 he had smashed his former season high for home runs when he launched his twenty-fifth homer. He had become the sixth American League second sacker to reach the 25-home-run plateau. Plus, he had already topped the 100-RBI mark for the first time in his career. In fact, he was now among the league leaders in countless departments, including batting average, runs, RBI, and hits.

Bob's view of the three-generation issue is that he's "proud of it, but my time's done, my dad's time's done—it's the kids, the brothers playing. And all that's great, but it really has nothing to do with the game." He candidly addressed a common question: Do players from baseball families feel any pressure to live up to the family name? "I think it's probably a cross that Matthew is bearing and that Bret's son is going to bear more than anybody else," he said.

Sometimes fans think something is more special than the players do. For instance, there are some players whose fathers were stars in the major leagues but to them it wasn't a big deal. They simply thought, "Hey, to me he's just Dad."

As much as baseball was his life, Bret said that as a child he never got into the collecting aspects of baseball, cards or autographs. "I was obsessed [with baseball], but not from a fan's standpoint, more from a playing standpoint—it's all I've ever wanted to do," he said. "I wasn't so interested in memorabilia or autographs—I just wanted to be out there playing."

So, to him, growing up around a major-league clubhouse wasn't exactly a thrill. He could, for example, have had players' autographs and even pieces of equipment. "I think when I was a kid I took it for granted. I didn't know anything else—I thought that was normal. But, looking back on it, I had a very special childhood. I got to do things that every kid doesn't get to do, and at the time I thought it was just a normal thing. If I'm fortunate to play long enough, I would like to give my son that same experience."

While rubbing shoulders with big leaguers may not have been earth-shattering, Bret did say that he liked all the players and had no favorites. "I just liked hanging around," he said simply. Whatever team his dad was on would become the team he'd follow, and that team's players were the ones he grew to like.

Bret told *Sports Illustrated* that his father "knows hitting." He added, "He was so good defensively that people don't think of him as a hitting guy. Because it wasn't easy for him, he says that he had to watch and saw more than most." With that in mind, Bob Boone gives his son advice through frequent phone conversations—even though at times Bret was hitting so well that tips hardly seemed necessary.

Bret felt that the sessions he and his father held together before Christmas of 2000 were extremely beneficial, maybe even more so than his weight lifting—although that may be impossible to measure. However, he feels that he can gauge his father's influence in the smoothing out of his stroke, and that has been huge for him.

Meanwhile, Brett's son, Jacob, who was born during spring training in 1999 (he also has one daughter, Savannah), has given him reason to believe that there is a very real possibility there will be a fourth Boone generation playing in the majors someday. Even though he couldn't realistically evaluate Jacob's talent at the time of our interview, Bret said, in typical proud-papa fashion, "I'm sure he's going to be good." Part of the reason he feels that way is that he clearly subscribes to the theory that a good bloodline is a major contributing factor to success in baseball.

Toss in the fact that the Boones are known for their strong work ethic, and this family could keep producing players for a long time. "My dad was a real hard worker, and this is a tough game," Bret said. "It's not easy, so you got to work hard to stay at this level and continue to be successful. I just think in order to maintain success, especially at this level, you do have to work hard." He said that Aaron has that same attitude as well.

However, Bret disagrees that players who come from a baseball family tend to play harder or automatically play better than others. "I don't think that's necessarily true," he said. "I think you grow up and you see how the game is played and how you're supposed to play it. I don't know how big of an advantage it is [coming from baseball stock], but I know it's not a disadvantage. To say just because you're the son of [a player you'll play the game right and succeed]—I don't know if that's true."

Bob responded to the issue by replying, "I think it depends on the person. All my kids do [play hard and hustle]. They've been raised that way; they knew they'd get a spanking when they were real young if they didn't. So they just know how to play the game, and they learned that from a very early age."

Chicago White Sox first baseman Paul Konerko seems to disagree with the Boones, though. "The guys who have fathers that played the game at the major-league level always seem to be smarter about the game, because they've been around it since they've been younger," he said. One example that quickly came to mind was Aaron Boone, a former teammate of his, and he'd get little argument from baseball experts about the diamond perspicacity of any Boone family member, for that matter.

In the meantime, Bret couldn't attest to his grandfather's work ethic firsthand, as he was too young to have seen him play. That said, he commented, "My grandfather was a big influence early in my life. He's probably the first one who put a ball and a bat in my hands." Ray also regaled Bret with "a zillion" stories about life in the majors.

That's not to say that his own father didn't share incidents and anecdotes. "It's just talk," Bret said. "You know, when you sit around you talk and there's stories we can all relate [to], because we all live the same life. It makes for interesting discussions."

In an article for Knight Ridder newspapers, Dave Cunningham wrote of an ongoing argument in the Boone family circle. Ray Boone would make comments like "The ballplayers were better in my era. Why, we had Bob Feller and Joe DiMaggio and Al Kaline." To which Bob would retort, "Naw, they were better in my era. What about Mike Schmidt, Pete Rose, and Steve Carlton?"

The three sons then replied, "The best are playing right now. Who was ever better than Mike Piazza, Tony Gwynn, and Greg Maddux?"

Aaron told Cunningham, "We have that argument all the time," also noting that he and Matt play third base like their grandfather, but neither of them catches, as their father did. "I guess we were either too smart or too stupid to be catchers," he quipped.

Ray also likes to joke that "sometimes I have to remind my son and grandson that 'old gramps' once led the American League in runs batted in." He did so in 1955, with 116 RBI. He also hit a then-record four grand slams in a season and homered in the 1954 All-Star game.

Just as Bret is proud of his grandfather, he is also proud of his father for a number of reasons. One, certainly, was Bob's durability. When he retired in 1990, no catcher had squatted behind the plate in more big-league games than he had, a staggering total of 2,225 contests—and that's a whole lot of squatting. "The one thing that sticks out about my dad wasn't what he accomplished on the field—and he had a lot of great things: several All-Star games, repeated Gold Glove winner, played nineteen years, . . . played on a World Championship team."

Instead, when he looked back at his father's career and his statistics, he commented, "Those things are great, and I have a lot of respect for what he accomplished, but I think the thing he taught me more than anything else, and what I respected the most, was how he went about the game and how he acted and how he carried himself. In my eyes, he epitomized what a professional is— that, more than anything, is what I got from him."

By the same token, Bret said, he believes that his father "is proud of what I've accomplished as a player because he knows what it takes to get to this level and be successful. I think he's just a proud father of his kids. He's just a wonderful father that did things the right way. He epitomized [the concept of being a] professional, and he was a great father to his kids."

Bret noted that there is a great contrast between the days of his grandfather and now where players' lifestyles are concerned. "It's a lot different," he said. "I think we're very lucky, in this day and age, to be able to do what we do and earn the living that we can earn. Back when my grandfather played, it wasn't that way. They made a nice living, but it wasn't the way we are nowadays. You know, he worked in the off-season. These guys were the pioneers; they were the ones who laid the groundwork to allow us to earn the kind of living we can.

"There's a lot that comes with that, but, at the same time, I think if you ask most major-league players, I think they'd say they feel very fortunate to be able to do what we do and live the life they live."

Bret said that his family has never teased him about the disparity in salaries, but he noted, "My dad, in his last couple of years, made a couple of million dollars, which, at the time, was considered quite a bit. That is not really an issue. My dad is happy for whatever I get, whatever my contract is."

The year 1998 was a special season for all of the Boones, according to Bret. "In 1998, we [his brother Aaron and he] were playing on the Reds together," he said. That gave his father and his grandfather the cherished opportunity to see both "boys" on the diamond at the same time. Bret recalled that San Diego is where his folks initially got to see the younger Boones in action. "I think we were in town, playing San Diego, and they were all there. It was the only time [season] I've ever played with Aaron."

Then there's Bret's "little brother Matthew—he's in 'A' ball with the Tigers [in 2000]." Like Bret and Aaron, Matthew is an infielder. However, Bret has never had the chance to be on the field with him. Perhaps not, but he did address their personality traits: "We're all different. Aaron and myself are four years apart, and Matthew is ten years younger than me.

"When Matthew was 8, 9 years old, I was going off to college. It was kind of a different relationship than I had with Aaron. Aaron and I grew up together and did a lot of things, played a lot of games together, and Matthew was real young, but he is a great kid—he's going to have a chance [at making the majors]."

Bob said of his youngest son, "He came along years later, so he was kind of the baby and he grew up a little different than the other two." Not only was Matt too young to compete with his older siblings but, Bob said, "He was more into trucks at an early age, where the other two had a ball. Matthew probably started a little later." Still, he also said Matt has a chance to make it, calling him "a nice player."

Years earlier, Ray Boone had evaluated both Bob's and Bret's baseball ability. In a 1995 interview for *Baseball Digest,* before Aaron had made it to the majors, Ray said, "I could just tell when both boys started to walk that there was tremendous athletic ability. Then, when I started playing catch with them, I knew for sure. I knew as early as when they were 3 or 4. It was more than just sheer ability. There was heart as well—that special intangible quality which is so important."

Tito Francona agreed. Not only did he know fellow big-league father Ray Boone but, he said, he "was traded for Boone." He added, "He was a swell guy. I was with the Chicago White Sox and he was with Detroit. At that time the Yankees always won the pennant every year, but the White Sox always finished second—they'd get second-place money. So I was traded for Boone, and every time we'd see each other he'd just put two fingers up to his cheek [to indicate] he was going to get the $2,000 that we get for second place, and I was out."

The Boone family history is packed with firsts, oddities, and ironies. On August 20, 1997, one of the peculiar events for which baseball is so notorious took place: the Cincinnati Reds surprised their veteran second baseman, Bret Boone, by sending him to the minors. Unhappy with his diminishing batting average, they felt that he would be able to work out his problems at Indianapolis. What made the move unique was the fact that Bret's spot on the roster was filled by his brother Aaron, who had been called up from the Reds' Triple-A club. That transaction is believed to be the first brother-for-brother deal of its kind in the history of the game. Again, the Boone family is clearly used to being part of famous firsts.

The Boones are, of course, the first family to put three consecutive generations into the majors. They are also special because so many members of the family have been good enough to play professionally. Bret, Aaron, and Matthew even have an uncle, Rodney, who was a minor-league catcher and an outfielder; he played in the farm systems of Kansas City and Houston from 1972 to 1975.

Bret gave his slant on playing on the same team as Aaron, saying it was special, "without a doubt." In all, Bret and Aaron played with the Reds for portions of 1997 and 1998. "We'd never played together because of the age difference, and to play together for the first time at the big-league level—I think at the time I was just a proud big brother to see that he had made it, and the fact that we were playing on the same team just added to it." Likewise, when they did things like turn a double play, the fact that they belonged to the same family made their accomplishments on the field all the more memorable.

In the Reds game of September 27, 1998, the entire infield was composed of two families—the Larkins and the Boones. Barry Larkin told team officials that he had always wanted to play with his younger brother, Stephen. So on the last day of the season it was arranged: Aaron was at third, Barry Larkin was the shortstop, Bret was at second, and Stephen Larkin played first.

This was the first time two sets of brothers had played for the same team in a regular season affair.

For that matter, in a 1997 game against the Expos the Boones squared off against the Guerreros, Vladimir and Wilton. This marked the first time two sets of brothers had faced each other in a regular season game since 1963.

Fans, as a rule, love such oddities, but do the players find them unique, special? Bob Boone opined, "It's no more special than anything else, than playing and just being a father-son or [part of a] grandson, father, grandfather. None of that changes. It's just kind of a neat thing, but other than that, they're more concerned with trying to hit that slider."

Back on May 11, 2000, Bret's Padres played Aaron's Reds and pyrotechnics ensued. Both Boones homered twice, marking just the second time in big-league history that brothers had homered against each other in two different games. The first time they did it was on September 1, 1999. The other brothers to do this were Jim and Graig Nettles, back in the 1970s.

On the first day of the 2001 season, another noteworthy event took place when Bret Boone and David Bell began the year as teammates in Seattle. Having two players who are each part of a three-generation family is indeed a rarity.

Then there was a wonderful footnote to the history of the Boone family. It also took place on Opening Day of the 2001 season. On April 2, the Bob–Aaron Boone duo made history as they became only the sixth father-son manager/player combination in the annals of big-league baseball. (Prior to the Boones, the last father and son to do this were Felipe and Moises Alou, in Montreal.)

As a side note, since Bob, Bret, and Aaron Boone have all been members of the Reds, as have several members of the Bell family, the Reds have had two sets of men who were part of three-generation families, which is also believed to be a big-league first.

Yet another oddity occurred on April 28, 2001, when Bob and Aaron were both ejected from a game by umpire Hunter Wendelstedt. According to information from the Society for American Baseball Research, the Boones are the third father-son combo to be kicked out of the same game. (Incidentally, Hunter Wendelstedt is himself the son of former major-league umpire, Harry Wendelstedt.) On May 12, 1993, the Giants' Barry Bonds and his father, Bobby, then a coach, were booted; and on August 7, 1989, Cal Ripken Sr., a coach at the time, and his son were thumbed from an Orioles contest.

In an April 2001 interview conducted by *USA Today/Baseball Weekly,* Aaron Boone spoke about playing with the Reds under his father. He told of how, that winter, he had heard numerous questions about what it would be like to play for his dad. He'd tell people that it was impossible to know prior to actually donning the Reds' uniform under the Boone regime, but he also conceded that he felt his father was "a good fit for this team."

He pointed out that his father "commands a certain level of respect, but at the same time he's really developed a relationship and communication lines between the players." He noted how Ken Griffey Jr. had already teased him about being the son of the manager. Griffey took to calling Boone "Gilligan" because his father is the "skipper."

Shrugging off the good-natured ribbing, Aaron told the publication that he enjoyed spring training a lot that year, as it also gave him a chance to spend time with his mother. "I can bring my laundry over to her, and get some chicken tacos—the family specialty," he said, sounding like a typical college kid home for break.

Furthermore, like that college kid, Aaron said that he and his father would spend some time together, of course, but that he'd also break away from dad. When the Reds are on a home stand, he said, he'd have his own version of a home stand, going to his folks' house for lunch from time to time. "On the road," he said, "I'll hang out more with the fellas. It's not going to be an awkward situation or anything. . . . If something comes up where we do something together, it's fine."

One issue Aaron did address, however, was the problem of what would happen if a teammate got upset about a managerial decision, as is inevitable, and began grousing (or worse) about his father with Aaron within earshot of such vitriol. "I think my teammates know that when it comes to something baseball-related these are my teammates first," he said. "I understand it's nothing personal. I'm sure they're not going to come to me and tell me my father is a jerk."

Bob added, "I think it's probably tougher on him than it is on me."

Back on August 8, 2000, there were some doubts about Aaron's health when he underwent season-ending surgery to repair a partially torn ligament in his left knee. Typical of the Boone family's attitude, Aaron said, "I'm looking forward to the challenge of overcoming this. My focus will be on playing in the 2001 All-Star game." Although he didn't make that squad, Aaron remains a solid player despite the fact that he had to go on the disabled list twice in 2001 after breaking his right wrist on two separate occasions.

Aaron says he delights in using his speed in situations where he can stretch a single into a double or perhaps score from first on a ball hit into the right-field corner. Again, he is a scrapper, like others in his family.

Meanwhile, Bob Boone displayed his modest, insightful attitude in a statement that he once made: "Catching is much like managing. Managers don't really win games, but they can lose plenty of them. The same way with catching. If you're doing a quality job, you should be almost anonymous." Actually, he was far from being nondescript: he won seven Gold Gloves for his defensive excellence. That total has him trailing only defensive geniuses Johnny Bench and Ivan Rodriguez for Gold Gloves received by catchers in the history of the game.

It's clear that Bob taught his sons his baseball philosophy. The Boones don't primp around the bases after hitting a homer. Their egos are sublimated to the game, just the way Bob would have it.

Because of their style of play and their personalities, the Boones are well liked. Big-league coach Ted Uhlaender commented on the family. "I think all three of them are different," he said, referring to Ray, Bob, and Bret. "From a third baseman to a catcher to a second baseman. I liked Ray real well, and Bob was a good guy, too."

Elrod Hendricks shared his thoughts on the Boones, too. "I played against Bob in winter ball and again once he joined the Angels, and I knew his dad when he was scouting," he said. "I met him way back, and we talked a lot. He was always talking baseball." He's convinced that Bob inherited his good baseball mind from his dad.

White Sox coach Joe Nossek said that of the father-son duos that he knew well, a couple of the "biggest ones were [the Boones and] Gus Bell and Buddy Bell, who I later had the privilege of coaching on the same team with here in Cleveland." He had watched Gus and Ray Boone play ball when he was still a boy. "It's interesting when their offsprings [David Bell and Bret Boone] came up and they were both class people—outstanding. And Bob Boone—though I don't know him well, I got to know him later on—he's a very bright guy also. That was something I took notice of. I had the pleasure of watching their dads play and also them."

Newly acquired New York Mets outfielder Jeromy Burnitz smiled at the mention of Bret. "Oh, yeah," he said. "I played with Bret on the USA team ten, twelve years ago and actually stayed at his parents' house and met his dad and both his little brothers, who are now playing. I didn't meet his granddad, but it's obviously a special thing when a family gets to carry on like that from one generation to the next. They definitely have a great bond and know what it's like to be a big-league ballplayer, and that's something that doesn't happen every day, that's for sure.

"I think Bret's a great guy, as well as Aaron—I don't know his little brother that well. And obviously people think highly of Bob. He's been in the game a long time; he's a manager again. So, yeah, I enjoyed them."

Early in 2001, Bret collected his 1,000th career hit. He said, "My grandpa had about 1,500 hits [1,260, to be exact], and my dad finished with about 1,900 [actually, 1,838]." Then, unable to avoid a playful jab, he added, "But my dad had to play 200 years to get them."

Chapter Three: The Bells

David Russell "Gus" Bell (1928–1975) played for the Pirates, Reds, Mets, and Braves in a major-league career that spanned from 1950 to 1964. A left-handed hitter, he hit .281 lifetime while hitting for power (311 doubles and 206 home runs). He had 23 triples in his first two seasons, and led the league in 1951 with 13. He once hit 30 home runs and had four 100+ RBI seasons. His entire career was spent as an outfielder, and in 1961 he appeared in the World Series with the Cincinnati Reds, who lost in five games to the New York Yankees.

Gus's son Buddy was born in Pittsburgh as David Gus Bell, but his family left the Steel City for Cincinnati when Gus was traded from the Pirates to the Reds shortly before the 1953 season. Like nearly all of the Bells, Buddy attended Moeller High School, Class of '69, and was the first of seven players from that illustrious school to go on to the major leagues. Some of the non-Bells to do so were Ken Griffey Jr., Barry Larkin, Bill Long, and Len Matuszek.

Buddy hit .279 over his lengthy career as an Indian, Ranger, Red, Astro, then Ranger again, when he called it quits in 1989. During eighteen years in the majors he owned 2,514 hits, of which 425 were doubles. Another 201 went for home runs. Plus, he drove in 1,106 runs and walked more often than he whiffed by an 836 to 776 margin. The Rangers named him their Player of the Year three times, more than any other man in franchise history whose name isn't Juan Gonzalez.

The Colorado Rockies Media Guide states that Buddy, a five-time All-Star, was, while playing, "arguably the best fielding third baseman of his generation." Furthermore, it said that most "historians consider him the best infielder taken in the middle rounds of the amateur draft which began in '65." He was the sixteenth-round selection in 1969, and needed only two and a half seasons before his first and only major-league promotion.

Both Gus and Buddy led their respective leagues in fielding. Gus did so in 1958 and 1959, while Buddy did it in 1980, 1982, and 1987, when he had only seven errors—a total that would have set the National League record if he had played in just eight more games to reach the minimum qualification. Bell's six Gold Gloves for a third baseman, all in a row, rank him behind only the great Brooks Robinson, who had sixteen such awards, and Mike Schmidt, who had ten. In addition, only five men ever played more games at third base than Bell's 2,186. His 4,925 assists as a third baseman is number five in the history of the game, and his 6,979 total chances rank third all-time.

Buddy, the winner of the 1988 Lou Gehrig Memorial Award, was also inducted into the Texas Rangers Hall of Fame that year. Then, in 1997, as the manager of the Detroit Tigers, his team won twenty-six more games than they had the previous year. That marked the largest improvement since the Orioles jumped 32½ games from 1988 to 1989 *and* the second-largest improvement in Tigers history, which dates back to 1901. He spent three years as the Tigers' skipper, coming in second in the voting for the Manager of the Year Award in 1997. Prior to his stint with Detroit, he had coached for six years, including a stay in Cleveland, where he briefly coached his son, David, in his debut season in the bigs. On October 20, 1999, Colorado named Buddy their third manager ever.

David Michael Bell entered the 2001 season at the age of 28, Mike was 26, and Ricky was just 22 years old. Ricky weighs 180 pounds, and Mike is a 210-pounder. Both stand 6'2", while David is 5'10", and weighs 195 pounds.

The story of Buddy's children is an interesting one. It starts with David. As a high-school player, David was elated when his Moeller High baseball team won the state championship during his junior season, 1989. From there it was a steady climb to even greater success. So far David has surpassed his siblings in pro ball, having spent six years in the majors. He began with the

Cleveland Indians organization back in 1990, when he was picked in the seventh round of the free-agent draft.

By 1994 David had demonstrated his durability, playing in every one of his minor-league team's contests, while also displaying his fine glove work in being named the league's best defensive player. There were three years in the minors when he led his league in a defensive category as a third baseman. In 1995 he made his big-league debut with the Indians before returning to the minors. When he first took the field at the major-league level, he made the Bells the second family to have three generations of big leaguers.

Later, he returned to Cleveland (where he hit an inside-the-park home run off Randy Johnson in his first at bat with the Indians), after a short stay in St. Louis, before moving on to the Seattle Mariners in late 1998.

Safeco Field in Seattle has been pretty good to him, as he's blasted 46 lifetime homers there. He enjoyed a burst of power in 1999, when he put up a career-high 21 home runs (20 as a second baseman) and 78 runs driven in—both represented team records for a second baseman. That year he and Alex Rodriguez set an obscure record when they combined for 62 homers, the most ever in the majors by middle infielders on the same team. Further, he was among the top-ten toughest men to double up, grounding into a mere seven double plays the entire season.

Versatile, he has played in the outfield, every position in the infield, and has served as a designated hitter. However, he seems best suited to play third or second base. In 1999 he actually led the American League with 313 putouts and 118 double plays as a second baseman. Clearly, he has extremely good, soft hands. A career .256 hitter prior to 2001, he stood out in the 2000 Division Series versus the White Sox. He hit .364, with an on-base percentage of .462.

David is yet another one of those players who, as the son of a big leaguer, is often introduced on the air by sportscasters as a man "who grew up in the clubhouse." It's true that when his father was with Texas, David did spend time inside the locker room around players. In one respect, that didn't help any when he broke in, though—he was treated like any other rookie. As a newcomer to a big-league team he was made to wear a dress, much to the delight of the veterans. In a way, though, he said that he felt lucky, because he was well aware that in days gone by rookies were treated far more harshly and "pranks" back then were neither entirely harmless nor well-intentioned.

Longtime baseball coach Joe Nossek says that when he runs into David, he'll chat for a moment or two, asking how his father is and to see if David has had a chance to talk to Buddy lately. Even though he doesn't know him well, Joe said, "You can tell he's the son of Buddy because he carries himself with the same class as Buddy does." He also said the family can be intense with a desire to win, calling them "great competitors."

Nossek said it doesn't surprise him that such traits are passed from one generation to another. "The bloodlines are weighed when scouts go out and look at sons of former players; they take that into consideration," he said. "I think probably they would have a little edge if two guys were comparable in numbers—the kid whose father played in the big leagues would probably have a little edge with scouts and organizations because of that fact."

In July of 2001, David displayed his family training. With just a few days to go before the deadline for the fans' balloting for the All-Star team, he was the top vote-getter at third base. David stated that if he beat out Cal Ripken Jr., who had already announced his retirement at the end of the season, he would step aside and let Ripken start the game. The point became moot when a flurry of votes for Ripken thrust him into the starting role. "It would be nice," David said, adding magnanimously, "I'd have been happy to go, but I'm happy for Cal. For all he's given to the game, he deserves it."

Still, Buddy commented, "David only cares about one thing—playing. And he is playing for one thing, and that's to win. Whatever happens above and beyond that is nice, but it is not important."

Listed as a 6'2", 210-pound infielder in the Colorado Rockies Media Guide, Mike Bell, born on the anniversary of Pearl Harbor in 1974, is another Cincinnati native. He also attended Cincinnati's Moeller High School, an athletic powerhouse, hitting .407 as a senior, which helped lead his team to a state title. And he lettered in basketball. Then it was on to pro baseball in the 1993 draft. Signed by Rangers scout Jim Dreyer, Mike made his debut in the Gulf Coast League, where he went on to lead all players in games, hits, and total bases.

Moving up the ladder, by 1996 he was in Double-A ball and led the Texas League in putouts, assists, total chances, double plays, and fielding percentage for a third baseman. In 2000, during his stay in Louisville at the Triple-A strata he hit a personal high of 22 homers.

In all, Mike has put in time with the Rangers organization, as well as with the Anaheim Angels, the Arizona Diamondbacks, the New York Mets, and the Reds. In 2001 he was united with his father's organization, the Rockies, in their farm system. If Mike moves up from Colorado Springs and plays for his dad as a Rockie, he will join that rare club of men who have played under their father.

Mike said that there is a picture of him, Buddy, and David that was taken in 2001 with them "in uniform and each one of us has it." He added, "It's another one of those things that, years from now [we'll look at and say,] 'Wow, that's pretty neat.' "

Going into the 2001 season Mike had forty-nine days of service in the majors, all with the Reds from July and September appearances in 2000. When the Reds first called him up, they were playing against the Rockies and his father, who was managing Colorado. However, Mike didn't see any action in that series.

September of 2000 not only found Mike in the bigs but also featured him becoming a father. His son, Luke Michael Bell, became the first grandchild of Gloria and Buddy Bell that month. Mike said of his son, "If he wants to play, that's something he wants to do [that's fine]. I'd like to see him be a doctor or a lawyer or something."

His logic was simple: baseball can be a difficult life. "It gets stressful," he said. "It's such a skilled game—you hit .300 and you're still failing most of the time. You have to learn how to deal with failure, and that can get pretty stressful at times."

All three of Buddy's sons are infielders. However, in the true Bell spirit, prior to the start of the 2001 season Mike told the Rockies that he was willing not only to play third base but to work out as a catcher in order to become more valuable to them as a multi-position player. Learning a new position may have involved adding stress to his life, but he was willing to take on the challenge.

The 2001 spring training was great for Mike in that, as he put it, "It was different at first, you know, working for your dad. I really enjoyed it, and I think we learned a lot about each other, too, which is nice. It was a time that I'll never forget."

He said that one way playing for his father was a different experience was that "usually I call him and tell him how I'm doing, and we talk about the game a little bit. But now, he's in a situation to kind of get on me a little bit, and that was kind of awkward at first, I think, but he handled me like any other player, which was the way I wanted it. At the same time, I could go in his office and we could talk like father and son."

As for learning about each other, Mike said, "I see how he is around other people and how he is at his job, how he treats people, which is just unbelievable. I knew from people telling me how much they enjoyed playing for my dad and how much they liked him that it was going to be good, but I never realized how good he handles players and people and the media. He does a great job, and he's fun to be around."

Of course, Mike was also around his dad at ballparks as a child. "I remember being at the ballpark every day," he said. "And I think I took it for granted as a kid. I thought everybody did that. Now I realize how lucky I was, just being around the park, playing with my brothers, hanging out with the players. I mean, we were so fortunate, and those are times in my life that I'll never forget."

He recognizes that he was also fortunate to have the name Bell. He said that he was treated specially at times. "I think so, and I don't say that in a negative way. I think when people first meet me sometimes that's the first thing they think about: this guy's dad is Buddy, or his grandpa was Gus. And that's fine with me, it's great. If they want to compare me to them, that's even better.

"I think that after they get to know me, they realize that I have my own personality and I'm my own guy. But hopefully they still think they can compare me to my dad, because that's a good person to be compared to."

Mike said that baseball helped him bond with his father "quite a bit just because we liked to go to the ballpark with him and hang out with him." He added, "I'm sure that helped us. I remember him being there more than he was away from us."

Buddy always made it a point to be with his family. "In spring training one year, he flew home to watch my brother play a basketball game after [he had played in] a day game," Mike said. "Then after my brother's game, he flew back to spring training." (For the record, the trip from his spring training site to Cincinnati was quite a long haul.) "I don't even know if he remembers it, but I know all of us kids remember all that stuff."

Mike said that he has never felt a need to live up to his family's illustrious name. "I'm very proud to be a part of this family, not even the baseball part, but just the kind of people that my dad and grandpa were and my brother," he said. "As far as pressure on the field? I put pressure on myself because I want to play in the big leagues, and I want to take care of my family. Those are the pressures that I feel, and every day I just try to put those out of my mind, because it's not easy to play thinking like that. But as far as because of my family? I've never really thought of that much.

"We go home in the winter, we really don't talk about baseball a lot. We watch a lot of basketball, a lot of football, and just hang out—go out with each other and have a good time."

Still, when it comes to being part of a three-generation baseball family, Mike says that definitely is something special. "Last year [2000] when I finally got in a game, we were the first three-generation family that put the same uniform on," he said. "I couldn't grasp that my grandpa had put this uniform on, too."

It was on July 23, 2000, that Mike became the fourth member of his family to collect a big-league hit. Since he did so in a Reds uniform, the Bells became the first family ever to produce three generations of players who played (and collected hits) for the same franchise. His father was a Red from 1985 to 1988, and his grandfather Gus, nicknamed "Ding Dong" Bell by some members of the media long before ESPN began coming up with such monikers, donned the Cincinnati uniform from 1953 to 1961.

Mike also spoke about another oddity. "My grandpa, my dad, David, and I hit a home run in Milwaukee, in that ballpark," he said. "Right now it's hard to grasp it, but probably in ten, fifteen, twenty, twenty-five years, when I'm talking to my son or my grandson about it, it's probably really going to have sunk in by then."

What will have sunk in is the fact that when Mike hit his home run in Milwaukee as a Red, the Bells became the first family to have three different generations (of four total players) hit a home run in the same park. For the Bells, the site of their homers was County Stadium, where Gus hit seven shots, Buddy added six, David had two, and Mike tossed in one. Mike's major-league relatives had all also homered at Wrigley Field, but Mike has yet to connect there.

Although being the son (and grandson) of a big leaguer is truly noteworthy, Mike said that when he runs into other players who share a similar background they don't really discuss their situation. "I really haven't. I've had a lot of people ask me, but I've never talked to those guys [like Aaron Boone] about it. I like Aaron, I consider him a friend, but it's just something we never got into."

Because the Bells are a close-knit family, Mike is in touch with what David is doing with the Mariners. "I see what he's doing just about every night," he said. "I either hear from my dad or see it on ESPN, and my wife keeps me updated pretty good. We all know what each other's doing."

Mike said his grandfather was a big influence in his life. "He was great," he recalled. "I'd talk to him quite a bit during the season. He would put it all into perspective really easy. I'd call him and I'd be struggling, and he'd just kind of laugh, because he knows how it was. He remembers and, at the same time, he knows that I'll be fine—I'll come out of it."

"I remember he used to ask me if I was swinging hard. He'd tell me, 'You gotta swing hard, if you want to hit hard.' Just little, simple things—instead of worrying about all your mechanics, let it go. And I still remember that."

It's pretty obvious that Mike thinks highly of his family. He said that his feelings for his father are difficult to put into words, but he then proceeded to spell them out in fine form. "Before my son was born," he began, "I started thinking about a lot of that stuff, about my dad and how he was with us. It scared me a little bit, because if I could be anywhere close to how he was with us, I'll feel pretty good about what I've done. He's just so caring and sensitive. He's not just that way with us; he's that way with his players and people he meets. I love my dad, and it's great having him for a dad."

Mike finished his interview by politely asking about the exact nature of this book. He asked, "Did you talk to my brother? I know Dave would probably like to do that." He then asked for my phone number, saying he would try to set up an interview, "because we like to do this stuff. Any time we can do something to remember my dad and grandpa [it's like paying tribute to them]."

The next Bell to flirt with a shot at the majors was the youngest member of the family, Ricky. He is also a Moeller grad, a third-round pick by the Dodgers in the 1997 first-year player draft. His four-year minor-league totals, through 2000, show a .243 batting average and 390 base hits. In 2000, he enjoyed a thirteen-game hitting streak, and in 1998 he became the fourth-youngest player ever to play in the California League.

Mike said of his brother's chances: "If you're playing, everybody has a shot. He's still young, he's still maturing and getting stronger. He's in Double-A, so he's two steps away. It took me seven and a half years, something like that, so it works different for everybody. You just got to keep playing and see what happens."

Entering 2001, the Bells had played in a combined 4,756 big-league games, ranking ahead of such families as the three Alomars, the Bonds duo, and the Griffeys, while trailing only two other famous baseball families. The Alous stand first, with 6,174 from Felipe, Matty, Jesus, and Moises; and the Boones are next, with 5,006 from their quartet of players. The Bells are hoping Ricky can help them pad their own family stats someday.

When Buddy Bell was the manager of the Detroit Tigers he put on a play that, as shocking as it was, typified the sheer guts that he (and his family) has had through the years. In just his second game as the Tigers' skipper, he gave the steal sign to the lumbering Cecil Fielder. No manager had ever given Cecil that sign; it's amazing to think that Fielder, who weighed 250-plus pounds, even looked for and recognized the signal. Further, it worked! What's more, Bell had the ursine Fielder steal yet another base later that year.

One managerial moment that was also special for Buddy, but at the same time was extremely upsetting emotionally, took place on May 25, 1998. It was then that Buddy, as the Tigers' manager, faced the Cleveland Indians, who featured a second baseman named David Bell.

That contest marked only the third time in the annals of major-league baseball that a father managed against his son's team. The other two occurrences took place in 1980, when Maury Wills of the Seattle Mariners went up against his son, Bump, of the Texas Rangers, and later when Felipe Alou managed the Montreal Expos against his son, Moises, who was with the Florida Marlins and later with the Houston Astros. At the time of the Bell confrontation there had been twenty-five games in which a father managed against his son, and the son's teams had won seventeen of those contests.

On the morning of the game, David went by the Tigers' hotel in Cleveland, picked up his dad, and drove him to the ballpark. "We were both a little uncomfortable about this day," David recalled. "We talked about everything but that. I'd been trying not to think about it because I didn't know how I would react. The big thing is we were looking forward to seeing each other. When we got here this morning, he said it was weird going to separate clubhouses."

Not only did the Indians win but David was instrumental in the victory. He had two hits, including a two-run double in the sixth inning that snapped a 2–2 tie game. Tigers outfielder Brian Hunter joked of the key hit, "That's Buddy's fault. He taught him too good."

Earlier that day Buddy had spoken of how he had done his homework before the Cleveland series and how peculiar it was when he read a scouting report on his son. When he was asked just how he would have his pitchers go after his son, Buddy said, "I know how to pitch [former Tiger and current Indian] Travis [Fryman] better than my own son."

David concurred. "He really hasn't seen me play a lot [in the majors]," he said.

Postgame comments abounded. Buddy, drained from the encounter, said, "I'm glad this one is out of the way. I had to fight myself early not to have any feelings about it." Meanwhile, David said of his feelings, "I'm so used to watching him on the baseball field, I found myself looking at him a lot. Hey, if your dad is in the other dugout, you're going to look at him."

David's teammates commented on how strange such a matchup was. Indians righty Charles Nagy said, "I have a tough time pitching with my dad in the stands, let alone in the other dugout."

One teammate, Billy Ripken, had a perspective that no one else had. Ripken, who had played under his father's leadership in Baltimore, said, "Basically, David wants to beat his dad, and Buddy wants to beat the Cleveland Indians. I would think if nobody was on base, deep down, Buddy would be pulling for David to get a hit. But with two men on, no way."

Recalling that crucial time at the plate, Buddy said of his mixed emotions, "The way I figured it, he is going to get another hit sometime in his career. It didn't necessarily have to be in that at bat."

The opposing manager, Mike Hargrove, chipped in: "I was talking to Buddy before the game, and he said, 'Grover, this is tough.' I would think a certain part of you has got to be thrilled that your son did well, but at the same time . . . I don't envy Buddy in that position."

It certainly was uncomfortable. And when a reporter mentioned that Buddy might eventually have to face his two other sons, he replied, "I hope the other two take their time. I don't want to have to do this too often."

Still, after Jacobs Field was empty and dark, Buddy and David tried to shake everything off and planned to go out for a late dinner. Would David, the victor, celebrate by picking up the tab? Buddy said, "I go back to being a father now. I'll probably pay."

As was the case with the Boone family, people who have been associated with the Bells are generous in their compliments.

In 2000, David's manager with the Seattle Mariners, Lou Piniella, said of his third baseman, "He is a good man. He's a hard worker, he's got a good attitude, and he's got determination. He's also got some pretty good skills." Piniella likes David's versatility as well, saying that while he plays second and third, he can also play first base and could even "play shortstop some." Perhaps above all else, he said, "We've enjoyed having him the last couple of years."

Piniella also knew Buddy and said, "He's a good man, too. He played hard—he was a solid player who played to win. I see a lot of the same traits in young David that I saw in his dad." And that's pretty high testimonial for any player, since Buddy was, by all accounts, a classy ballplayer who knew how the game was played.

David's contemporaries think highly of him, too. All-Star first baseman John Olerud said, "I really like David. He's quiet, he works hard, and has a very businesslike approach, but at the same time, I like his personality. He's got a great sense of humor, so he's a fun guy to be around."

Meanwhile, Orioles coach Elrod Hendricks said, "I played against Buddy. Buddy never says an awful lot, but he's serious about baseball. As a player, I remember him playing [with Cleveland] and moving from the infield to the outfield." He played hard at the position where he spent most of his career—third base—where he became, according to Hendricks "an excellent third baseman." Further, Hendricks remembers him diving over the outfield wall at Cleveland Municipal Stadium after balls.

Hendricks's take on David was to the point: "He's rather intense when he's out there playing; he's very serious out there on the field, and very short-tempered also." He said that Buddy, an equally intense player, was capable of having a short fuse at times. "Buddy was [short-tempered], trust me," he said. "Oh, yes. It was a little quiet demeanor he had, but he could get as upset and angry as anyone I've seen."

Despite pointing out such similarities, Hendricks felt that, as a rule, the children of big leaguers are often different from their fathers. "I'd say they're all [somewhat] different, probably because they grew up in a major-league atmosphere; they grew up in the clubhouse, and as kids they could run around, have free range around the clubhouse and the field. And it never changed once they became professionals, even though their dads may have been a little bit more reserved. I know watching Buddy and his dad, they *were* a lot alike, but the kids are different."

It is noteworthy that the famous Bell and Boone families have much in common. Bob Boone observed, "Our families parallel each other. Three generations—Buddy and I were employed by Cincinnati at the same time, he managed Detroit when I was managing Kansas City, so we have a lot of similarities. And the kids played together. Mike played with Aaron in [Cincinnati]. David, of course, is playing with Bret right now. And Ricky was drafted the same year Matthew was."

Bob said that he and Buddy don't dwell on the similarities between their families. "We talk about the kids and their playing, but it's just the way we live, it's nothing unusual for us." He agreed that it's more of a big deal to the media and the fans than it is to them.

The Bells truly seem to be universally respected. Art Kusnyer, who was coaching with the Chicago White Sox in 2000, said that he played with or against, or knew many of the father-son duos in baseball, including the Alomars, the Bells, and the Boones. "All the kids seem to be like their dads [in how they played the game]—smart, good people, and they come to beat your butt every day when they come to the ballpark."

Major-league coach Ted Uhlaender, who was very concise, said quite simply and accurately of Buddy, "He's a class guy."

Clyde Wright, who once threw a no-hitter and is the father of Cleveland Indians pitcher Jaret Wright, observed that there seems to be more and more sons of baseball dads on the scene of late. "There weren't that many when I played," he said.

However, Wright did recall Buddy Bell. "Buddy was a good third baseman," he said. "He looked like he was [always] even-tempered. He was just a good, decent baseball player and a good, decent human being."

Tom Grieve, once the Texas Rangers' general manager and the father of Tampa Bay Devil Rays outfielder Ben Grieve, commented, "Buddy's kids are about the same age as my kids—he's got more of them than I do, but his oldest son, David, who plays in the big leagues for Seattle, played against my son Tim in the Arlington West Little League, and his son Michael played *with* Ben on a ten-year-old Little League All-Star team in Arlington. So they have very similar experiences.

"I had a long conversation with Buddy's wife, Gloria, in Colorado last year after a ball game. She was asking me how my kids were doing, and I was doing the same. At the time, Tim had stopped playing professional ball and was a scout, so I only had Ben playing professional baseball. I was talking about how nerve-racking it is, and then I started to hear her talking how nerve-racking it was for her because she had three kids playing: David, in the big leagues; Michael, I believe at the time, was in Triple-A with Cincinnati; and Ricky was in 'A' ball with the Dodgers.

"So she's trying on the Internet, and every way she can, to follow all three kids on a daily basis and, at the same time, take care of a family and a husband who's a big-league manager. I knew how nerve-racking that could be," Grieve said with a strong dose of empathy. "Talking to Gloria, I saw the same things running through her mind go through my mind.

"I think Buddy was probably a lot like I was. Watching him with his kids—Buddy, as a matter of fact, was a player with the Rangers when I was a farm director and a general manager, and I used to watch him pitching balls to his kids and saw how positive and supportive he was with his kids."

Former big leaguer Tito Francona said that his son Terry "and Buddy Bell are very close. They became close friends when Terry was with Buddy at Cincinnati." He was glad that Terry had picked such a good friend, as he considers the Bells to be "a very good family." The baseball world agrees.

Chapter Four: The Hairstons

Jerry Hairston Jr. is not only the son of a former player but also the grandson of a man who played professional baseball for the Cincinnati and Indianapolis franchises of the Negro American League from 1945 to 1949 and who later made it into Major League Baseball as a catcher with the Chicago White Sox in 1951. Jerry's father was an outfielder whose big-league career was the longest of any Hairston family member thus far.

Jerry Jr. had two uncles who played pro ball, and one of them, John, made it to the majors as a catcher/outfielder with the Chicago Cubs. The other uncle, Sam Hairston Jr., was a minor leaguer in the Chicago White Sox organization.

Jerry Jr. is a 5'10", 175-pound infielder (he has played second and shortstop in the minors) who was selected by the Baltimore Orioles organization in the eleventh round of the free-agent draft in June of 1997. He broke into the majors by 1998 for a cup of coffee. The 1999 season found him at the Triple-A level and in the majors, where on three occasions he enjoyed four-hit games with the O's. During his fifty games with Baltimore he handled 269 total chances without one miscue, and he is well known for his great range on defense. In fact, the 2001 survey conducted by *Baseball America* to select the best players based on various skills ranked Jerry Jr. the third-best defensive second baseman in the American League.

In 2000, once more he split time between the minors and the majors. He started the 2000 season on Baltimore's roster but did not play in any games before being optioned back to "AAA" Rochester. When he got the call back up to the bigs in August, Jerry Jr. homered in his first major-league at bat of the season. In Rochester he was named the International League's best defensive second baseman by *Baseball America* for the second year in a row, and by 2001 he had won the starting job as the Orioles' second baseman.

A lifetime .303 hitter over 365 games in the minors, Jerry Jr. was on the all–Chicago area team in basketball and became a two-time All-State selection in baseball. He then attended Southern Illinois University and was named Missouri Valley Conference Freshman of the Year while also earning All-Conference honors.

Since Jerry Hairston Jr. comes from such a long line of athletes, it wasn't a shock to hear Mike Hargrove, who took over the Baltimore Orioles' managing position at the start of the 2001 season, refer to him as the best all-around athlete on his team.

Like many offspring of baseball players, Jerry Hairston Jr. grew up in several locales. "I grew up some in Texas, but mostly in the Chicago area, in a city called Naperville, Illinois," he said. His birthplace is listed as Des Moines, Iowa, and he says his immediate family "lives in Arizona now, in Tuscon."

No matter where he was, though, baseball definitely helped him bond with his father, he said. "You know the father-son bond is strong; it should be, anyway, but when you have a special, common interest, like we do with baseball, it really kind of solidifies that bond, so to speak. Especially with fathers who have played themselves, because they know what we're going through now—they've been there, and you go [to him] for advice. You talk and that really helps the father, and it helps the son as well. It really strengthens that bond.

"It's one of those things where I watched my dad grow up being around the game," he continued. "That was a big plus for me. You get to experience what big-league life is. You appreciate it, but at the same time when you're doing it yourself, you kind of appreciate it more. You realize it's really difficult. It's not easy to get up here, and you have a new appreciation for the game."

When his father played for the Sox at the original Comiskey Park, Jerry Jr. would tag along. He remembers the grounds crew letting the players' kids play twenty-minute games on the field after White Sox victories.

"K. C. Fisk [Carlton's son], Ryan Luzinski [Greg's son], all of us being around the game—we used to have our own little game after [their fathers' game]," he said. "It was one of those things where it helped us. One day I said, 'I'm going to be playing in this park.' Obviously, I couldn't play in the old Comiskey Park, but playing here [as a visitor in the new Comiskey Park] is just as good."

Although Jerry Jr. had the opportunity to collect tons of baseball memorabilia, he said, "I never was an autograph seeker. It was more like [the players] were my father's teammates—you had respect for them that they were major leaguers, but at the same time you saw them as just people because that's what we are. We're just normal people that play a game and have fun with what we do."

His baseball background left him with many figurative bits of memorabilia, and while he said there was no single moment or memory that stood out, he loved going to the park with his dad. "He'd come to the ballpark early, and he'd take me along and I'd get a chance to hit on various fields—whether it was in Boston, Milwaukee," he recalled. "I really did get a kick out of it. I remember hitting batting practice in Boston when I was, like, 10, 11 years old. That's a pretty good feeling."

Digging deeply, Jerry Jr. came up with his earliest childhood memory of his father and baseball. "When my dad was in Mexico playing in winter ball—I was probably about 2 or 3—I had this cute little uniform. I remember picking up the ball and throwing it. I was playing catch with one of my dad's teammates. He was throwing the ball high, and I was catching everything; he couldn't believe it. Finally, he threw one *real* high and it hit me in the head."

He credits both his father and his grandfather with starting him on the path that quickly led to a love of baseball. "It started from as far back as I can remember," he said. "I was around the ballpark [because] I just wanted to be around my dad. And being here, what better way to spend time with your dad than at the ballpark?"

Having a father like Jerry Hairston Sr. was a benefit, too, in that much of his father rubbed off on Jerry Jr. He analyzed points of comparison and contrast between his father and himself. "Probably, the only similarities we have are how we go about our business," he said. "I think our work ethic [is the same]. We aren't the biggest guys, so we always had to work harder. I always saw him work hard. He always was in there getting extra hitting; always in there making sure he was ready to play.

"You always want to make sure you're ready to play. You're not going to play well sometimes, but at least you know you prepared yourself. I'm very much like that. That's the only way I know how to approach this game.

"We play hard and we play aggressive, but I'm a little bit of a different player than he was. He was an outfielder and a D.H., and I play second base, so our defense is slightly different. I'm an infielder. I hope I'm a little better defensively. I've got more speed. I'm more versatile. He was more known for his bat—the way he could hit. I'm trying to get to the point where he was. He was a great pinch hitter later on in his career. Hopefully, I can develop into a hitter like him. He was an incredible hitter, and I'm just trying to get better and one day be as good a hitter as he was."

Perhaps Jerry Jr. was being overly modest. His father was a career .258 hitter who once hit as high as .294. However, he did excel as a pinch hitter. For four successive seasons from 1982 to 1985 he led the American League in pinch at bats, and during the final three years of that skein he also topped the league in pinch hits, with 17, 18, and 14. His lifetime average as a pinch hitter—a difficult task, to be sure—was .260 (three points better than his average as a non-pinch hitter). Over a three-year period he hit .291 as a pinch hitter. Then, in 1984, he hit .305 in the role of a pinch hitter and nearly matched that in 1986 (with a .304 mark).

Longtime major-league coach Tom Trebelhorn said of Jerry Hairston Sr., "We used to have trouble getting him out, that's for sure. Jerry was a good left-handed pinch hitter and got a lot of big hits.

"I think that athletically Jerry Jr. is more gifted than his dad. Junior is very gifted—speed, bounce, spring in his legs, agility. His athleticism is excellent, but I think growing up in the game certainly helped his career."

At any rate, Jerry Hairston Jr. also noted that a father who has played the game can even relate to baseball's negatives. "They know what it's about—everybody's gone through slumps and they know how hard it is," he said. "My dad gives me a call every now and then, and I give him a call. Sometimes you've got to learn by yourself, but other times you have to go and get Dad's advice."

He could have thrown other family members into the equation. "My grandfather, Sam, played many years in the Negro Leagues, and he was the first black player to play for the Chicago White Sox," Jerry Jr. said. "He was with the White Sox organization for over forty-five years as a player, coach, and scout. My uncle, John, played briefly for the Chicago Cubs until a knee injury. He and my father were the first blacks that had two generations in the major leagues. My father played twenty years professionally, fourteen years in the big leagues [almost exclusively] with the Chicago White Sox [but a little bit with the Pittsburgh Pirates]." In truth, of Jerry Sr.'s 859 contests played, he wore the Sox uniform in all but fifty-one of those games.

For the record, Minnie Minoso signed with the White Sox two weeks before Jerry Hairston Sr. did to break their color barrier, but he is officially listed as being Cuban-born.

Jerry Jr. said that he can remember his grandfather. "I knew him very well. He was great to be around. He knew so much about life in general. He was the oldest of, I think, fourteen or fifteen kids, and we were very close at the time of his death. He died in '97."

Jerry Jr.'s grandfather shared stories with him, such as the time he caught Satchel Paige in an All-Star game and the times he played with such stars of the Negro Leagues as Josh Gibson and Jackie Robinson. "Actually," said Jerry Jr. of his grandfather, "he was a veteran when Hank Aaron was coming up in the Negro Leagues. Willie Mays was a rookie when he was on the Birmingham Black Barons. He got a chance to play with those guys."

While the Hairstons were years ahead of, say, the Griffeys, as a two-generation family, few people are aware of that fact. And, as thoroughly as the game is covered today, with minutiae abounding, it is incredible that few people know that this family has joined the Bells and the Boones as baseball's only three-generation families. Even though Sam and John played in the majors for only one year, the Hairston family baseball tradition is, in many ways, as rich as that of the other illustrious families.

Longtime Oriole Elrod Hendricks has a theory concerning this lack of recognition. "I knew his [Jerry Jr.'s] dad and his granddad," he said. "He hasn't established himself as yet; those other guys [Boones and Bells] have. For example, the Boones were well documented before they even got to the big leagues, but Hairston will make a name for himself soon. He's a pretty good-looking young player, and he's going to get better."

In 2001, Jerry Jr.'s manager, Mike Hargrove, echoed some of Hendricks's thoughts. "I knew Jerry's dad; they're very dissimilar players," he recalled. "I played against his dad—a very good hitter, ran well, maybe a little more stocky than Jerry is. I never quite made that [three-generation] connection with them, as opposed to the Ripken connection or the Bells— what a great family that is, fantastic." He attributes the lack of recognition where the Hairstons are concerned to "just a matter of people not publicizing it, that's all."

Hendricks continued the Hairstons' comparison, saying, "Dad was more on the quiet side, rather shy, and the grandfather was basically the same way—he didn't say much. Jerry, on the other hand, is a little bit more outgoing.

"The grandfather was a catcher and Jerry's father was a catcher-slash-utility player, but mainly a pinch hitter. Defensively, I would say the son is much better than his dad." He said that the young Jerry is good both defensively and offensively.

Joe Nossek then picked up the commentary: "I was coaching with Chicago when Jerry was pinch-hitting for us, and [serving as] a part-time player. I haven't met his son, but he played against us [in 2000] and did well against us—seemed to enjoy playing against us to prove a point, I guess by asking, more or less, why didn't we sign him? Which is a good question; we let him get away."

Nossek also pointed out that the Hairstons had a connection with Chicago that goes back to the grandfather, Sam, who "was a player in the old Negro Leagues, then played briefly with the White Sox and then spent the rest of his life in the White Sox organization, and he was a good friend who I knew well over the years. He'd help us in spring training every year, the big club. Then we'd go out and help the Double-A team where he lived. He passed away a couple years ago.

"Jerry's dad was also a White Sox guy, as was Jerry, and it seemed to kind of follow that Jerry's son would also go with the White Sox." Instead, he signed with the Orioles, where he wound up playing well against them, rather than for them.

"I think Jerry, the dad, was another class act that I had the privilege of being around, and one of the best pinch hitters that I've ever been associated with coming off the bench.

"And Jerry Jr. looks like he's got a chance to put some time in, in the big leagues. How big he's going to be would be tough to say now. I'd say he compliments a team real well. I'd hesitate to put a star tag on him, but he's a fine ballplayer and great competitor, like his dad was."

Unlike Hendricks, Jerry Jr. says he can't really explain why his family has been overlooked. "A few generations is a lifetime—it's a long time so maybe it gets lost in the shuffle a little bit, but that's O.K.," he said. "We're proud of it as well as the Bells and Boones are. We're a proud family."

Interestingly, his grandfather not only played ball but also indulged in a moment of prophecy. "My grandfather said when I was 2 years old that we'd be the first black three-generation family, and I guess he was right," Jerry Jr. said.

Often, intense familial pride is accompanied by pressure—the pressure to live up to the family name. However, Jerry Jr. commented, "I don't think it's too much pressure. I've always been around the ballpark; it's something I've always wanted to do. My father said that the first word out of my mouth was 'ball.'

"My parents never forced me to play this game. I had to make my dad—force him—to put me on a Little League team. He really wanted to make sure that this was what I wanted to do. He always supported me; he was always there, especially at an early age. He never suggested anything to me about the game. He was there to answer any questions, but as I got older, and he could see I really wanted to pursue this, he was always there for suggestions and to help me out."

Like his grandfather, Jerry Jr.'s father was also somewhat prophetic—actually, more accurately, he merely had an eye for talent. He knew early on that his son was very talented. Jerry Jr. said his father foresaw a future in the majors. "The one thing he did say was he knew it at a young age for me," he recalled. "I was always able to hit the baseball, and I always had that love for the game. That's something you need first. Besides working hard and playing well, you have to have that love for the game. There are going to be times when you're not going to play well, you're going to have some tough periods in this game, but that love for the game keeps you coming back and keeps you going."

While some sons who are exposed to baseball at an early age may, in fact, get fed up with the game, Jerry Jr. says he hasn't seen that. In fact, the articulate Oriole said that his experience has been that early exposure is great. "I never heard of it [a son rebelling against the game]. I've never run into anybody like that," he said. "I know Cal [Ripken Jr.] here [in Baltimore]. He's come from a baseball family and he brings his son, Ryan, to the clubhouse. That's good for him, and he loves the game. It's just something that, as a young boy, you want to do what your father does. You follow him—whether it's mowing the lawn or painting the house or what have you. It just happened to be that my father was a baseball player, and I loved it."

So it was hardly surprising that Jerry Jr. was baseball's equivalent of basketball's "gym rat," a term that sounds negative but has positive connotations. Youngsters like Ben Grieve, his brother Tim, the Alomars, and a slew of others delighted in "hanging around" the clubhouse, the dugout, and the field.

"I was always around the ballpark," Jerry Jr. recalled. "I always hung around with Harold Baines—it's kind of ironic that I played with him [in the majors], and I used to hang around with him all the time when he was a young player and I was a really young kid. He was my favorite player." He added that when Baines was with the Orioles and it became known that he had been playing so long that he had known Jerry Jr. as a kid, "a lot of the guys in here [the clubhouse] used to get on him."

Interestingly, just before the All-Star break in 2001, there was only one Baltimore player who had appeared in every one of his team's games—and it wasn't "Iron Man" Cal Ripken Jr. It was Jerry Hairston Jr., a man who, according to the writer Brad Engel, of the Naperville newspaper *The Sun,* was showing "his durability, defensive solidity and energetic approach to the game."

Hargrove seems to agree with Engel. "Jerry comes to play. He got that from his father," he said. "Jerry's intelligent and a hard worker, and he'll get things squared away. Jerry, offensively, will get himself into good hitting counts and then swing at a bad pitch, which happens to a lot of young players. And the older players do it, too.

"Kids that grow up in the game," Hargrove continued, "know how to respect the game. I think that's probably what they learn from their fathers."

Jerry Jr. is polite and soft-spoken, yet intense on the field. He has also shown signs of humility off the field. He told *Sports Illustrated* of his being baptized a Jehovah's Witness in July of 2000, and of how he now goes door to door in Baltimore to speak of his faith with as much anonymity as he can maintain.

When observers said he was being a bit ostentatious after he slammed his bat on the ground after popping up during an at bat versus Roger Clemens, Jerry Jr., demonstrating the form and understanding Hargrove spoke of, replied, "I meant no disrespect to Roger." He said he was merely upset with himself and, because he's a passionate person his emotions burst through. Hargrove said that he had no problem with the incident, as Jerry Jr. is indeed a fiery player who "plays to win."

Hargrove continued his Hairston synopsis. "Jerry's a very talented player," he said. "He's a nice guy—typical young kid, though. He has a tendency to get a little full of himself at times, but I think we all do that. But you can tell that Jerry has been around the game and talked the game."

It seems safe to predict that the future for Jerry Hairston Jr. will be at least as luminous as it was for his father when he was a young big leaguer, if not a whole lot brighter.

Chapter Five: The Griffeys

Ken Griffey Jr. was the first overall pick (out of 1,263 players) in baseball's June 1987 free-agent draft. His father was a fine player himself, but to illustrate the contrast between the two Griffeys, the elder Griffey noted, "When I got drafted I was the last one drafted by the Reds, period." Needless to say, his slarary back then wasn't much, while his son got a signing bonus alone of $160,000. Despite such differences, both men gained considerable fame.

In fact, Junior's spiral toward greatness began with his being the No. 1 pick and has been a rapid and virtually nonstop ascent to stardom. He is one of the most highly recognizable people in the game. He's even appeared on television shows such as *The Fresh Prince of Bel-Air,* and he made his big-screen debut in *Little Big League.* Barely in the majors for a year, he had a candy bar named after him (despite being allergic to chocolate).

This is a man who began his pro career at the age of 17 and won his first Gold Glove in the majors just two years later, becoming the second-youngest man ever to win that award. When he made his first out in Little League, he cried so hard they took him out of the game. Only about a half-dozen years later, he was playing ball professionally.

Many fans are aware of the accomplishments of this charismatic figure, but even some of his obscure statistics are simply staggering. For example, for his first ten years in the majors he hit more home runs than any hitter in the history of baseball (for a ten-year period), with the exception of Eddie Mathews and Ralph Kiner. Further, only fifteen men managed to drive in more runs than he did over his first ten seasons. Griffey averaged 35 home runs and 101.8 runs driven in during those years. As of the end of the 2000 season, sixteen men had averaged at least one run batted in for every five trips to the plate; Griffey was one of those elite sixteen. And, over his last ten years played entering 2001, his 400 homers were the most by anyone in the game.

He was the youngest player to reach the 350, 400, and 450 home-run plateaus. He got to No. 450 in 2001 at the age of 31 years and 261 days, some fifteen days younger than the previous best of Jimmie Foxx. Griffey's 438 homers entering 2001 ranked him twenty-fifth on the all-time list, and he is one of just four men to hit 40 homers in five straight seasons. Plus, only three men have driven in 140 runners for three straight seasons: Babe Ruth, Lou Gehrig, and Junior. Two of the most prodigious single-season home-run totals belong to him as well. In all, he has 1,270 RBI.

A famous feat took place in 1993, when Ken Jr. hit a home run in eight straight contests to tie an astonishing major-league record. That torrid stretch caused one American League manager to mutter, "He's so hot he could hit a home run off Superman."

Other honors include being the youngest member of Major League Baseball's All-Century Team and being named the Player of the Decade for the 1990s. He won the 1997 MVP Award unanimously. Three times he's won the All-Star game's home-run contest, and in 1994 he received an all-time high of more than six million votes for the All-Star balloting.

A 1999 survey with an illustrious panel of men such as Tom Lasorda, Tony Gwynn, Larry Bowa, and Jack McKeon picked Ken Griffey Jr. as the best defensive center fielder of the last twenty-five years. While they admired others, like Garry Maddux, Paul Blair, and Andruw Jones, Griffey got the nod. Through 2000, he owned ten Gold Gloves and is also a member of the Gold Glove Award All-Time team.

In May of 2001 Ken Jr., already the father of a 7-year-old son, Trey Kenneth (Kenneth is the actual middle name of his father and grandfather, whose real first names are George), and a 5-year-old daughter, Taryn, announced that he and his wife, Melissa, were considering adopting a child. Although the adoption process fell through on that occasion, he said he was leaving future attempts up to his wife, who had herself been adopted. Their love of children apparent, fans couldn't help wondering if yet another male Griffey would someday appear on a diamond.

Although Junior's statistics and accomplishments outshine his father's, Ken Sr. had a stellar major-league career. It's just that playing in the Reds' star-studded lineups of the 1970s, and not being overly demonstrative, the senior Griffey didn't stand out. Nevertheless, his list of highlights isn't shabby at all.

In 1980 he led the National League to a 4–2 win in the All-Star Game with a key, two-out home run. For his efforts he won the MVP of the mid-summer showcase. Incidentally, his son also won an All-Star Game MVP, and, coincidentally, both their trophies were won for contests held in San Diego. The fact that they both homered in those games didn't hurt their MVP chances at all. That not only made them the first father-son duo to homer in the All-Star Game but also the only ones to cop the MVP in All-Star play. Senior was a .750 hitter as a three-time All-Star. His son, for the record, hit .435 over 23 All-Star at bats through 2000.

Meanwhile, Ken Sr., drafted in 1969, had seven seasons in which he topped the coveted .300 plateau (not counting his initial season, with his .384 in 86 trips to the plate), including a personal high of .336 in 1976. That was the season he nearly copped the batting crown, finishing second in a photo finish to Bill Madlock, who hit .339 in a race that went down to the very last game of the season. In both the 1975 (.305 with 95 runs scored) and 1976 seasons, his Reds won the World Series. No National League team had captured back-to-back titles in more than a half century prior to the Reds. They also won six division titles during the decade of the 1970s.

When Junior was still a relative newcomer to the league, Sparky Anderson, manger of the "Big Red Machine" said that Ken Jr. would have a long way to go to match what his father had done. He praised Ken Sr. as a fine, underrated player.

In nineteen seasons—more than 2,097 contests—Ken Sr. sported a career batting average of .296. (Oddly, that was exactly the same average his son had through the 2000 season.) Meanwhile, his League Championship Series average stood at a lofty .313. In the 1975 World Series, the gem against the Red Sox, he hit .333. His lifetime homerun total stands at 152, he drove in 859 runs, and scored 1,129 times. Stolen bases were rather plentiful (200 career), and his hit total was 2,143. Make no mistake, this was one fine baseball player.

Even toward the end of his career, Ken Sr. hit well. In 1987, with the Atlanta Braves, he was a .611 hitter in the role of pinch hitter (11 of 18). In all, he was with the Reds, Yankees, Braves, back to the Reds, then on to the Mariners.

In 1990, when he signed on with the M's on August 29, he joined his son with the team. Then, two days later, he and Ken Jr. made history by becoming the first father and son ever to start a major-league game. A more dramatic father-son moment came on September 14 that season, when both he and his son connected for back-to-back home runs off Angels pitcher Kirk McCaskill, yet another big-league first. When Ken Sr. finally called it quits, he had homered against every big-league team with the sole exception of the Cleveland Indians.

A gifted athlete from his youth, in high school he not only lettered in four sports but excelled in each. Ken Jr. played baseball for four years and football for three years at Cincinnati Moeller.

Ken Sr. entered the 2001 campaign, his fifth as a Reds coach, assuming the duties of the team's hitting coach after also spending time as their first-base and bench coaches. Earlier, he had also coached for the Mariners and the Colorado Rockies. After he retired in 1991, he even spent some time as a television analyst with the Mariners, where he was sometimes called upon to critique his own son, then in his third year in the majors. That season he must have had lots of show-stopping moments to observe, as Ken Jr. drove in 100 runners for the first time and hit his career high of .327. The former right fielder for the Big Red Machine has even managed in two winter leagues.

Ken Sr. and his wife, Alberta, have another son, Craig, who spent some time in the Seattle Mariners organization, and a daughter, Lathesia, born in 1972. Ken Jr. was the firstborn in 1969, while Craig came along two years later. Both Ken Sr. and Ken Jr. now reside in Orlando, Florida.

Ken Sr. and his son have combined for more home runs (590 entering 2001) than any father-son twosome other than Bobby and Barry Bonds. They stand ahead of the Perez family (416), and the Bells and the Berras (tied at 407).

On May 21, 1993, the Mariners played the Kansas City Royals in a "turn back the clock" day. Players dressed in team uniforms from bygone days. As a tribute to his father, Ken Jr. wore jersey No. 30, the one Ken Sr. had worn for years with the Reds.

It seems clear that one reason the Griffeys are so close is that Ken Sr. and his father weren't. In fact, he barely knew his own father, Buddy, who had left the family—his wife, Ruth, and six children in all, and had been a baseball teammate of Stan Musial's in Donora.

If someone is really interested in what it's like to be the son of a big-league baseball player, he might head directly to Ken Griffey Jr. After all, he has witnessed the major-league level for several decades already *and* from several unique perspectives.

While he did hang around the Cincinnati Reds' clubhouse as a child, he dispelled a long-standing media myth. For years it's been said that he virtually grew up inside the locker room, running around on his father's turf while learning the game from such members of the illustrious Big Red Machine as Pete Rose, Johnny Bench, and Joe Morgan. In addition, he was said to have gained more insight by absorbing the words of wisdom from his dad.

Not totally true, says Junior. "No, he just told me to go out and play, and I wasn't in the clubhouse that much. Very seldom was I in the locker room." His father verified that. "He wasn't there that much," Ken Sr. said. "He wasn't allowed in the locker room; he wasn't allowed on the field. People always take it for granted, but Kenny was not allowed on the field at any time except for when we played the father-and-son games, and that was it.

"Other than that, he wasn't in the cages; he wasn't taking batting practice—all that stuff we did, we did at home when I had the opportunity to go outside and throw him batting practice in the backyard or catch with him. Those kind of things happened at home, not at the ballpark."

He conceded that his son was in the locker room on some occasions. "He was in the clubhouse when we won," he said. "The biggest thing about him being in the clubhouse and everybody seeing him there all the time was that after games if we won, the kids could come into the locker room. That was mostly when they'd seen him, because we won a lot. Between 1973 and 1981, in Cincinnati's uniform, we won a lot. But everyone always thought he was there [before games and virtually all the time]. He came to the ballpark when his mother came."

Still, Ken Jr.'s father and the game of baseball were, of course, major influences on the boy who, even as a grown-up, would carry a youthful moniker, "the Kid." Years after his infrequent days in the clubhouse, he still recalls some words of wisdom that his father gave him. "My father always told us, 'Don't be anybody else. Just be yourself.' " Because of that, he said, he never really had a baseball hero. When, for example, he collected baseball cards as a child, he did so with one purpose—to simply have fun with them. "We just bought the cards for the gum and to play a little flip game into a hat." Perhaps his father's words about being himself helped him emerge as a star, instead of being overwhelmed by the shadow of his famous father.

Ken Sr. said that he certainly did not push his son into the world of baseball. "When he was growing up he played football, basketball, he ran a little track, so I didn't really push him into baseball—that's all he'd seen me play. He didn't know I was an All-State football player. He didn't know I was an All-Section basketball player. So he had no idea until he read the 1968, 1969 yearbook. That's when he found out that I played all the sports, but he just knew I was a baseball player because that's all he knew me as, as a professional baseball player."

"He was probably about 15, 16 years old when I started trying to teach them how to play basketball and a little bit of football, and they looked at me like, 'You don't know anything about basketball and football.' That's when I told the youngest one, 'If you want to find out, just look at the yearbook, and you tell me if I don't know anything about high-school basketball and high-school football. And he did, and he came back, and he was a little surprised that I had set all kinds of records."

His son's love of baseball, Ken Sr. went on to say, "was always that way. He picked up a ball when he was able to pick up a ball and start throwing it. When he got older, Craig, my youngest son was there, and they always picked up a ball and threw it. He's always had a ball around him. I didn't start to really develop things about the game until he got to be around 9 or 10."

When did Ken Sr. recognize skills in his son that would allow him to shoot beyond his own records in baseball? Ken Sr. asserted, "I knew he was that good when he was 12 and 13. That's when I went to New York [the Yankees], and he used to get himself in trouble because he was doing a lot of stuff. And when he got in trouble they sent him to me for the weekends. That's when he really started developing, because I was able to take him in the cages, teach him a lot of stuff about hitting, about catching, and those kinds of things. But that was just for weekends."

If Junior seems to have a mischievous smile on his face from time to time now, it probably goes back to the time his father referred to, when he got in trouble. "Which was all the time," Ken Sr. said, smiling. "Every weekend I had him, just about. He just stayed in trouble; he didn't get in real bad trouble. He was a mischievous kid. He did a lot of stuff to his grandmothers, but he wasn't a bad kid."

Ken Sr. said back then he knew his son had talent because of his quick hands and "how well he handles the glove, batting—when he got about 14, I couldn't strike him out, and I never told him what I was throwing. We went to batting practice and we took it just like he was in a game. It was always game scenarios that we went through, and I never told him that I was going to throw him a curveball, change–up, slider, whatever. As he got better and better by recognizing pitches, by the age of 14 I knew that he could handle himself pretty good."

It had to have helped Junior, too, that his father was going lefty-on-lefty with him. Many young left-handed hitters have a difficult time solving the riddle of left-handed pitching, but not Junior. His dad said, "It was straight up [left-handed pitching]. That's all he saw, so that's why left-handers really don't give him that many problems. He saw me throwing to him left-handed, and I was throwing breaking balls and everything else. At that time, I could throw pretty good."

Junior's ability against left-handed pitchers has been nothing short of amazing. In the history of the game, a left-handed hitter has homered off lefties 20 or more times in a season only a handful of times. Ken Jr. has done this twice and is tied with Stan Musial, with 21 for the most ever in a season. Musial did that once; Junior did it in 1996 and again in 1998.

"As he got older, he started to develop his own tools in terms of playing high-school ball and Legion ball," Ken Sr. said. "Midland was one of the better clubs that he played for. It was a traveling squad for 14–15-year-olds and 16–17-year-olds, and they traveled all over the country. He was on the 16–17-year-old team when he was 13 and 14. That's when he really developed, but mostly when I had him in New York during the summers."

Moving to New York and the Yankees from the Reds was a difficult decision for the Griffeys; they decided to let the children continue their schooling in the Cincinnati area, with Alberta staying there, too. Ken Sr. was used to being around his children from his minor-league days on, but ultimately the switch to the Yankees was one he felt he had to make. At the end of each month, it wasn't unusual for Alberta to peel open the phone bill, gaze at the bottom line, and see a figure of $500 or more.

When Ken Jr. was playing amateur ball, his father got to see him from time to time. "To be honest, he couldn't get a hit in front of us for six years," Ken Sr. said. "From age 12 till he was 17 years old, he didn't get a hit in front of me in about 30 or 40 at bats. He struck out more than half [the time]; he was pressing, especially when he got older, between the ages of 15 to 17, right before he got drafted. Every time I had an opportunity to see him play, he wouldn't even make contact.

"Finally, I had to tell him, 'You show off in front of your grandmothers and your mother.' It was after his first pro season, in the Instructional

League, and he was in Arizona. Birdie [his wife's nickname] and I drove out there to watch him, and I told him, 'I'm going to park this RV out here. I'm going to sit behind this thing, and the only ones here are your mom and you and your grandmother, because you just seem to show off in front of them. So I'm not here.' He got a base hit. I said, 'Now, was it that hard?' He said, 'No.' After that he never stopped hitting."

Ken Sr.'s other son, Craig, was no slouch as an athlete, either. "Craig made it as far as Triple-A," his father said. "And, as a matter of fact, he was one, two days on the big-league roster. He made it to the big leagues; he was on the roster with the Mariners, and Kenny was there. This was at the beginning of the year. He made the team, but they didn't know what they wanted to do with him, so they had to take him with them [up with the big club as they broke camp]. Then they sent him back, and he was at Triple-A for a while. Then he was playing for five, six years in the minor leagues, and then he called it quits." One souvenir of the Griffey brothers' playing days was a baseball card a company put out featuring them together in their Mariners' uniforms.

"He was an outfielder," Ken Sr. went on. "His tools were a little different because he stopped playing at 8. He was a football player, period. He went to Ohio State two years, and they promised him a scholarship and didn't give it to him. He was a walk-on, and if he made the team as a defensive back, he would get a scholarship, but they found out who his dad was, so they kind of blew that out of the water and didn't give it to him."

Ken Jr.'s background of early excellence notwithstanding, one would expect, with the endless highlight films on him, that there would be moments when even Dad shook his head in bewilderment and said, "Man, I can't believe he made that catch!"

"Well, those are the things," Ken Sr. said. "All his catches are amazing. I mean, I knew he could run, but the biggest thing I was impressed about him was his jumps on balls—his knowledge of knowing where the ball is at before it comes down and getting to the fences quicker than anybody else to get up to make the play, like jumping on top of the fence.

"Just watching him at that young age at 17, 18, and 19—the first time I saw him play, he was up in Western Hills when he was playing against [their] high school, when he was still at Moeller. It was his junior year, I think, and a guy hit a ball to left-center field and all of a sudden he [Junior] just took off, and I just didn't know he had that type of defensive ability. I knew he could hit; I didn't worry about that, but the [defensive] ability and then the arm, which was another thing—when he caught the ball, he turned and fired and got a guy out at second—was totally different. He likes to play defense just as well as offense, and that's a big plus for him."

Ken Sr. said that one advantage his son had was that "he just had short-cuts, people don't understand that. He was taught what to look for. I didn't have anybody to teach me anything in terms of high school. Our high-school thing was, 'You're on your own.' I had Harry Haywood and Dave Munoz and those [non-high-school coaches] guys that were teaching me, but in high school I had Mr. Gidick, who was just an art teacher.

"When I got to the minor leagues it was the same scenario; I didn't have anybody to teach me outfield play or anything like that. I had to learn it all. And learn how to hit; I had to do that all on my own.

"He [Ken Jr.] at least had somebody there who knows exactly what to look for. When he got [to be] 17, I had eight, nine years in the big leagues, so his experience was what I was teaching—the experience I learned. So he had shortcuts in terms of understanding exactly what to look for, in terms of at the plate, what to look for, what the pitcher is doing so he can watch the catcher move in and out and he has an idea what the pitch is going to be, de-fensive prowess—those things you can teach him, and that was the biggest [advantage]."

Ken Sr. may not have had shortcuts, but he had some good luck that saved his life shortly after he was drafted by the Reds. "Everyone thought I was going to play football," he said. "If I went to play football, I'd have gone down in that plane crash with Marshall [University, where he had been recruited]." Ironically, a high-school teammate of his at Donora High was on the team at Marshall but "got kicked off the team the week before [the crash]. I would've probably been on that football club, though."

He then reiterated how he was taught "nothing" in the farm system. "Nobody taught me how to hit but me," he said. "At that time you either do it or you don't, and I figured it out myself."

Ken Sr. played on all grass in the minors, but he knew that his game was predicated on speed. "My game was bunting, but when I got to the big leagues my game was making good contact and hitting the ball on the ground and running because of the Astroturf. So I had to change my game completely once I got to the big leagues.

When I was in high school sitting the bench, watching Ken play for our Donora Dragons in 1969, he used his speed to roam the outfield and used his power to hit long shots. Ken Sr. said, "I didn't bunt at all. I knew I could run, but I didn't really develop my speed until, like, between '69 and '70 in the off-season, when I would go up to Donora High School and run sprints. I'd run 30-, 60-, and 90-yard sprints, 10 of each every day after I got home from work. Then I developed into going down to first from 4.1 [seconds] to 3.2 or 3.3."

Donora has produced tons of fine athletes, and Ken Sr. said that during his period of playing high-school football there were two or three other kids in his age bracket who were faster than he was. Still, just a few years after being able to rank only third or fourth best in his own hometown, he became one of the fastest players in the major leagues, and a great deal of that can be attributed to his hard work running sprints.

Many years passed before Ken Sr. and his son began sharing marvelous baseball moments together, but when it happened, it was outstanding. Prior to spring training in 1989, Ken Sr., still with the Reds, told his Mariner son that he had a feeling they had a chance to play in the majors that year. That would, of course, make them the first father and son to play in the bigs at the same time.

"I figured he was kidding at first, but he was serious," Ken Jr. said. "It was something I could give him after all he's given to me." Realistically, back then the odds were rather long, but Junior made the team and history was made.

The ultimate father-son baseball experience would have to be both players appearing together in the World Series. That being the case, the Griffeys had several penultimate experiences. It was on August 31, 1990, at Seattle's Kingdome, that both men pulled off another first when they played in the same game together—the 40-year-old father in left field, flanking his 20-year-old son, who was in center. Although both Griffeys felt it was great that they were the first father-son combination to play at the same time, suiting up together as teammates in the Mariners' clubhouse had been much more special to them.

Interestingly, the Mariners talked things over with Ken Jr. before signing his father, because they wondered if the father-son scenario would make him feel awkward. He told them they shouldn't hesitate for even an instant.

Looking back on his first game with his son, Ken Sr. said, "The first time that we ran on the field together, I had to kind of put the situation in perspective by thinking, He's 12 years old, and go through it that way. That was the only way I could handle it at that time. It was a lot of fun; I enjoyed it.

"The opportunity was presented because the Reds [where he had been playing] had released me and gave me the opportunity to go up to Seattle and play with Junior. At first, what they did was kind of force me to retire. Then it came about where if I retired I had 60 days where I wouldn't be able to play and it was August, so I wouldn't have been able to play with Junior. So they reversed it [the retirement] and released me to give me the opportunity. But it was just a strange feeling. Very strange, because I didn't think he would get there at that time and I didn't think I'd be around that long in order to even get an opportunity to play with him."

He said he knew his son would make it to the majors but felt it would take him about four years to do so. "He only had 400 at bats [actually, 465] in the minor leagues, so I figured [he'd need] at least 1,500 to 2,000 at bats, but he surprised a lot of people." Ken could have added that his son is *still* surprising a lot of people with his prowess.

The Griffeys' debut as Mariners was a resounding success when they collected back-to-back singles in the very first inning. "I had a hit up the middle," Ken Sr. said. "And the strangest thing before that happened is that the first time up I was getting ready to hit, and I'm hearing from the on-deck circle— probably no one else would hear that—'Come on, Dad.' That kind of shocked me," he said, smiling.

"I had to step out and re-gather my thoughts in order to go ahead and swing the bat. I had to take all my concentration on doing what I was doing, and that was to get a base hit somehow, and it worked out, but it took a little doing, a little tussling."

Ken Sr. said that his son's comment made him feel as if their roles had been, if only for that moment, reversed. He noted, "I used to say, 'Come on, kid,' but I wasn't in the on-deck circle, I was in the stands. It was just a strange phenomenon then, to even hear that coming from the on-deck circle.

"I got a base hit, and he got a hit right behind me. The rest is history on that part of it, until we went back-to-back home runs, and that was different.

"That was amazing, there. We were hitting two and three—Harold Reynolds was one. Harold was on when I hit my home run and we went up two to nothing, then he hit his on a 3–0 count. The pitcher wasn't trying to pitch to him; he was trying to pitch around him, and he got a fastball away from him. And he hit it to left field, which, to me, is a difficult task, because if you're getting a 3–0 count you want to pull the ball, hit it hard that way, but he hit it hard to left field and it went out. When I hit mine, when I rounded third base and he was the first one to meet me, I knew he was determined he was going to hit one. That kind of put it all in perspective."

Naturally, he said, the emotions were "running real high. I can't even remember exactly, but I was proud of just the opportunity of playing with him, and then we get back-to-back home runs was probably the No. 1 thing in my baseball career."

Ken Sr. also said that, like many events, the Griffeys' accomplishments had the greatest impact in retrospect. "After all, this was all over and done," he said. "At the end of the year, that's when it probably caught up to me the most, when I really figured out, 'First father and son, first time up we both got hits, first time back-to-back home runs'—it was just the whole basic scenario that may or may not ever happen again. It may not." Furthermore, should another father and son replicate their feats, it would never again be *the* first time. "We'll always be the first."

When his father collected that first hit as a Mariners teammate, Griffey Jr. commented, "When I saw him get that hit, I wanted to cry. He'll always be the best to me." The father and son shared a celebratory postgame hug and much media attention before moving on to other accomplishments.

One company that produced posters of sports figures decided to put out a large poster of the Griffeys. This was hardly surprising, as Ken Jr. was highly charismatic—as far back as his days in Class-A ball, a poster night had been held for him. The father-son poster showed the two together in a locker room. Ken Sr. was in his Reds uniform, Junior in his Mariners outfit, leaning on his father's shoulder.

My mother, who was still living in Donora back then, bought the poster for me, and I promptly placed it on the back wall of my classroom. It's still there today (although when I mention to my class that I attended the same high school as the elder Griffey, I am invariably greeted with scoffs of incredulity).

When the Griffeys were reunited in Cincinnati in 2000, when Junior came over from Seattle in a trade, they were able to spend some time together during spring training. However, Ken Sr. said, "I don't see him on the road. Nah. Every once in a while he'll call me and see what I'm doing, but 95 percent of the time he's hanging with the fellas, which I don't blame him. He'll say, 'Dad, you want to go out to dinner?' We'll do something like that, but other than that, no, I don't see him that much. I see him more in the off-season, because we live in Orlando."

Now, Ken Sr. says if there is one thing above all others that he finds admirable in his son, it is simply his "just being himself. That's what I'm most proud of," he said. "That's the most important thing. His private life is never his, and he's handled it pretty good. Some people say he can be a monster sometimes, but I've watched other superstars that are the same, if not nastier."

He realizes, of course, that to outside observers his son is Ken Griffey Jr.—Superstar. However, in his mind, Ken Sr. said as concisely as possible, "He's my son." Still, does he think of him at times as his "little boy"? No. "He's not my little boy, he's my son, and that's more important than anything," the elder Griffey said. "He's my son first, before he's this superstar, this baseball player, and that's the way he feels. He was always, 'That's my dad.' "

Ken Sr. drifted back to stories of his son, especially one that concerns Junior's birth. "The first time I saw Junior? Well, it took a little while to get there. Birdie got to the hospital, but the strangest thing—what happened was we were laying in bed and she said she was having contractions, like I knew what that meant." He laughed, admitting that he had no idea what his wife was saying to him. After all, he was a mere 19-year-old at the time.

"I wasn't even thinking about that," he went on. "I was asleep. I said, 'What are those?' She said, 'Labor pains. I'm ready to go to the hospital.' I said, 'Woah.' So I got in the car, went upstairs and got her mother—we were staying down the cellar at Curly's house [her father]. Her mom got dressed; she was in a full evening gown with sneakers. So we took off." Then he delivered the punch line: "We left Birdie on the steps; we forgot her."

He continued to describe a scenario that might have been taken straight out of an old sitcom, such as the classic *Dick Van Dyke Show*. "I had to back the car up to get her. She got in the car; she was almost ready to have Kenny at that time. So when we got to the Charleroi-Monessen Hospital, he was just about ready to come.

"When he came out all I looked at was he was a big kid—that was all I was worried about. I wouldn't even touch him." Was he afraid? "Yeah," he said, his voice rising, as if to say, "You better believe I was afraid."

The reason he was intimidated, he said, was "my hands weren't that good. I figured I might drop him. It took me about a week before I picked him up." Here was a man unafraid of big-league pitching or of picking up a hard-hit ball sizzling off Astroturf, but shivering at the prospect of picking up a tiny bundle of a baby. He said he was so nervous "being that was the first one." (Interestingly, Junior was born on November 21, the same day as Donora's pride, Stan Musial.)

Even players whose father didn't play in the majors have fond thoughts about this father-son duo. Frank Thomas said, "I've seen the Griffeys—that's special. I played against his father at the end of his career the time he was here [in the American League], so that's very special."

Manager Art Howe goes back so far that, he said, "We baby-sat Griffey Jr. in winter ball. I played with his dad and we baby-sat him when he was 'yo' big and he used to go swimming with my kids. My wife used to keep an eye on them at times.

"Griffey Sr. can play; he was a great teammate, and his son—" he stopped short of saying the obvious. Many experts feel that not only are the Griffeys among the greatest father–son duos of all time but they are, in many ways, the most unusual.

Ted Uhlaender, a longtime baseball man, said he felt that the Griffeys were "a little bit similar hittingwise." That concise comment can be construed as a compliment to both father and son.

In the meantime, Elrod Hendricks says it's pleasurable to be around the game long enough to see the second (and third) generation of players roll along. "I've marveled at Ken Griffey Jr., for example. You know, I remember him running around the clubhouse in New York [when Hendricks and Griffey Sr. were with the Yankees] and on the ball field in Puerto Rico as a youngster."

Hendricks has also seen Diego and David Segui and Jose and Danny Tartabull, watching the sons grow from infancy to adulthood. "Sometimes I say to myself, 'You can't be that old,' because it's like I don't expect them to grow up."

But grow up they do, and Junior now has a family of his own. In fact, aside from his family there is only one thing that is extremely important to Ken Griffey Jr., and that is baseball. Just prior to spring training of 2001, he told the press that about one week after the previous baseball season had ended, he was ready to play ball once more. "I'm bored," he said. "I don't have any hobbies, except baseball." So it's a safe bet that just as baseball helped him bond with his father, it will help cement his relationship with his own children.

Nevertheless, there exists a huge contrast between the Griffeys. Ken Sr. grew up in a small town, where he attended a high school whose graduating class was well under 200. His rise to the majors was routine, and although he was a solid star, he was largely unheralded. His personality was somewhat low-key, and he was far from flashy on or off the field.

Junior attended a prestigious high school, Moeller of Cincinnati. His fame was established before he was 20 years old. By the early 1990s, when he was still with the Mariners, he lamented his high visibility, and commented that he couldn't even leave his house to shop. That was certainly a problem his father never had to endure. Junior has a flair on and off the field, and is recognized as one of the most interesting and colorful figures of the game. His dad got the job done without much fanfare.

Ken Sr. said of the Griffey fame, "It doesn't bother me. I don't get swamped, he does." The elder Griffey may never have had to worry about being inundated with mail, but his son gets more mail than many small-town post offices.

Actually, Junior once estimated his haul at more than 300 items of fan mail per week. It's reached the point where, he says, "A secretary screens my mail, sorting out bills and fan mail." It is impossible to respond to autograph requests. "We have to send [baseball cards] back [unsigned] with a form letter."

Junior became so popular so quickly that he was almost instantly considered to be a highly recognizable, a.k.a. "high profile," celebrity. In 1994, he said that for him privacy was an impossiblity, especially in his home city. "I don't go anywhere when the team's at home. I haven't gone to a mall in Seattle in years." However, he added somewhat wistfully, "You get used to it."

Furthermore, it's not easy for a star of Ken Jr.'s caliber to kill time on the road. The notion of his going incognito is almost inane. He said what he will do "depends where I'm at." Sometimes in the early 1990s, he said, he managed to go to the mall without being mobbed, but that soon became another impossibility. At the time of this interview, in the early part of the 1990s, he said that his fiancée, now his wife, did "all my shopping for me, but I don't have to twist her arm," he added with a grin.

One aspect of fame, though, that Ken Jr. feels strongly about is the fact that he believes fans should try "to understand and learn that we are humans and we have lives, too. Just because sometimes we can't sign [autographs] for them, you can't get an attitude and call us names, because that just makes it worse for you and other people. If you're nice and polite, then usually we sign, but if you're not, well, you know . . . ," he said as his voice trailed off.

He added, "You got some rude people out there. Guys don't appreciate that. When you're rude, guys on the team tend to see that and get rude back at them." In other words, he simply wishes fans would follow the Golden Rule.

Ken Sr. said it took him some time to gain some savoir faire, to learn how to handle his fame. "It took a little while. I didn't say much in high school, nobody knew who I was." In a way, he was right—we all knew him, but there was a group of athletes who were more outgoing, even rowdy, and they drew most of the attention at our school. There were "guys who were forceful and fighting, and I wasn't into all that," he said. He could have added that, unlike those guys, he had succeeded in life.

"As I got older, I learned," Ken Sr. said. "I took a couple of communications classes. I went to the Connecticut School of Broadcasting in the off-season." He mentioned that he spent some time in the Seattle broadcasters' booth after he retired from the game. "I liked it, but it was just that I wasn't polished enough to understand what I needed to do at that time. I was just coming off the field.

"At that time I had two jobs—I was still the roving hitting instructor for them, so I didn't get a chance to do any of my homework like most broadcasters do. They go to the games two or three days before the one that they're going to announce. They got an opportunity to sit down with the fellas and get little bits and pieces, but I wasn't able to do that because I was on the road, helping the kids in the minor-league system."

So he did the announcing job for a year, making commentary on his son and the other Mariners, before giving that up. What he most relished about his work in the booth was that it allowed him to stay near his son.

Because Ken Sr.'s own father left the family behind when he was young, Ken vowed not to repeat that mistake with his own children. As a result, family has always been of paramount importance to the Griffeys. For instance, there was the time Ken Griffey Jr. was in Cleveland to play the Indians at the old Municipal Stadium in September of 1992. His cousin Darrell Harding, a running back at the University of Cincinnati, was playing at home that afternoon.

According to Ken Sr., Harding had broken rushing records in Pennsylvania as a high-school player, racking up somewhere around 5,000 or 6,000 yards. "It was an ungodly number; he was a heckuva football player," Ken Sr. said. "He didn't play much once he got to the University of Cincinnati, because the coach that recruited him got fired in his second year and they made him a defensive back."

In any event, Ken Jr. wanted to visit his cousin, but the only way he could squeeze the gridiron game into his hectic schedule was chartering a jet to Cincinnati. No problem—the superstar center fielder plunked down $1,000 and flew in and out of Cincinnati, supporting his family. Admittedly, the money he dished out to make the trip was nothing for a multimillionaire, but the time, effort, and concern for his cousin were typical of what his father had instilled in him.

Likewise, that same year I was sitting with my family in the section of seats that the Indians reserved for the families of players and media members. At one point, I turned around and spotted several people I knew from the Griffey family. They told me they always made the trip from Donora to Cleveland (nearly 400 miles round-trip) when Seattle was in town. Now that Junior plays for the Cincinnati Reds, family members have it easy, as nearly the entire clan has relocated to the Queen City area.

At one time when Ken Jr. was young, I had the impression the Griffeys' batting stroke on warm-up cuts was somewhat similar, but I was later informed that I was wrong. When I interviewed Ken Sr., he told me their swings had never been alike, not even in warm-ups. He said his son always had "his own way of doing things." Perhaps I saw a similarity when they stood in the box simply because I wanted to see one. At any rate, another point about the Griffeys' cuts came from Uhlaender, who said, "Griffey [Junior] has changed from when he first came up to now."

Joe Nossek saw Ken Sr. at the end of his career, and Ken Jr. from his first days with Seattle to the present. I asked him to evaluate their swings and styles, just to get another point of view. He said, "I never really thought that they were very comparable with their swings. Junior was geared more to a home-run swing, where Senior was towards the tail end of his career [when Nossek observed him in the American League], so he was more trying to put the ball in play and make contact. He went the other way much more [than his pull-hitting son]."

A look at an old videotape I had seemed to confirm that although father and son do have some similarities, such as their approach to the game and their tendency to keep things low-key, there are considerable differences between them. However, the situation wasn't totally resolved. And I felt somewhat vindicated when I later heard Griffey Jr. say that he did get his swing from his father.

At any rate, Ken Sr. (we called him Kenny in high school) was a three-letter man on our high-school football, baseball, and basketball teams, and he ran track for two years. At our school, baseball wasn't a major sport, and it got relatively little publicity compared with football and basketball. Kenny did well, hitting better than .300, but that was spread out over just nine games. (The team went 3–6 despite Kenny's presence.) The schedule was always truncated because of the inevitable nasty Pennsylvania weather each spring. Kenny hit many a towering home run, but he paid the price with fairly frequent strikeouts.

He changed his game in the pros, but his son has seemingly had a home-run swing forever—even though throughout most of his career he claimed, with a straight face, that he wasn't a home-run hitter, despite having put up some monumental totals.

The power contrast is sizable, as Junior shot by his father's career home-run total in just his sixth major-league season, at the tender age of 25. Likewise, Ken Sr. won only one Player of the Week Award during his big-league stint; Junior won two in his first month in the majors.

At any rate, back to the elder Griffey's hoop career. His three years on the varsity were interesting, in that he was a guard during his sophomore year, switched to forward for his junior season, and wound up playing center while being listed as a mere six feet tall in his final year at Donora High School. During our talk in 2001, he confided that he certainly *wasn't* six feet tall back then. Yet he set school records for most points in a game (40) and for a career (just under 1,000 points in three years). His rebound records still stand—27 for a single contest and 307 for a season. He even helped the Dragons rattle off a record 22 straight wins one year.

When he was asked if he was as good a high-school B-ball player as his dad, Ken Jr. replied, with a chuckle and that Junior grin of his, "No. I had no outside shot."

There are, of course, many similarites between the Griffeys, too. The yearbook entry for Ken Sr. read: "Sports is his life . . . Masculinity personified . . . Popular . . . Fun to be with." Sounds like Junior, too.

The old cliché "Like father, like son" is a cliché because over the years it's held true so often that it was repeated ad nauseum. And although Ken Sr. wasn't exactly an extrovert in high school, I have since seen him on shows such as David Letterman's and Arsenio Hall's. Maybe in this instance the father took after the son, as they are both highly poised and as comfortable in front of an armada of cameras as they are on a baseball field.

Kenny's classmates felt that he was a better basketball and football star than baseball whiz. Still, he could hit for power and he could run, covering ground in the outfield with ease and stealing bases effortlessly. More than anything, it was his sheer speed that attracted a Cincinnati Reds scout. Baseball experts use yet another cliché to describe the benefit and allure of speed in young players: "You can't teach speed."

His climb from the Gulf Coast League to Indianapolis and then for two "cups of coffee" with the Reds was a steady ascent. Finally, by 1975 he was a bona fide member of the Big Red Machine, hitting .305 for the World Champion Reds while scoring 95 runs. He had truly arrived.

By the time Ken Sr.'s career had ended and his son's was still in its relative infancy, legendary Reds skipper Sparky Anderson said he felt that both Griffeys were of Hall of Fame timbre. Although the leader of that Big Red Machine was known for his use of hyperbole, it was flattering to the Griffeys to hear such kind words.

In the early 1990s, Anderson said, "If Ken Jr. does what his father did, he'll have done a lot." He may well have been alluding to the fact that the father owned two World Series rings to none for his offspring. He also praised Ken Sr. for possessing a great work ethic. Junior was truly following in some big footsteps, according to Anderson. Around that time, Junior agreed with

Anderson's assessment. "I want to surpass my father, because then I'd know I accomplished a lot," he said.

Even before Anderson's evaluation, Ken Sr. had spoken of his son with pride. "I think he's going to be a better player than me," he said. "I enjoy watching him play."

The Griffeys still find family to be very important in their lives, and they still manage to get back to Donora to visit, although this happens much less frequently now that there is only one brother living there. Ken Jr. has also seen the Little League field in town, which is named after his father (as well as the one that's named after Musial).

Junior's father must have taught him tolerance and how to fit in. Ken Jr. said it's all part of being a teammate. "It's easy to get along with others. You've got different guys from different parts of the country, but you just try to get along." Back in the early 1990s, when the Mariners were a young team with budding stars, Ken Jr. noted, "We're learning about each other."

Now that he has become a megastar, I find it difficult to think back to the first time I saw him on my old Zenith TV set. What I do recall is that back then—and now, too—when I saw him, I could see the physical traits of both Alberta (everybody still calls her Birdie) Littleton Griffey and Ken Sr.

Clyde Wright, who knew Ken Sr., said, "Griffey just looks exactly like his dad, but I don't think they even come close to hitting like each other." I disagree, because I knew Birdie, too, and can readily see her genetic influence. She was a fine athlete, too, so who knows? Maybe Ken Jr. hits like *her*.

Like Sparky Anderson, Bret Boone is a Griffey admirer. He said that when it comes to "a Ken Griffey Jr. or that level of talent, there's only a handful of those guys. They probably don't have to work as hard as the rest of us. It would be nice to have his swing, but there's only one of those." If that's true, then it seems that Junior truly got his swing simply from "being himself."

Finally, here's a great Griffey story that dates back to 1989. It displays the love between father and son, which glows even under the guise of a little macho teasing. At that point Ken Sr. was still with the Reds, and his son was a rookie. Someone asked the elder Griffey if he thought that someday he and Junior might play together on the same team. With a broad, bright smile, he replied, "No way! He'd drive me nuts."

Chapter Six: The Ripkens

With all the lore associated with the Ripken family, it's surprising that by now the public hasn't heard a television announcer blaring out, "This Sunday, the feel-good story to end all. A story of family love and devotion on the movie of the week, *The Ripkens: A Baseball Legacy*."

If they did develop that movie, the producers would quickly find that there was more than enough material to turn it into a miniseries. Start with the eldest Ripken. Cal Sr. was a baseball "lifer," having been around the game for decades. He never made it to the majors, but he did spend seven years in the minor leagues. One of his two brothers also played professional baseball, but, again, not at the big-league level. Cal Sr.'s greatest fame, aside from producing two major-league sons, was achieved during his days as the manager of the Baltimore Orioles. He took over the club's reins for two games in 1985, on an interim basis prior to the team's rehiring of legendary skipper Earl Weaver. Then, in 1987, he took over the job full-time, compiling a won-loss record of 67–95.

It wasn't so much his record that gained him headlines that season. It was the fact that he, Calvin Jr. and Billy were all on that same team. That made the father the first man to be the manager of two of his sons simultaneously in big-league, regular-season history. There are two more Ripkens, Fred and Ellen Leigh, but obviously they never made it to the majors.

When Cal Sr. made history managing his sons, he took it in stride, almost stoically. He said to the media, "I hate to disappoint you guys, but Billy is just one of the twenty-four players." Billy sounded delighted to join the

Orioles, saying, "I drove down [from the minor-league team in Rochester], but I guess you could say I flew in."

When Cal Sr. first coached Cal Jr., he had taken an approach that was akin to the concept of separation of church and state. He loved his son, but on the field he would show no favoritism. In fact, when Cal Jr. was 22, reporters wanted his father's take on the situation: Was he beaming with pride over his son, the big leaguer? Cal Sr. replied, "Am I proud of him? Well, sure I'm proud of him as my son. But as a ballplayer, ask in fifteen years."

Upon arriving in town Billy went directly to his brother's house, then on to Memorial Stadium. There his father first greeted him with an old family nickname: "Hi, Bub." He then penciled Billy into the lineup, explaining, "In all my years as manager, I've always put somebody who was just called up right into the lineup."

The 1988 season began with an abysmal thud, with the Orioles going 0–6, which led to Ripken's dismissal. Ironically, when Frank Robinson replaced him, he and his O's would see the losing streak run to 21 before it mercifully came to an end.

Whether as a manager or a coach, Cal Sr. remained a part of the Orioles picture seemingly forever. As a matter of fact, in all, Cal Jr. played in parts of twelve seasons in which his father was in the Orioles' uniform as either a big-league coach or a manager. Cal Sr.'s actual ledger with the Orioles includes fifteen years on their coaching staff, dating back to 1976.

Officially, he was listed as their third-base coach for thirteen and a half of those seasons. In addition, he managed at the major- or minor-league level for another fourteen-plus years. Of that time, thirteen-plus years were spent in the Orioles' farm system, longer than that of any man in the history of that franchise. The only level he never spent time in was the Rookie League.

The Orioles and the media hailed him as, according to the Baltimore Media Guide, "perhaps the best teacher of young players in Orioles history. As a young player in the Orioles system he was a catcher, although he also played at third, in the outfield, and even as a pitcher. No wonder he understood the game inside out.

His best season was at Fox Cities, in Appleton, Wisconsin, as a player under Earl Weaver. The next season he became the player-manager of that squad. Little did he know then that more than thirty years later, in 1996, he would be inducted into the Orioles Hall of Fame.

Shortly after that, during spring training of 1999, Cal Sr. succumbed to cancer. The Orioles "family" honored him by wearing his jersey number, seven, on their uniform sleeve for the entire season. They also painted that number in orange in the third-base coach's box at Camden Yards, where it, too, stayed for the whole year.

Billy Ripken never got the recognition that his brother did, because he just didn't have the same skills. Still, he carved out a decent career, which lasted from 1987 to 1998 with four different teams. His minor-league career dated to 1982, when he was selected by the Orioles in the eleventh round of the free-agent draft. By 1986, he was leading the Southern League in double plays turned by a second baseman and total chances. Late in his career (in 1995), he even led all American Association shortstops in fielding percentage, assists, and double plays. His offensive highlights would include the .308 he hit over 234 at bats with the Orioles in 1987 and his numbers with them in 1990, including 28 doubles to go with his .291 batting average.

He and Cal Jr. played together for five and a half seasons, from July 11 of 1987 through 1992. They became the fifth set of brothers to play up the middle at second and short. The others were Granny and Garvin Hamner for the 1945 Phillies; Lou and Dino Chiozza of the 1935 Phillies; Milt and Frank Bolling with the 1958 Detroit Tigers; and Eddie and Johnny O'Brien, who were teammates with the Pittsburgh Pirates in 1953 and again from 1955 to 1956. Many times when the Ripkens formed their team's double-play combination, they gave the Orioles fine defense, as Billy was certainly a good second baseman with the glove.

In 1990, the Ripken brothers combined for just eleven errors, the fewest in major-league history by a double-play duo (while performing in the necessary, qualifying number of games played). Their record is two better than the mark Toronto's Tony Fernandez and Manny Lee achieved in that same 1990 season. Of the brothers who have played second and shortstop together, the Ripkens also played in more games than any other duet, 663 (with 287 double plays to their credit), and they even teamed up to help turn a triple play versus the Yankees on June 15, 1989.

One year and three months later, to the day, they each homered in a game—a thrill for the entire Ripken family. That made them the first brother act to homer in the same game since Graig and Jim Nettles did so in 1974, but the Nettles were opponents. The Ripken blasts came against Toronto's David Wells and marked the fifteenth time brothers had homered in the same game, but just the fifth time they did so in the same inning. The last time that had happened was way back on July 12, 1962, when Hank and Tommie Aaron both connected.

Billy returned to the Orioles in a utility role in 1996, and both he and Cal homered in a game again, this time with Cal drilling three in Seattle's

Kingdome. Going into 2000, even though Billy hit only 20 home runs, their combined total of 422 had them ranked No. 7 on the all-time roster of home runs hit by brothers. (Hank Aaron, with 755, and his brother Tommie, with 13, stand as No. 1.)

According to CBS SportsLine, when the three Ripkens were all in Baltimore uniforms together, it marked only the fourth time this had been done by three men from the same family. In 1973 Jose, Hector, and Tommy Cruz all suited up for the St. Louis Cardinals. Ten years earlier the three Alous, Matty, Felipe, and Jesus, made history when they manned all three outfield positions for the San Francisco Giants. And CBS stated that back in 1876 George, Sam, and Harry Wright were together with the Boston franchise of the National League.

The list of Cal Jr.'s accomplishments is seemingly infinite. When he played in his 2,131st game in a row back on September 6, 1995, not only did he break Lou Gehrig's long-standing record but he captured the heart of the baseball world. Well, most of the baseball community, anyway. When Tom Goodwin was with the Kansas City Royals, Cal Jr. made a couple of nice plays on him, one in particular that robbed him of a sure hit. Goodwin grumbled, "I wasn't too thrilled when he made that play . . . I was thinking, Why doesn't he take a day off?"

Cal Jr.'s consecutive games-played skein spanned an incredible seventeen seasons. When it began, on May 30, 1982, the Dow Jones Average stood at 819.54. By the time he ended the streak—at 2,632 games on September 20, 1998—it had soared more than 7,000 points, to 7,895.66! By July 1, 2001, Cal Jr. ranked among the top ten players in history for games played; only three men had ever played in more games for a single team. Only Carl Yastrzemski, Hank Aaron, and Stan Musial topped him in that department.

In 1999, he was voted to baseball's All-Century Team as the only shortstop other than Chicago Cubs Hall of Famer Ernie Banks. He was a part of the Series-winning Orioles club of 1983, and he is one of just seven men to hit 400 homers while banging out 3,000 or more hits.

Cal Jr. is so widely revered that when umpire Drew Coble ejected him during a 1989 contest, Coble said he felt as if he were "throwing God out of Sunday school." Years later, when another ump, Al Clark, thumbed Cal from a game for arguing balls and strikes, Clark was asked if he felt the way Coble had. He replied jokingly, "I'm Jewish. I don't go to Sunday school." Nevertheless, Cal Jr. clearly has the respect of the baseball community, and he has earned it.

Cal owns two Gold Gloves, the 1982 Rookie of the Year Award, two MVP trophies, with one of those coming in a year when his team played below-

.500 ball (something that had happened only three times in the history of the award). Counting his final season, 2001, he was selected to the All-Star team nineteen straight seasons, with his seventeen consecutive starts being a record. He was also given the MVP Award for the midsummer classics of 1991 and 2001.

The list continues: only ten men have hit twenty or more home runs in each of their first ten full seasons, Cal Jr. is one of those men; he is believed to have more extra base hits than any shortstop ever; and his home run total easily passed Ernie Banks (who had 277) for the most ever by a shortstop. Entering the 2001 season, Cal had smacked 345 home runs as a shortstop.

In all, he has more than 400 homers, with more than 1,600 runs and 1,600 runs driven in for his lifetime of toil. Entering the 2001 season, only seventeen men had more than his 3,070 hits. He is one of only eight shortstops to reach the 30 home-run plateau in a single season. His most recent landmark came in April of 2001, when he became the fifteenth man to amass 5,000 total bases.

The Baltimore native born in Havre de Grace, Maryland, is a graduate of Aberdeen High School, where he earned All-State honors. He had accumulated (owned or shared) eleven major-league or American League fielding records by 2000, including a fielding percentage of .996 in 1990, which ranks as the greatest ever by a shortstop for a season.

That year he also set the mark for committing the fewest errors at short, a mere three. The league record for most consecutive errorless games at shortstop is also his, at 95. All 95 were in one season; since then, over a two-year period, Cleveland's Omar Vizquel also played that many straight games without an error.

He led his league in double plays by a shortstop eight times, yet another record. All that from a man who was drafted in 1978 after forty-seven other players were selected, including three by the Orioles (Bob Boyce, Larry Sheets, the only fairly recognizable name of the three, and Edwin Hook).

Along with his wife, Kelly, Cal Jr., who had been groomed from early on to become a quality person by his parents, has given to the community time and time again. He was involved in a plethora of charitable organizations throughout his career, including the donation of a quarter of a million dollars to help Baltimore's adult-literacy campaign. To commemorate Cal's breaking of Gehrig's streak, the Cal Ripken, Jr./Lou Gehrig ALS (amyotrophic lateral sclerosis, the disease Gehrig had) Research Fund was established at Johns Hopkins University, in September of 1995. The Orioles and local businessmen seeded the fund with $2,000,000, which was raised by the sale of special on-the-field seats for Cal's historic record-breaking game.

Cal Sr. once said that he never lived his baseball life vicariously through his sons. However, he did notice from an early age that Cal Jr. was indeed going to live a life full of baseball. Cal Jr. always had a ball in his hands, and was always up for a game of baseball.

Cal Jr. said that his most lingering memory of his father dealt with all the time they spent together in the minors when he was growing up. They would don their uniforms, trot onto the field, and Cal Jr. would shag flies in the outfield.

In *Baseball Fathers, Baseball Sons* by Dick Wimmer, Cal Jr. commented that he would always remember his father "tappin' me on the leg and sayin', 'You wanna go with me today?' Seemed like the highlight of my day. I waited for that."

Elrod Hendricks, who has a history in Baltimore that's nearly as long as anyone not named Ripken, has been an Orioles player and coach for an eternity and has, in truth, probably witnessed the Ripkens just about as much (or more) than any person outside the Ripken family circle. He teasingly said that Cal Jr. was "a little brat, but he also had an awareness of the game and a respect for the game."

He remembered how Cal Jr. would respect the players, too. "Watching them practice, you'd see him sitting in the dugout watching Brooks [Robinson] field ground balls, watching [Mark] Belanger field ground balls. He'd just focus on those two guys the whole time that they were out there working.

"Ironically enough, when Cal started playing, those habits that they had, going out there taking 150 ground balls and doing the right things, he still does it twenty-one years later," Hendricks continued. "It's good to see that; that unlike a lot of the young ballplayers today, he watched the older guys and went out and did just what they did. That's probably what helped him play as long as those guys did."

Hendricks said that he can vividly recall families like the Griffeys, the Tartabulls, and, of course, in even greater depth, the Ripkens. "I saw Cal's dad in his last year playing. Then he became a manager in the minor leagues. I watched Cal in this clubhouse—watched him turn into one heckuva person and player."

His reaction to seeing Cal Jr. going from being a child running around the Orioles' facilities to becoming a modern-day legend was simple. "Sometimes you feel a little old because you never expect them to grow up," he said. "You expect him to be a little boy still. Cal is 40 years old, but he's still a little kid inside, and I think that's good, because that's what this game should be all about—you should have a lot of kid in you to play this game and really enjoy it."

As a resident expert, Hendricks observed, "Billy was in the shadows of his brother. He tried to live up to that, which was unfair to him because he was always being compared to Cal. He had good abilities; he was good at second base, but everyone expected him to hit like his brother, which was not fair at all. At times, he'd try to do that, and he became very frustrated. I think if Billy had had an injury-free career, you'd have seen some numbers put up.

"Defensively, he was outstanding. He could turn the double play and he was a very smart player. And he wasn't bad with the bat, too, except for when he'd try to hit home runs." Hendricks was certainly correct about Billy's defensive side. In fact, Billy and Cal turned quite a few double plays when they were together.

When it came to describing Cal Jr., Hendricks gave a deep, affectionate laugh and said, "Cal's Cal. You know there's only one Cal, and he was a great player for us and for the game. He single-handedly, in '95, brought the game of baseball back, brought people back to the park. Now it's McGwire and Sosa that are getting all the accolades, but back in '95, when we came back off the strike year, Cal was the one that led everyone back into baseball." That comment says volumes; it puts Cal on the same pedestal as Babe Ruth, in that Ruth, too, was seen as a savior of the game after the Black Sox scandal of 1919.

Cal Jr. didn't see himself as a messiah, or, for that matter, as an idol. "I never perceive myself as a hero of any kind," he said modestly. "I'm just a baseball player." However, he added, "If you are put in a position to influence people's lives, why not do all you can to cast it in a positive light?" So if there was a burden to carry during baseball's bleak years, he certainly helped lift that load.

Meanwhile, Billy Ripken can be a funny man, a great guy to have in a clubhouse. Billy sees himself as a Casey Candaele type, who, Billy said, provided comic relief but was "not a prankster." He added, "I had the pleasure of playing with Casey in Buffalo last year [1996]. I'll go down on record as saying Casey is *the* funniest human that I have ever met."

Yet many feel that Billy was—and still is—in the same ballpark. For example, he came up with this quip: "Errors are part of the game, but Abner

Doubleday was a jerk for inventing them." Billy feels that it is vital for a team to stay loose during the long, demanding major-league season. "I think that everybody who plays this game has their moments," he said. "There are very few people that I would go out and say are normal. When you're with every-body, everyday through the course of the season and you're playing 162 games in 180 days, I think it has a tendency to weigh on you a little bit." And *that* is his motivation for joking around and keeping things zany at times.

When Mike Hargrove managed Billy in Cleveland, he praised him, saying, "He's just got a good sense of humor. Brian Giles and Bill were running buddies when they were playing Triple-A a couple of years ago, and Giles is about a half bubble off sometimes."

Candaele agreed, labeling Billy a "true flame," a colorful guy. "He's great. He's funny, a character. He's good out-of-control, a good flake. It's hard to explain." He added that Billy Ripken, to be appreciated, had to be seen day in and day out. With Billy, he said, comes "the joy you get to come to the park and see that guy and the things he's going to say [and do]."

Candaele also appreciated Billy because, he said, even when it's good to be flaky "you have to know when to stop, when it's time for business." And Billy always knew when it was time to play ball and when the team needed an injection of humor.

By way of contrast, Hendricks harked back to the days of Cal Sr., who was a presence in the Baltimore dugout and a figure Hendricks simply called "a baseball man." He added, "He was a very serious man once you got on the field. He was all baseball—a very hard worker. You played by the book with him. It was baseball all the time when you were on that field. The moment you get to the ballpark, you better start thinking baseball with him, because he did not put up with the lack of hustle and all that.

"Even more so, he hated mental errors. He knew that physical errors would come but mental errors he hated, and he stressed that I don't know how many times. I've oftentimes heard him say, 'If I have to tell you a thousand times, maybe the thousand and first time you'll get it right, but we're going to do it until you get it right.' I mean, that's just the way he was."

At times, though, Cal Sr. would flash the Ripken humor. As the Ori-oles' manager in 1987, he said, "The doctor said I should do a lot of walking. So I walk to the mound nine or ten times a game."

The public perception seems to be that Cal Jr. takes after his father, in that they lean toward the serious side, while Billy is more fun-loving. But Hendricks dispelled that theory. "It again goes back to [Billy] trying to live up to his brother, so he tried to get his own demeanor," he said. However, he also stated, "Cal Jr. was not always that calm as you see him. He was a little wild kid himself. As a matter of fact, he was—and still is—a prankster, but rather subtle, as opposed to Bill, who's more vocal. Once Cal established himself, then he toned his act down," Hendricks concluded.

In other words, it appears that once Cal became a star and was thrust into the public eye, he evolved into a more mature persona. Interestingly, Hendricks has had a chance to observe Cal's children around the park in Baltimore and, he says, they are "a lot like Billy. Actually, like Cal was as a kid, too. Just having a lot of fun and enjoying being out at the ballpark." He said they were, in fact, nice kids, but that Cal's son, Ryan (whose middle name is Calvin), was a bit more outgoing than his sister, Rachel. "She's more quiet, like the mom or like Cal is now, but his son is just like Cal was, a bottle of energy—he never gets tired, he's out there all the time. He's tireless; he could be out there for an hour and he wants to go for an hour and a half."

Does Ryan, who was conveniently born on July 26, 1993 (an Orioles off day, enabling Cal Jr. to keep his famous streak alive; his sister was born in the off-season), show talent to go with his boundless energy? "It's too early to tell," Hendricks said. "He's still just a baby; I think he's, what, 7 years old and he's at the park quite a bit with Cal, so it's no different than when Cal used to come out with his dad. The difference is that on the field Cal spends more time [with his son] than Senior did, because Senior did not think, or feel, that once you got out to a major-league park kids should be there. Cal [Jr.] came, but he sat and watched."

It is certainly true that Ryan is now permitted to be around baseball in ways Cal Jr. couldn't be a generation earlier. During the 2001 All-Star Game Ryan, and other sons of stars, was permitted to sit in the dugout during the game. Until recently, that would have been unthinkable. It's a safe bet that Cal Sr. would never have been responsible for such a change in baseball's mores.

Cal's manager in 2001, Mike Hargrove, noted, "Baseball is much more tolerant [now]. I had a manager one time, and Alan Bannister and I were playing together in Cleveland. His wife, Vicky, was having a baby when we were in Milwaukee. He went to the manager to ask for permission to go home for the birth. The manager said, half jokingly, *half jokingly*, 'What are you, a doctor?' And that, at that time, was kind of the prevailing attitude in baseball. If you left the club, it was because somebody in your immediate family was sick or had died and you were going to the funeral.

"I remember my father-in-law died when I was playing with the Rangers in 1976. I almost didn't get permission to go home for his funeral. So it was one of those things where I asked for permission, and it was reluctantly given, but it was also one of those things if it wasn't given, I was going to go anyway. So, yeah, baseball is a lot more tolerant of stuff like that, and of wives going on the road with husbands. I think that's a good thing."

In other words, family has always been important to the players, but not to the front office. Now, many people find it refreshing to see a son like Ryan nestled beside his father on a special day, such as Cal's final All-Star appearance. Television cameras captured the two sitting together in the dugout while the game was still in progress and no one seemed to mind one bit.

And what an All-Star Game it was for the soon to be retiring Cal. Not only did he start the game but, at the prompting of manager Joe Torre and the man who had been voted into the game as the starting shortstop, Alex Rodriguez, he even made a token appearance at his old spot, shortstop.

Rodriguez had set the whole thing up ahead of time, and had suggested the tribute to Torre, who immediately approved. Cal Jr. commented, "I must have been the only one on the whole planet that didn't know. I thought, This isn't the time or place to go back to short. I haven't played it in so many years. But Rodriguez said, 'No, everybody is expecting you to do it. Go on over there.'

"I was secretly wishing that Roger [Clemens] would strike out three guys and I wouldn't have a play to make. But with two outs I started thinking, Yeah, I'd like to have a play, like to see what it feels like again."

While that was a nice, sentimental gesture, Cal's home run and his winning MVP honors were sheer baseball drama. He also became, at the age of 40, the oldest player ever to homer in All-Star competition.

Clearly, Cal Ripken Jr. has earned a great deal of respect over the years. Another tribute came in 1990, when Todd Benzinger, a major-league infielder, said, "I don't admire guys who hit the ball a mile or steal bases the way I admire people like Cal Ripken . . . it takes a lot of character and mental toughness to go out there and play every day, no matter how you feel."

In August of 2000, when Cal turned 40, one "gift" came when he learned that a youth-baseball organization, Babe Ruth Baseball, had renamed one of its divisions after him. He told *USA Today/Baseball Weekly* how he first got involved with the group. "When Dad retired, he was very interested in teaching clinics," he said. "Babe Ruth [Baseball] came aboard and brought him in for a couple of events. That's when our rapport started. They really liked the substance Dad taught, and the honesty and pleasure that he showed. They could also read our passion towards teaching. We saw Babe Ruth as an opportunity to use our 'celebrity' name to help drive this."

He was also asked if he would like to someday manage, as his father had done. He replied, "My immediate interest for the next eight to ten years is not in managing or coaching."

He said that he wanted to have more freedom and flexibility with his personal schedule. "The job of a manager or coach requires you to live the same baseball schedule that I lived through as a kid, as an adult, and as a parent," he explained. He concluded by stating that maybe he'd possibly take up managing at some future point but "at this moment, I don't want to miss that window of time to be with my kids."

On June 18, 2001, Cal Jr. made it official—he would retire at the end of that season, his twenty-first. He reiterated that he wanted to spend more time with his family and to devote more time to his youth-baseball involvements. "It's inevitable that you can't play forever," he said. "[Baseball] has given me a lot of joy and happiness and satisfaction. I'm proud of what I've been able to do. But I'm ready to do other things. I'm ready to be home and available to my kids and family." He again addressed the topic of a future baseball job when he stated that he hoped to eventually run a big-league team.

A June 26, 2001, Knight Ridder article told of how Rachel, then 11 years old, had shown her father a cartoon from *USA Today* that depicted Cal Jr. standing at an ironing board. His wife was approaching him with a load of clothes, saying, "Here you go, 'Iron Man.' " Cal laughed when he saw the ribbing that was directed at him and joked, "On occasion I iron my shirts in my hotel room, with no success. So I will not do that."

He also told reporters that he "thought my 7-year-old boy would be a little more upset because's he's so crazy into baseball. But he saw the opportunity that I would be home. I talked to him a lot about that. It's important for me to be home."

The first city to say adieu to Cal Ripken Jr. was Chicago. On July 1, 2001, the White Sox honored him, and he rather reluctantly accepted the accolades. In the second inning, when he strolled to the plate for his first at bat, he received a standing ovation, but he didn't respond to the crowd—not this time, no way. He remained stoical and serious on the diamond. As a result the cheering lasted only about thirty seconds. I covered the game, and I couldn't help thinking that if, say, Reggie Jackson had been in the batter's box for *his* farewell tour, he would definitely have responded to the crowd so that he could milk the applause.

In Ripken's final at bat the crowd, once more, cheered, wanting to say goodbye to the legend. This time he relented. Leading off the ninth, he removed his helmet and waved to the fans, then quickly stepped back into the box. "For my last at bat, I said to myself, 'Well, the game has been going on for so long. . . .'" He said it as if to apologize for the slight delay. (The game had pushed, or at least nudged, the four-hour mark.) No apologies were necessary. He even popped out of the dugout after the contest to sign autographs for a pocket of faithful fans, a small percentage of the 34,588 who had originally been in attendance.

After the game, opposing manager Jerry Manuel commented, "For me to watch him play was like art. He wasn't the fastest guy or the one with the most power, but he was always in the flow. It was like poetry or artistry, really. We'll miss that."

Former teammate Robbie Alomar tossed in more praise. "It was an honor to play with one of the best shortstops in the game of baseball," he said. "He is one of the smartest guys I ever played beside. He knows every player from other teams and how to play them defensively. When you play beside him, you learn a lot about baseball."

Cal's teammate Jerry Hairston Jr. concurred. "He's a great person and a great teammate, and he's fun to be around," Hairston said. "He jokes a little bit too much once we're in the clubhouse, but he's a very humble person. He's handled his success and fame as well as anybody can. He's great to be around.

"First of all, people don't realize how hard he works," Hairston continued. "Of course, he has the 'Iron Man' persona, but when he comes to the ballpark he's always willing to work, learn. He's been playing twenty-one years in the big leagues, and he's always trying to learn new things. Those are the things that rub off on the other guys; we're always trying to learn and better ourselves."

Orioles coach Tom Trebelhorn said, "I played in the Southern League in Birmingham, and Cal was the batboy in Asheville when his dad was managing. His experiences in baseball at the professional level started very young. He had great schooling by his dad. His dad was a taskmaster who knew the game, and taught the game, and lived the game. That's what Cal came up through. His dad wasn't as good a player as Cal, but as far as his getting Cal ready to play, Cal couldn't have had a better instructor or mentor.

"Cal Sr. was just a good ol' baseball guy, and humor's always part of baseball so I think he was a very serious baseball man, but within the context of the game you also have to have a certain amount of humor and a certain amount of fun. And Cal Sr., in his career, had a lot of things to laugh about and a lot of stories to tell, but he knew how he wanted the game to be played and how he felt it should be played. Within those guidelines he coached and managed, but he was a human being and a really good baseball guy."

Davey Lopes, manager of the Milwaukee Brewers in 2001, said of the Ripkens, senior and junior, "Oh, they were extremely close. I think Cal's work ethic was learned exclusively from his father. His father was a workaholic, very dedicated to his job and his organization, as well as Cal is. There are a lot of characteristics—I'm sure he has a lot from his mother, but his father probably stands out a little bit more because I've seen his father and been around him and Cal, and see a tremendous amount of similarites."

He said Billy also had the Ripken work ethic. "Their father was just a regular Joe Blow—a hard, blue-collar work guy that put in a lot of time and energy and loved what he did. He left the world a little too early."

Meanwhile, Hargrove added, "Cal and his dad had a lot of the same features. Cal's obviously a much bigger man than his dad was, but as far as facial features and their eyes, they're the same.

"But I also think they have the same work ethic—it was like father, like son; and how they were respectful to people are the things I saw as much as anything. They respected the people in the game, and out of the game, but they also respected the game."

When Hargrove opposed Cal Jr. during his playing days, what he remembered, other than the similarities between Cal's mannerisms and his father's, was Cal's talent: "It's easy to spot talent like that. I don't think that you think, Gee, that guy's a Hall of Fame guy. That develops over time, but you could see that he had the talent and he really epitomized his father. You knew then that if hard work would make him a very good player—he was always a *good* player—then the hard work would be there because he was so much like his father."

As for Cal's streak, his peers are simply in awe of what he did and how long he lasted. Only eighteen men who were active in the majors at the start of the streak were still around when it came to an end. Defensive standout Omar Vizquel was asked what baseball record impresses him the most, and he shot back, "Cal Ripken. There is no doubt. To be able to go on the field every day, day in and day out, for fifteen years is not easy to do. Especially at shortstop, where there are so many things that can go wrong: a pulled groin, get hit by a pitch, have a headache, stomachache, feel bad. I mean, there are *so* many things [that can stop a streak]. That's the hardest record to break.

"It's especially tough in these days [to keep a streak alive], when guys are getting a lot of money and they like to take care of themselves. If they feel they have a bad arm or leg, they don't want to push it too much," the Cleveland shortstop concluded.

Yet another shortstop, Ozzie Guillen, concurs. "I don't think anybody's *ever* gonna' break that," he said. "I think that record is my No. 1 pick [as the most unbreakable record of all]."

Prior to Mark McGwire's home-run explosion, Matt Williams said he believed Ripken's record was safer than Roger Maris's 61 homers. Williams predicted, "Nobody's hit over 61 homers, but every year it looks like it's in jeopardy. Somebody can do it. It's not out of reach."

However, when it came to Cal and his record, Williams said, "It's amazing. You're lucky to play one year without something that's going to keep you out of the lineup, let alone fifteen seasons."

As a final note to put Cal's streak in perspective, consider this: when his string of games played had reached 2,350, the next longest active streak was held by Houston Astros second baseman Craig Biggio, at a very modest 256.

Although the streak brought Cal Ripken Jr. fame, it also brought out some nit-picking critics. If Cal wasn't playing up to what was expected of him and the Orioles slumped, some members of the media blamed him for the team's losses, saying he should take himself out of the lineup.

Billy defended his brother in a *Baltimore Sun* story. "In the past, I considered the emphasis on the streak to be an assault on him," he said. "There was an awful lot of blame pointed his way whenever something went wrong with the Birds. Usually, it was because he was tired and wasn't helping the team. It was venomous, I thought."

More painful than media attacks was the death of Cal Ripken Sr., which hit the family hard. He died about a week before the season opener in 1999. Cal Jr. told *Baseball Digest,* "It was devastating, losing a father. It was a horrific experience. I know everybody has to go through it, but that doesn't make it any easier."

Chapter Seven: The Bonds Duo

Taken separately, the lifetime stats of both Barry and Bobby Bonds are impressive. Together, though, these two men own virtually every major record involving a father and son in the history of the game. They've done it all, with power and with speed. Entering the 2001 season, their combined 826 homers (Bobby contributed 332) is not only No. 1, it ranked 236 ahead of the second-place Griffeys. They are also trailed by the Bells (453 HR), Boones (409), and Berras (407; of which 358 were owned by Yogi).

The runs driven in list is also headed by the Bonds duo, with 2,429 (Barry had 1,405), followed by the Bells at 2,262; the Boones with 2,247; the Griffeys at 2,129; and the Berras, who check in with 1,708.

Finally, stolen bases. This time the list reads: Bonds, best of all time, with 932 (Barry led his father by 10, with 471 as of this writing); 782 by Maury and Bump Wills; 589 by the Alomars; 381 by George and Dick Sisler (even though Dick swiped only six bases); and 373 by the Griffeys.

Barry was tabbed the Player of the Decade for the 1990s by *Sporting News*. All he did for that ten-year period was average 109 runs, 107 RBI, and 36 homers a year while hitting .302. The homers and runs batted in total stood third best among all players for the 1990s.

He had also compiled 30 or more home runs in each of his previous nine years, something only five men have managed. In 1993 he became the first man ever to capture three MVP trophies over a four-year span. For that matter, only eight men have won three MVP Awards ever.

Among players with 4,000 or more career total bases, Barry Bonds owns the sixth-highest slugging percentage of all time, at a robust .567, ahead of such luminary power hitters as Stan Musial, Willie Mays, Mickey Mantle, and home run king Hank Aaron. Once, over a period of several days, Barry reached base fifteen straight times to tie a National League record.

It's no wonder he's feared by pitchers everywhere—the proof is his 320 intentional walks drawn, more than any man to ever lace a pair of spikes. In the next year or so, he could also rank as high as No. 6 in the all-time walks-drawn department.

His dynamic burst to start the 2001 season, which lasted not just for a hot spell of a week or two but for months, culminated with his breaking the all-time single-season home run record, with 73. In the month of May he posted a slugging percentage of 1.035—becoming only the second man in the last twenty-four seasons to top the 1.000 level for a month, joining Todd Helton of the Rockies.

Bonds has even appeared in a few movies, the most notable being *Rookie of the Year,* in which he played himself. He is also a member of the Screen Actors Guild, and is quite active in a number of charities.

Barry was born in Riverside, California, a community that also produced his father, Anaheim Angels second baseman Adam Kennedy, former Seattle Mariners star Alvin Davis, and Dusty Baker, Barry's manager with the Giants. As a kid growing up, the only baseball hero Barry had other than his godfather, Willie Mays, was Mickey Mantle. Apparently, he favored sluggers from childhood on.

Barry has three children: a boy, Nikolai, and two daughters, Shikari and Aisha Lynn. His aunt, Rosie Bonds, was a member of the 1964 Olympic team and once held the United States women's record in the 80-meter hurdles.

Bobby Bonds, once a hitting coach with the Giants (and also with the Cleveland Indians), lasted fourteen years in the majors. He now lives in San Carlos, California, and is still on the Giants' payroll as a special assistant in player personnel. He began his career with a big bang. On June 25, 1968, in his first major-league game, Bobby smacked a grand-slam. In all, the well-traveled elder Bonds played for seven organizations: the Giants, Yankees, Angels, Rangers, Indians, Cardinals, and Cubs.

In 1981 Bobby joked of his nomadic ways, "I would like to find a home in baseball. The only thing I've been a part of the last six years is American Airlines." Still, he was a star who could even shine on defense in the outfield, like his son. Bobby Bonds owns three Gold Glove Awards of his own, making him and Barry the only father-son duo to have earned those trophies.

When he retired in 1981, he held the record for the most home runs hit to lead off a game ever, at 35—a record that lasted until Rickey Henderson broke it in 1989. He epitomized the speed-and-power game, foreshadowing what would come in the package of his son years later. For example, Bobby had a total of 793 homers plus steals. His 332 homers with 461 steals makes him one of four men to reach 300 or more steals with 300-plus homers. Since his son did this as well, they account for half of the men in this exclusive statistical group. (The other two are Willie Mays and former Expos and Cubs standout Andre Dawson.)

The temptation to say that baseball helped Bobby Bonds bond with Barry Bonds is strong, especially since that statement happens to be true.

Bobby has stated that his son began swinging a bat at the age of 1 and added, perhaps with only slight exaggeration, that he had perfected his swing by the time he was 2.

By the time Barry was 4 years old he was, according to the Giants Media Guide "a regular visitor to Candlestick Park [home of the Giants, his father's team then]." His mother, Pat, would drive Barry and his brother Rickey, five years younger, to the park. There the boys lived the dream of millions of youngsters. They would go "to the stadium on game days and they would play catch with Barry's godfather, future Hall of Famer Willie Mays." The children also "would shag flies and run around the clubhouse."

Barry has said that from his early youth on, he was spurred in his drive to make it to the majors by two factors: 1) he wanted to impress Mays and, 2) he wanted to impress his father with his prowess. When Barry was in junior high, he felt that he was indeed destined to play major-league baseball. That, said his father, was something he had known for nearly a dozen years.

When Barry began playing Little League at San Carlos, California, and later in high school at Serra High in San Mateo, it was Bobby's turn to become the spectator. As the Giants Media Guide put it, "He seldom sat in stands for fear of stealing [the] crowd's attention." Instead, he would park his car behind some trees and gaze at his boy's feats. Among those accomplishments was a .467 batting average in 1982, Barry's senior season, which helped him become a prep All-American.

After Barry graduated from the same high school that produced Pro Football Hall of Famer Lynn Swann, former big-league player and manager Jim Fregosi, and former big leaguer Gregg Jefferies, it was on to college. His prodigious high school stats allowed him to write his own ticket. After all, a three-year varsity batting average of .404 wasn't exactly shabby.

So Bonds elected to attend a school with a fine baseball program, Arizona State. There he played for three years, compiling a career average of .347, with 45 homers and 175 RBI. He was named All-Pac 10 for each of his three years and a *Sporting News* All-American during his junior season of 1985. Only the year before, he had tied an NCAA record with seven consecutive hits in the College World Series. His dad relished every moment of his son's success.

On opening day of the 2001 season, Barry Bonds hit yet another homer to close in on the venerated 500 plateau. As he crossed home plate, he was met by a 10-year-old batboy. Bonds bent down and tenderly placed a kiss on the child's cheek. That batboy was, of course, his son, Nikolai.

Give Nikolai another ten years or so, and he might be the one circling the bases. Right now, though, he's enjoying his duties even while acting nonchalantly, not unlike his father, some would say. As for his special job, he simply replied, "It's just something we [he and other players' children] do."

That may be, but in the All-Star Game of 2001 Nikolai got to do something very few children do. He not only sat in the dugout during the contest but was also interviewed on national television while the game was in progress.

In July of 2001, Nikolai was on his second Little League championship team. His father congratulated him, yet couldn't resist a moment of ironic humor. "That's great, son, I love you," Barry said. "Dad will get one [championship] sooner or later." Barry also commented that championships are, of course, "something Dad wants real bad. He's won more than I have."

Nikolai, who bats lefty and throws righty, was a batboy in the 2001 All-Star contest in Seattle. He also plays second base, in addition to playing his father's position in left.

If Barry's son does wind up following in his father's footsteps, there is no assurance that he will hit like, or even look like, his father on the field. Even if a father has a big influence on his son, they may not have similar styles when it comes to the game of baseball. Ed Spiezio said he sees no points of comparison between the batting stances of Bobby and Barry Bonds. "They seem to have their own styles," he said.

Maybe so, but when it comes to combining power and speed, they have few peers. As of the end of the 2000 season, only two men had compiled

30 or more steals and homers in a season more than three times (and only one other man, former Mets infielder Howard Johnson, did it in three seasons). Both Bobby and Barry accomplished that feat an incredible five times.

Perhaps the ultimate sign of respect came from Barry's opponents when, on May 28, 1998, the Arizona Diamondbacks elected to give him an intentional walk—with the bases already loaded. With the Giants down by two runs and with two men out, Arizona manager Buck Showalter walked Barry, allowing—make that, forcing—the potential winning run to move into scoring position. The move paid off in a Diamondback win, but this doesn't diminish the fact that it was prompted by the fear that Barry's opponents have of him.

As Barry approached his 500th home run in early April of 2001, he was besieged by a blitz of media attention. In many of these interviews, he decided to hold court. He told the story of his first big-league homer versus the Atlanta Braves. After hitting that initial blast, he called his father, who couldn't resist a playful dig. Bobby teased that his son had a mere 331 home runs to go before he'd tie him.

Barry spoke, too, of his godfather, the legendary Willie Mays, who had given him some fatherlike advice on his chances of chalking up impressive statistics, provided he managed to stay healthy, and thus build some longevity in the game. Mays also said that no matter how long Barry lasted, there was still no guarantee that he would win a glistening championship ring.

Barry knows that's true. He told *Baseball Weekly*, "I just want a World Series ring. Then, I can retire and leave this game. Really, that's all that's left." He added, "That's why I'm in this game. If you don't have that as a goal, why play?"

That quest has, in fact, kept Barry hungry throughout his career. Entering 2001, among players with no World Series appearances, only Ernie Banks (with 512 home runs) had more home runs than Barry did. By early 2001, Barry stood alone in that realm. Incidentally, another son of a major-league player, Ken Griffey Jr., with 438 homers, was also looking for his first shot at the Series. Only three men who have never played in a Series rank higher than Griffey on the all-time home-run list. Somehow, being the slugging son of a player loses some of its luster if that man never sees a single World Series at bat.

Appearing in the October classic is also important as a matter of pride. After all, Barry has been denied a shot at the Series partly because he hasn't done well in postseason play (partly because enemy pitchers give him little to hit, according to some experts). Going into 2001, he appeared in postseason play four times while compiling a pitiful .196 average and a meager 1 homer in 97 at bats.

The elder Bonds, a nine-time All-Star, was proud that for years only he, Mays, and Andre Dawson had 300 or more stolen bases with 300-plus homers, making for a highly exclusive club. Barry, though, has now created his own club, with 500 or more homers and more than 400 stolen bases. Plus, Bobby realized that, even as he spoke, his son would soon take it to 500 homers and 500 steals as well.

Of all the men in the 500 home run circle, the closest to Barry in steals is Mays, with a distant 338. And, of the men with 500 or more steals, the top home-run hitter was Rickey Henderson, with an even more remote 282. Such accomplishments as Barry has racked up certainly cause a father to shake his head in amazement, as if to say, "My little boy has done all that!"

On April 17, 2001, Barry achieved his dream, hitting his 500th career shot versus the Los Angeles Dodgers. He became the seventeenth member of the ritzy 500 home run circle when he connected off reliever Terry Adams in the eighth inning. In each of his at bats leading to the historic homer, the crowd rose and chanted, "Barry! Barry!" Imagine how he and his father must have felt at those moments.

The ball had barely settled into McCovey Cove, beyond right field, with a resounding kerplunk and the drama of an astronaut's splashdown, when Barry crossed home plate. He was greeted by his father near the plate, where they embraced. Moments later, the fence in left field swung open and out popped Mays and McCovey, fellow 500 home run hitters, who then golf-carted their way to honor Barry.

Barry spoke to the Pacific Bell Park throng (41,059 fans were packed into a park that lists its capacity at 40,800), and he showed everyone what his priorities were when he said, "First of all, I'd like to thank my parents for having me." It took thirty-six years since his birth to reach 500, but in 7,501 at bats he was actually the eighth quickest to attain that milestone. (McGwire, in 5,487 trips, was the quickest.) After the game, he again paid tribute to his parents. "I wanted to run off the field," he began, "and hug my wife, my dad, my mom, and to thank the Giants organization. Then I started looking for Willie [Mays]."

When Barry hit his fifty-third home run in August of 2001, he again invoked the name of Mays, this time teasingly. He got in a jab at Mays because his homer broke the Giants' team record set by "the Say Hey Kid" when he starched the ball to the tune of 52 home runs back in 1965. Said Barry, "He'll probably congratulate me. But I've got a couple of things I need to say . . . like 'Gotcha.' "

In the meantime, Tom Trebelhorn called Bobby Bonds "the best player I ever saw come up through the [Pacific] Coast League. I was a kid—

maybe I was in college when he came through and played for Phoenix. He was the best Triple-A player I ever saw. And Barry has done more than Bobby. Great careers."

Gary Ward, an American League coach in 2001 and himself the proud father of a major-league son, said that he seldom ran across the Bonds family. "Barry's father was in the league as a coach with Cleveland when I was a player, and I watched a lot of the drills that he would take his players through. I sort of copied them and did them for myself; they helped me out quite a bit."

While he wasn't sure that Bobby used those same drills to instill proper technique in his son, Ward said, "As good of a swing as he has, and growing up with players like Willie Mays and Willie McCovey, I'm quite sure they all had a piece of the pie to put in it, and he just put it all together for himself."

Not only is Barry a great offensive threat but he has collared eight Gold Gloves. Tony Gwynn, who has made a lucrative living by hitting the ball to the opposite field, paid Bonds a high compliment. "I want to hit the ball to left field, but if they [pitchers] come inside, I have to pull it," he said. "The majority of balls I hit do go to left field."

If that's the case, he was asked, then why don't the left fielders cheat on him and play shallow where he often swats the ball and thus steal many singles from him. Gwynn then paid Barry a compliment, saying, "It's funny, but every team is different [in how they defense him]. Some try to take hits up the middle away from you, or take away something else. Barry Bonds tries to take it away from me [in left field], but it takes guts and talent to do that. Bonds is the only left fielder in the National League who has the guts to come in and say, 'I dare you to hit it over my head.' In my career, I only did it once. I kid him all the time: 'I'm gonna' burn you.' It took me going off the wall to burn him. If I don't hit the wall, he'll catch it."

Gwynn isn't alone in his praise of Barry Bonds and his defensive skills. In 1999, *USA Today* ran an article listing the greatest defensive players of the last quarter century at each position. Although Hall of Famers Carl Yastrzemski and Dave Winfield were well liked in left, Barry was chosen as the best.

Hall of Fame left fielder Billy Williams said that in his prime Rickey Henderson was the quickest at getting to the line in left to deny doubles. Then he noted, "But when you look at Barry playing the outfield, he's worked hard . . . he charges the ball and makes great plays in the outfield. I think with his experience now, knowing where hitters hit the ball, he gets himself in good position to make the plays. He's just become a great left fielder."

Chapter Eight: The Alomars

The same *USA Today* survey that praised Barry Bonds's defensive talents also tabbed Robbie Alomar as the greatest glove at second, ahead of such great flashers of the leather as Ryne Sandberg, Frank White, Willie Randolph, and Harold Reynolds.

Robbie, of course, is another player who comes from excellent stock. His father, Sandy Sr., played the game for fifteen years from 1964 to 1978, finishing with the Rangers after also playing for the Yankees, Angels, White Sox, and the Braves in both Atlanta and Milwaukee. In 2001, he was coaching for the Cubs, but in the off-season after the 2000 campaign he coached a winter-league team in Puerto Rico. His designated hitter was his son Robbie, who wanted a tune-up before reporting to spring training.

Sandy Sr. appeared in 1,481 games, over which time he hit .245. Never a great hitter, he was a valuable player nevertheless. He switch-hit in all but two of his big-league seasons and played all over the diamond. Mainly a second baseman, he also played shortstop, third base, first base, outfield, and spent some time as a designated hitter. He was a highly efficient base stealer, too, succeeding in almost 74 percent of his attempts.

Former catcher Art Kusnyer agreed with so many people around the game who said that Sandy Sr. "was a good man and he was good on the ball club. He played hard, and he was one of those guys who came to beat you, like his two boys do."

The 5'9", 140-pound native of Salinas, Puerto Rico, had to be overjoyed when his two sons played on the same team. That happened first, on the professional level, in 1985 at Charleston, Class "A." It occurred again in "AA" at Wichita in 1987 and 1989; Triple-A ball in Las Vegas in 1988; with the San Diego Padres in 1988 and 1989; and, most recently, as members of the Cleveland Indians in 1999 and 2000.

In 1999, the Alomar brothers bought twenty-seven tickets for each of twenty-seven Indians home games. They had the tickets distributed to youth organizations in the Greater Cleveland vicinity. The reason they chose twenty-seven for the number of tickets they bought was that their jersey numerals added up to twenty-seven.

Robbie, born on Hank Aaron's birthday (February 5) in 1968, in Ponce, Puerto Rico, is a deep thinker when it comes to baseball. He pursed his lips as he thought through virtually every question during our interview, showing the same intensity and intelligence that have made him perhaps the greatest second baseman in the history of the game. He is engaged to tennis star Mary Pierce. Should they have any children, it's a given that their genetic background would give them a head start in athletics.

Robbie's glove work is unparalleled—he owns nine Gold Gloves through 2000. Only Ryne Sandberg has won as many as a second baseman. From June of 1994 through early July of 1995, he put together a streak of 104 errorless games at second, the longest in American League history at that position. His five errors in 1992 share the league record for the fewest miscues in a season at second base. Most impressive of all, his .98644 fielding percentage is the greatest in the history of the American League.

The eleven-time All-Star has also won four Silver Slugger Awards as the best offensive player at his position. In 2001, when he was named to yet another All-Star Game, he said that when he was a boy he used to dream of making it to one All-Star Game—he did a lot better than that. He also said, "I will always remember the first one. I was in San Diego, Sandy was in Cleveland, and my dad was the coach. That was a real moment to remember, for myself and for the family."

During the ten-year period from 1991 to 2000, only Rafael Palmeiro and Mark Grace had more hits than Robbie. Acquired via trade during this most recent off-season by the New York Mets, he owns a career batting average of .304 for his stints with the Padres, Blue Jays, Orioles, and Indians. The fine switch-hitter has also driven in 918 runs, with a season high of 120 in 1999. His personal best for home runs is 24, also done in 1999, and on four occasions he had 40 or more doubles in a year, proving that *some* second basemen can certainly put a charge in the ball. Furthermore, his lifetime batting average for each of the three rounds of postseason play that he's been in are all above .300, including a .347 average in World Series play.

Call him a "five-tool player," because the man can run, too. In 2000 he became the thirty-sixth man, since the rules for stolen bases were established, to reach 400 burgled bases. Twice he's topped the 50 level for steals, and he doesn't appear to be slowing down; he stole 39 while being caught just four times in 2000, at the age of 32—good for a torrid 90.7 percent success rate.

His 1999 showing vividly displayed his five tools: 40 doubles, 24 homers, 120 RBI, 37 steals, a league-leading 138 runs, and a season full of dazzling defensive plays that earned him yet another Gold Glove. That year he became the first Indian in the team's 99-year history to top 20 HR, 100 runs, 30 steals, and 100 RBI in a season.

Meanwhile, as Sandy Jr. patiently fielded question after question from me about his family, he stared directly ahead into his cubicle in the clubhouse of Jacobs Field, back when he was still with the Indians. As he responded to questions about his father, he seemed to be gazing at the picture of his dad that was prominently on display. A woman had given him the shot of his father in an Angels uniform, and he was so taken with it that it became a permanent fixture in his locker.

Born in 1966, in Salinas, Puerto Rico, Sandy Jr. signed with the San Diego Padres as a free agent at the tender age of 17. He was named the Minor League Player of the Year by *Baseball America* in both 1988 and 1989, the same years he won the MVP of the Pacific Coast League.

By 1990 he had impressed the experts, winning the Rookie of the Year Award and his one Gold Glove Award as well. A six-time All-Star, Sandy won the MVP in the 1997 All-Star Game in Cleveland, becoming the first man to win that award in his own home park. He also appeared in two World Series, in 1995 and 1997, as a member of the Indians.

The year 1997 was one of those enchanted seasons for him, a season in which everything clicked. He smacked the ball to a .324 tune, drilled 37 doubles, 21 homers, and drove in 83. He set personal highs in virtually every offensive category and also compiled an incredible 30-game hitting streak, the second longest in big-league history by a catcher. For the capper, it was his September 26 home run that won the division for Cleveland.

When the postseason rolled around, he, too, rolled. He had 5 homers, a postseason record for catchers, and 19 runs batted in—a new postseason mark for ribbies. He was the fifth player in World Series history to compile 10 RBI and the first since 1960. He also became the first man ever to hit a home run in his home ballpark in both the All-Star Game and the World Series.

After hitting .316 in the '97 Division Series, he went on to belt out a .367 average in the Series.

Overall, he owns a .276 lifetime batting average to go with 93 home runs in 993 big-league games.

He has two children, Marcus and Marissa.

Testimonials for the Alomars are far from rare. The consensus seems to be this is a family with a ton of baseball insight. Plus, they play the game with intensity and a high degree of skill.

Charlie Manuel, Robbie's manager in 2001, praised his second baseman, saying, "He's as good a baseball person as I've been around."

Cleveland coach Clarence Jones said that Sandy Sr. was "a pretty good player at second and short and had real good hands." He added, "He was a pretty good hitter, too. I knew him well—he's a good man. He did a great job with Sandy and Robbie. I guess he stayed on them pretty good—they turned out to be fine players."

Art Kusnyer, who was coaching with the Chicago White Sox in 2000, said that he played with or against, or knew many of the father-son duos in baseball, including the Alomars, the Bells, and the Boones. "All the kids seem to be like their dads [in how they played the game]—smart, good people, and they come to beat your butt every day when they come to the ballpark."

Clyde Wright said that of the sons of players he recalls from when they were young "the ones I remember really well were the Alomar brothers. They were down in Puerto Rico when I played with their dad. They used to come in the clubhouse all the time. Oh, God, they were little brats." Actually, he amended his teasing, saying, "They were just normal kids.

"Let me tell you a funny story," he continued. "I used to tell them to leave, run them out of the clubhouse, right? And when my son [Jaret] signed with Cleveland I went down [to the clubhouse] and Sandy comes walking over towards me. Six foot five, about two-thirty [pounds], something like that—and he looks at me and says, 'Now run me out of the clubhouse.'"

Needless to say, Alomar was joking. He does indeed stand 6'5" and weigh 220 pounds, but he is as gentle as he is big. Furthermore, he is media-friendly as well as fan-friendly—a classy guy. When it became apparent that the

Indians weren't going to sign him for the 2001 season, Clevelanders staged a mini-uprising. Even Charlie Manuel, his Indians manager, commented on how the loss of Alomar hurt him and spoke of how much he would be missed.

Fans concurred. The American League schedule just happened to feature the Indians hosting the White Sox, Alomar's new team, to open the 2001 season. It was a celebration of the first game ever played in the American League that featured the Sox versus the Indians. At any rate, spectators greeted Sandy Jr. with a standing ovation when he was introduced, and continued to cheer and support him in every subsequent appearance.

"It was just fun to see them," Wright concluded. "Then all of a sudden, later on, they're playing in the big leagues and you played with their dad." He added that Robbie truly did love hanging around the parks more so than Sandy. "He was there *all* the time, but they both loved the game [and were] there all the time with their dad."

Meanwhile, in March of 2001 the general manager of the Chicago White Sox, Ken Williams, was glowing after he acquired Sandy Jr. from the Indians. "I played with Robbie and, after seeing Sandy this spring, I think I'm going to call Sandy Sr. and ask how he raised two such fine sons," he said. "I hope I can do as well."

With Sandy in Chicago, and his father serving as a Cubs coach, the two would have a few more chances to get together, but not as much time as many fans might think. As a rule, when the White Sox are in town the Cubs are on the road and vice versa.

As important as the game was—and still is—to his family, Robbie says that he and his father would have been close even without baseball, "because he's my dad—I always have a good relationship with my dad." While baseball wasn't *necessary* to their relationship, again, it was constantly a part of their world.

"He taught me a lot of baseball. He taught me everything I know about the game," Robbie said. "But he never pushed me to play the game and he did nothing to hurt my feelings," adding that his father, back then, wasn't really too strict with him.

He said that being the son of a big leaguer was a great experience, allowing him to hang around stars and grow up with the game. Baseball was always his dream, and now he feels that he's living that dream. He also stated that he subscribes to the theory that having a father who went through big-league battles helped him make it to the majors.

There can be no doubt that his dad taught him well. Robbie perennially wins an honor, such as being among the top three players listed in *Baseball America*'s yearly polls for top bunters, best gloves at second, and best base runners. As recently as the publication's 2001 survey, Robbie took first place in the categories of best bunter, best hit-and-run batter, and best defensive second baseman. He also came in second for the best base runner. That poll is prestigious because the people surveyed are big-league managers. Robbie is easily one of the smartest men in baseball when it comes to analyzing the game and taking advantage of other team's mistakes. One of his former managers, Mike Hargrove, once commented, "He sees a lot of things that other players can't, or won't, see."

Sandy Jr. is a baseball thinker, too. Once when he was catching for the Indians against the Mariners, a runner off first base got such a good jump on the pitcher that Sandy instantly knew he couldn't throw him out. Instead of holding the ball futilely or gunning it to second, risking a wild throw without any real chance of catching the base burglar, Sandy concocted a plan on the spot.

He purposely lobbed the ball high over the infield in the direction of second baseman Carlos Baerga. Alomar was hoping the runner would be deked into thinking the ball had been hit, resulting in a lazy pop-up. If fooled, he would have to scamper back to first base; he would lose his sure stolen base. The decoy didn't work, but it demonstrates how clever this family is, constantly thinking on the diamonds.

Despite his realization that his father was a big leaguer, Robbie never felt that this made him or his family special or better than anybody else. He said simply, "He's my dad. I didn't look at him as a baseball player or as somebody famous. I just looked at him as my dad. I always enjoyed being with him, and I will always enjoy his company."

For the record, Robbie says his father did get some special attention in his native land of Puerto Rico after he had made it to the big leagues. "A little bit. The people knew who he was. He was, I think at the time, the only professional baseball player there." Naturally, the folks in their hometown of Salinas were proud of him.

Of course, it's not unusual for standout ballplayers to be treated like gods on the island of Puerto Rico. "Every time there's a celebrity, people treat you differently," Sandy Jr. said. "I guess they're proud of you for what you accomplished for the country, that you represent Puerto Rico. Yeah, you're pretty much treated a little bit different, but it's all good—they're just proud of you performing at a major level. They're hoping their kid will do the same thing."

Likewise, Sandy Jr. says he's proud of his family. "Oh, definitely. I'm proud to be Puerto Rican, proud to be doing well, and representing the country well."

One of Robbie's first tastes of baseball, he said, was when "I used to go to the games in winter ball and in the States when we weren't in school during the summer. We'd go to the United States to see him play. I remember, because I was born in 1968 and he retired in 1978, so I was old enough to remember.

"I got to meet a lot of the players he used to play with," Robbie continued. "I remember all of them, but my dad was my hero all the time." Many players take their fathers for granted and select other players as their favorite. Not Robbie. He said, without a split second of hesitation, that his dad was clearly his favorite player of all time.

As a youngster, Robbie saw many great Puerto Rican players, and while his dad was No. 1, he added, "I liked Jose Cruz a lot, and I saw a lot of Americans—Thurman Munson and others."

As kids, the Alomar boys played a game Sandy Jr. called "paper-cup baseball." "You put one cup inside another one and squeeze and compress them into a ball," he explained. Once they had the makeshift ball, their hands became their bats. They played this game a lot when Sandy Sr. was in Texas, in 1978. Joining them there during the summer, after school was through, were Barry and Ricky Bonds, since their dad, Bobby, was also with the Rangers back then.

"We used to play in the hallways at Arlington Stadium," he said. The paper-cup game was an ingenious one, in that at the time the children weren't "allowed to take any object like a bat to the park." Thus they learned how to improvise.

"And at Anaheim [Sandy Sr. was there from 1969 to 1974] we used to hang around in the concourse playing that game. When we lived in a rented apartment, we played outside pretty much all day. We used to bat in the backyard with tennis balls and Wiffle balls."

Because Robbie has such a sterling heritage, one would expect him to feel some pressure to live up to his family name or to his country's expectations. "Not really," he said. "I figured I had a God-given talent and just took advantage of that talent."

Robbie's father has seen him at every stage of his career, from Little League up through the professional ranks. Some fathers who are active coaches see their sons play only when their teams meet, sometimes only in spring training. In Robbie's case, his dad was on the scene from day one of his big-league career.

"He was my coach [in San Diego] my first year," Robbie said. "It was a lot of fun. I played with him in the minor leagues—he was my coach in the minors, and when I came up to the big leagues he was my coach, too. To me it was fun, because he helped me a lot, and when you're young you make a lot of mistakes and having a dad there who played the game and *knows* the game—he can help you a lot."

That was especially true in the case of Sandy Sr. because he spent 1,156 of his professional contests at second base. In all, he played only forty-seven times at a position other than the infield during the course of his fifteen-year career.

After being with Robbie at Charleston, South Carolina, in 1985, Sandy Sr. moved to the majors as a coach. Robbie took a little longer to get out of the Padres' minor-league system. But, he said, "eventually I caught up to him in the big leagues," and they were both ecstatic to be reunited.

Sandy Jr. also had his big-league debut in front of his father with San Diego. "He had the opportunity there to watch me play; so did my mom," he said. "It was great for our family that we were together and everybody got to watch everybody. It was fun."

While Robbie's father taught him a great deal about playing the infield, Sandy Jr. noted that, unlike his brother, being a catcher "we were in a different situation. My dad let the catching instructor pretty much dictate and tell me what to do, because he was [just] in charge of infielders. Naturally, he helped Robbie more than he helped me baseballwise. But, [dealing with] mental errors and stuff like that, yeah, he was good with me and Robbie, and he helped me that way."

While some fathers had a direct involvement in their son's money matters, Sandy Jr. said, "In our family we never talk money—we were never that kind of family. My dad gave me advice about how to play the game, but not about money."

Likewise, he said that some fathers who played the game would warn their sons about the dangers of life on the road. At times shady characters try to get close to players, but Sandy Jr. said he believes "it's something every player should realize and learn on his own." He added, "You should know who are the good people and who are the bad people. You [should] always associate with good people so you'll be fine. We are [always] around good people. In baseball, the organization gives you a lot of help."

Sandy Jr. now has a son who's just a few years shy of his teens. Marcus already loves the game and has shown a flair for it. Specifically, he has the uncanny ability to mimic the myriad batting stances of famous big leaguers, including, of course, his father and his uncle Robbie. He became so good at it that he was featured in the national media, a point of pride for his father.

So, too, is Marcus's ability. In 2000, Sandy Jr. said, "He's playing Little League. He pitches and plays first and second. He likes to emulate other players. He's shown some athleticism; he's been in *Baseball Weekly* emulating the different players. Yeah, he has some talent."

Marcus "has matured a lot and he has done a lot of things that he sees on TV from baseball players," said Sandy Jr. "He's watching games, and he's very smart about the game. He keeps asking me questions about different situations all the time.

"When he watches a game, he calls me and says, 'Dad, how come this guy did that?' And I get to explain some situations to him. You don't want to overload his mind, because he's still a kid. I mean, just go out there and play ball and have fun."

Sandy Jr. said he is surprised at how incisive his son's questions are. "They're pretty smart questions. A couple of times he asked me, 'How come the guy slides early into second base on a double play?'

"I said, 'Because if he doesn't they'll take his head off.' They [kids] don't know that—that the shortstop's going low [with his throw] and if you don't slide early they hit you pretty hard. It's stuff like that; it's stuff you don't think a kid is going to ask you." He was impressed that a youngster would watch a game and be able to observe a nuance such as a runner sliding "way ahead of where they normally slide." Most kids tend to notice only flashy moments, like home runs.

The identity of Marcus's favorite player is easy to figure out. "He always likes his dad," Sandy Jr. said with a grin. "He always tells me that, but he likes other guys, too. He likes his uncle, and Barry Bonds—[he's a] front runner."

As for the days of his own youth, Sandy Jr. continued, saying that his father was his favorite when he was a boy, and "because I enjoyed catching, I always liked Thurman Munson. I liked Jeff Torborg and most of the catchers—Johnny Bench, I used to watch him when I was a kid. But my dad was always my hero."

"We always hanged around my dad pretty much," he went on. "Robbie did more than I did. He was the most [dedicated] baseball freak that I ever saw. I did other stuff with my friends.

"On one occasion we were supposed to go to school, not go to a Winter League game. Robbie hid in the backseat until my dad was halfway to the game, then he popped up. My dad said, 'What are you doing here?' Robbie said, 'I want to go to the game.' He knew if he asked my dad, he never would've taken him. He just liked to go to the games, but my dad couldn't take him every day because we had to get up early to go to school."

There is no doubt in Sandy's mind that baseball has helped him bond with Marcus, just as it helped him get closer to Sandy Sr. "Oh, definitely," he said. "Baseball is kind of a language of communication for us. We are a big baseball [family], and sometimes that causes problems with your family because you have to learn how to divide time, and not always be [dealing with] baseball."

In the off-season he tries to let baseball taper off as the focal point of his days, but, he said, "Still it's always there, and when you go in the street, people always ask you questions about baseball."

When Robbie was asked to sum up in one sentence his thoughts and feelings for his father, the superstar second baseman succinctly replied, "I always love my dad no matter what."

Sandy Jr. spoke of how his relationship with his father didn't change much when he left childhood and became a grown-up. "Actually, our relationship is pretty much similar. We have the same communication as when I was a kid. Now, he talks to me like I'm an adult—I am an adult, but it's pretty much the same [as always]. It's always been a great relationship.

"He's not afraid to say anything he has to say and, at the same time, because I've been a rebel in the family, I'm not afraid to say, 'Hey, Dad, you're wrong about that.' Definitely, he respects my opinion a lot more [now] because I'm a catcher. I've been in baseball for—this is my twelfth year. He knows that I've learned a lot. But pretty much it's pretty good. He's easygoing, and we still talk about many things in life."

Sandy Jr. further said that his feelings for his father border on the indescribable (then proceeded to do a fine job of expounding on the subject). "You can't explain it," he said. "First of all, he gave me life, brought me to this world with my mom. My mom deserves much of the credit, but my dad—I love my dad. He's been a total guide for us."

Chapter Nine: The Seguis

David Segui was born on June 19, 1966. By then, his father, Diego, had already spent four full seasons pitching for the Kansas City Athletics. Diego, born in Holguin, Cuba, had subsequent big-league stops in Washington (1966), another in Kansas City in 1967, followed by a stay with the Oakland Athletics (after the franchise shifted to the West Coast in 1968), and a year with the fledgling Seattle Pilots. He was 12–6, with a dozen saves for the expansion Pilots—quite an accomplishment for a team that went on to win a mere sixty-four games that season. That works out to Diego's having been involved in nearly 40 percent of the team's victories, counting his wins and saves.

The journeyman pitcher also spent some time with the St. Louis Cardinals and the Boston Red Sox before finally topping off his career as a member of the inaugural Seattle Mariners squad of 1977. His status as the only man ever to play for both big-league clubs in Seattle made him the answer to a trivia question that every Washington native could answer instantly. Plus, as an oddity, he pitched for both teams for just one season, both their respective first seasons in existence.

Diego's other career highlights include a one-inning hitless, scoreless stint in the 1975 World Series with the Red Sox; his tremendous longevity, pitching in the big leagues until he was 40 years old; and his 1970 earned run crown, earned with Oakland when he came up with a sparkling 2.56 ERA. In fact, from 1967 through 1973, his ERA never rose above 3.35 and was sub-

3.00 on three occasions, including a personal best of 2.39 in 1968. In all, he won ninety-two big-league games over fifteen seasons.

David also gives his mother, who coached both him and his two brothers, a lot of credit. One brother, Dan, went on to play in the minor-league systems of both the New York Mets and the Minnesota Twins from 1987 to 1990 but never broke into the major leagues. His other brother attended Kansas State University, playing baseball there.

David credits his mother for his baseball instruction, but his overall diamond education was a family affair. Taught to switch-hit by an uncle who was an All-American at Missouri Western, David has put together quite a career. He played for the Baltimore Orioles (as their eighteenth-round draft pick in June of 1987), New York Mets, Montreal Expos, Seattle Mariners, Toronto Blue Jays, Texas Rangers, and Cleveland Indians before finally returning to the Orioles in 2001.

More important, he led the National League in fielding percentage in 1994 (at .996) and led the American League with a .999 fielding percentage in 1998. Then, in 2000, this slick-fielding first baseman went the entire year without committing a single error despite handling 617 total chances. Entering 2001 he shared the record for the highest fielding percentage in the history of the game for a first baseman at .996.

He can hit, too. For his eleven-year career through 2000, he owned a lifetime batting average of .292. His single-season highs were .334 in 2001, when he finished sixth in the race for the batting title at the age of 34; .309 in 1995; .307 in 1997; and .305 the following season. Thus he has hit more than .300 four times, and did so over a six-year span. (The only year during that stretch that he did not top .300 were 1996 and 1999, when he hit . 286 and .298, respectively.)

If David is indeed getting better with age, his 2000 season seems to serve as testimony. That year, he topped the 100 runs driven in plateau for the first time in his career (with 103), while scoring 93 times and racking up 192 hits, two more personal bests. In fact, he finished in the top ten in the league in four major offensive categories, not counting the league best .429 he hit during day games. Not only that but, he's a clutch hitter with a career batting average of .370 in bases-loaded situations.

Charlie Manuel managed David Segui for part of the 2000 season, and "knew David's dad when he was a pitcher from hitting against him," he said. "I used to talk to him every now and then, and he was quite a competitor as a pitcher. David Segui's an intense player, a hard-nosed player. Hustles, really loves to play the game, and I see a lot of similarities to them."

It was as if David was destined to become a big leaguer. "All I ever wanted to do was play baseball," he said. And his baseball memories go back very far—he says he can recall being in Municipal Stadium in Kansas City when he could barely walk. Despite being that young, he can still recall what the grandstands looked like.

While he loved baseball, there was obviously one aspect of the game that he loved the most—hitting, of course. "I have always loved hitting," David said. "My dad was a pitcher, and I pitched in high school and a little into college, but it just didn't suit my personal mentality."

David said that having a father who played in the majors "doesn't make it easier [for him to also succeed]; you still have to perform on the field, but the part I thought it helped me most [with] was knowing the lifestyle. When I did sign and started playing professionally, it wasn't a shock to me. I was used to living out of suitcases and traveling all the time—being away from home and from my family, all those things, dealing with those pressures."

While the average fan doesn't think of those aspects of the game, David says it's simply because they don't think things through. Fans tend to think of players as not having a life of their own off the field, much the way young schoolchildren think their teachers are more robotic than human. His deep voice booming, David said, "They just think, Players make a lot of money, they're not supposed to be human."

His father did teach him "inside baseball," as well as inform him about the inside story of the world of big leaguers. "Oh, yeah, when we'd sit home and watch a game he'd tell me about what the pitcher's trying to do to the hitter, setting him up—that kind of stuff," David recalled.

Does that sort of instruction make a player a better hitter? David thinks so. "It makes you realize from an early age that the guy's not standing on the mound just throwing the ball over the plate," he said. "There are a lot of people who watch TV, grown-ups even, who don't realize there's a whole cat and mouse game going on, changing speeds. They see a guy throw a ball up, high and away, and they wonder, What's he doing? How could he miss by that far? Well, he's setting something up. So you realize that there's actually another whole side of the game you don't see going on."

Not only did David watch *with* his dad but he was also able to watch his dad live. "I clearly remember seeing him play," he said. "I think he played till I was in college," he said. The fact that his father stayed around the game up to the age of 40 in the majors and then continued to play elsewhere helped; many children of players have dim, if any, memories of seeing their fathers play. Diego, who was born in 1937 in Cuba, was still in the majors with the expansion Seattle Mariners in 1977. By then, David was 11 years old.

"He was playing year-round," he said of his father. "After [his last year in the majors], he played [about] another ten years in Puerto Rico and Mexico. He'd play summer in Mexico, then he'd play winter ball in Puerto Rico."

David was amazed at Diego's longevity and durability, agreeing that his father must have had a rubber arm. "I don't know how he does it," he said. When he was asked how old his dad was when he finally quit the game entirely, David replied, "Geez, probably [when he was] mid to upper forties.

"I think I could play into my forties like my dad if I wanted to, but I would rather be home and watch my kids grow up," he continued. "That's something that no amount of money you make can ever replace. Nobody understands the time you miss away from your family. Fans don't see that or understand how much time we lose away from family and can never get back.

"It gets to the point where it is not worth it, as much as I love the game. The choice between being with your kids growing up or playing baseball is an easy decision on my part. And believe me, I love the game."

In fact, he feels that, as much as he loves every aspect of hitting, he would probably not decide to become a hitting instructor. At least not, perhaps, until "after the kids are grown up." His children are Cory, who was born in 1991, and Haley, who came along in 1994.

Since David was aware of his father's special talent at a young age, his pride in his dad began early and continues to this day. However, he believes he would have been proud of Diego no matter what he did for a living. "It's like any other kid, I think," he said. "You're always proud of your parents."

As for Diego teaching his son more than baseball, David said, "He was strict, not overly strict. I mean, we had rules we had to abide by in our household." In that respect, Diego sounds somewhat like a baseball manager who is fair and establishes rules he expects to be adhered to.

Furthermore, just as there is frequently a strong bond between a player and his manager, baseball helped tie a strong knot between David and Diego. Interestingly, though, because his father played ball virtually all year long, David believes the baseball bonding process took place more when he became an adult than when he was a child.

"Now it [baseball] does [bond us]; it's different now than when my dad played," David said. "He didn't make the money we make now, so he was gone all the time. The game took him *away* from us. I didn't even *know* my dad until I was in college and he finally came home. I don't know how they stayed married—I don't know how they did it, because he was gone all the time.

"But now it seems like the game has brought us together. Now. But for so long it took him away, and you don't get that time back, either—that's what people don't understand. That's all time lost," he concluded.

It sounds as if David could relate to a player like Ryne Sandberg, who left the game early partly to spend time with his family. For that matter, Matt Williams, who left Cleveland to play in Arizona, where he could be close to his children, also comes to mind. David said one thing he looks forward to about his retirement is the fact that "my kids will still be home when I'm done playing baseball, and I'll be able to enjoy them even more."

Today's players can afford to quit early if they want to because of their financial security. Even though he says baseball is a personal passion, and he enjoyed a great season in 2000, it would not be at all surprising to see David do the walk away from the game and into the arms of his children.

When it came to his peers, David said having a father who was a celebrity didn't cause him to get special attention. His friends apparently didn't create a clamor by begging for autographs. However, he did get treated differently, but "only on the baseball field," he said. "People expected you to be head and shoulders better than anybody else, which really isn't fair. But that's just the way it is."

Sometimes in baseball when an opponent knows that a player has a famous father, he might give that player a hard time, challenge him. David said he didn't openly experience that, but, he added, "I'm sure there were times where other kids resented it."

David isn't at all surprised that many of his peers are better players than their fathers were. He said one reason is that each generation is bigger, faster, and stronger than the previous one. "There's no doubt about that," he said. "Just look at football. The little guys now are bigger than the big guys when my dad played." Even though he said his dad was "known as one of the strongest guys when he played," when he comes in the clubhouse now he's not astonished to see monsters like Mark McGwire on the scene.

"My dad's a strong guy," David said. "He's six feet, 190, but now that's what the little middle infielders are. You look at every other sport, and they seem to embrace that theory—it's not even a theory, it's fact. But for some reason in baseball, whether it's history or tradition, people don't want to let go of the fact that the guys now might be better than they were twenty-five, thirty years ago."

One thing David didn't have to learn directly from his father was the dangers of being on the road as a baseball player. There are, in fact, some shady characters who try to sidle up to players for numerous nefarious reasons.

"I saw that on my own just watching him, watching his career, watching how many people act like they're his friend," David said. "Or, how many people who, when he was playing, were around and then when he wasn't playing anymore or wasn't in the big leagues, how many of those same people were never around anymore. That's just human nature, how people are around anybody who's successful—that's just the way it is. It's really sad, but that's the way it is."

David said enough confidence was instilled in him so that he never felt he had to live up to his family name or follow in his father's footsteps. "Never. Ever since I was little I wanted to play baseball—that had nothing to do with my family name. I'm sure it had a lot to do with growing up, watching my dad play, but I never felt like 'I'm a Segui and I need to be a baseball player.' That's what my passion is, and that's the only reason I do it."

But don't get David wrong when it comes to family pride. "Of course, I have pride in the type of person my dad is. I'll never be the man he is," he said, reflecting the feelings many sons have expressed. "He's a far better man than I'll ever be."

Quite candidly and extremely sincerely, he added, "We're very much alike, so we butt heads a lot. We're both very impatient. Probably as much as we disagree, there's nobody else that I'd ever want to be my father."

At the time of the interview, in August of 2000, David spoke of his son, Cory, then eight years old, and of how Cory's favorite player is Bobby Bonilla. "He likes Bobby Bo from my Mets days, when Cory was little." David smiled, knowing that Bonilla was his son's favorite player but that his favorite man was, of course, David.

Like any father, David loves to be with his son and enjoys passing down some tips. He said that on his next day off he already had a trip planned to be with Cory and catch a baseball game his son was to appear in. "He's just like I was when I was little—in here [the clubhouse] all the time," he said. "He carries a bat around. He just loves baseball. He lives and breathes it. It's kinda scary to see how much alike we are."

If Cory is indeed *that* much like his father and, by extension, his grandfather, a third-generation big leaguer could be in the offing. In fact, Cory would probably have been at his father's side, helping with the interview, had it not been for the fact that his school "season" had started early that year.

David continued, "When I think back about how I was when I was a kid, it's the same with him [regarding the love of the game], so I don't have to push him; I would *never* push him—he has the drive already in him. Whether that takes him anywhere, we'll see."

David says he can't actually remember the first time his father saw him play in the majors, as "he didn't watch that often—it's hard for him to sit in the stands and watch. He gets too nervous."

As for his memories of seeing his dad pitch, he said that when his dad did have an occasional bad outing on the mound, he never felt like, "Oh, poor Dad is getting hit hard today." However, he said with a chuckle, "You knew it was going to be a quiet ride home that day."

As a grandfather, Diego, according to David, is "probably more proud of him [Cory] than he was of us as kids. It's pretty cool. He coaches him and practices with him when he's home. They live in Kansas City, so whenever he gets a chance he'll work with him. It's nice that he's able to spend time with my son, time that he never got to spend with me. It works out nice."

While thinking back to the days of his father's career, David said it was impossible to pick a memory or two that stand out. "You can never pinpoint one thing," he said. "It's just like a mass or flood of memories you have, not one you could pick out."

If he could, perhaps the day Diego wrapped up his 1970 ERA crown would have stood out. With a microscopic ERA of 2.56, he captured the title over such pitching luminaries as Baltimore ace Jim Palmer, Fritz Peterson, fire-baller "Sudden" Sam McDowell, and Jared Wright's father, Clyde.

When David was asked if his father is prouder of him as a person or as a player with big-league prowess, he laughed while poking fun at himself. "I don't know—with a tongue ring and the bleached hair, who knows?"

Going beyond the obvious difference in the positions played by father and son, Clarence Jones offered a deeper analysis of Diego and David Segui. "Diego was a pitcher known for his forkball—he had a real good one." Jones said. "He threw pretty good, and he had pretty good command of it. He had respect from everybody; he was a great guy on the field and off the field.

"I just got a chance to meet David a couple years ago, and he's another fine ballplayer. He's a student of the game. He knows every pitcher who goes out there, and he knows what he's going to do when he goes in the batter's box. He stings the ball," Jones said.

Ted Uhlaender was a coach with the Indians when David Segui was with the club. He observed that while many father-son duos are alike, others are very different. He remembered David's father, pitcher Diego, and said, "I faced him. He made a living off a split pitch, and his son's a first baseman." A bottom line detected was the fact that they were both fine players.

Cleveland teammate Jim Thome had praise, too. "He's a guy that prepares every day and plays very hard," he said of David. "And whether he has aches and pains or whatever, he's still out there." Aches and pains, indeed. David Segui plays with a broken metal plate in his left foot, but he never complains.

Elrod Hendricks also had recollections of both Diego and David Segui. "I watched him [David] grow as a kid, a little shy kid. And all of a sudden, here he is in the big leagues. Wow, how fast he grew.

"His dad was very quiet, but a very strong-minded person. I caught him in Puerto Rico. He was all baseball. When he was pitching, what concentration he had—oh, yes."

Finally, Joe Nossek said that he played with Diego and found him to be a "fine man, strong as a bull—that's one thing I remember about him, and David is, too." He also thinks David is a "quality guy," adding, "Both are talented individuals."

Chapter Ten: The Spiezios

E d Spiezio had the chance to accomplish many things in his life, but perhaps two stand out more than all the rest. The first was something many men have done and are proud of: he produced a fine son. The second feat is something millions of men have dreamed of but only a few have managed: he made it to the major leagues. According to one source, in the annals of baseball only about 15,000 men have played at the big-league level. Considering the population of young men in the world who aspire to make it to the majors, the odds against such success are astronomical.

Once in the bigs, he did something else every pro baseball player has yearned to do: he stepped into the batter's box during a World Series contest (his career average in the Fall Classic is .500 based on one hit in two pinch appearances). He owns two World Series rings, having been on the championship teams of the 1964 and 1967 St. Louis Cardinals. He went to the Series again in 1968, but his Cards lost to the Detroit Tigers. Thus in his five years with St. Louis, he was on three pennant winners.

Perhaps the highlight of his career would be when, he said, during the 1968 World Series, he "hit a line shot against Mickey Lolich, who was really tough, for a pinch hit. I must have fouled off 15–20 pitches—it's funny the things you remember. It [his at bat] went on and on and on. He won three games in that Series to beat us," he said.

A year earlier, in his only other Series at bat, he was robbed when, according to Ed, Boston's Joe Foy "made a diving catch to his left on a line drive." Had it not been for that defensive gem, Ed would own an unblemished 1.000 career batting average in World Series play.

Another great time in his career came "I think it was in San Diego, I'm guessing, in June of 1970," he said. "I hit eight home runs in—I think it was [in] ten games." He likened that hot spell to what Barry Bonds experienced in 2001.

"I know what he's going through, although I never hit 38 home runs before the All-Star game." Then he added with a laugh, "Or 38 at all, for my career." For the record, he hit 39 for his major-league lifetime of 554 games. Bonds hit his thirty-ninth for the 2001 season on June 23, breaking the old high for home runs before the All-Star break of 37 set by Mark McGwire in 1998 and Reggie Jackson in 1969.

In all, Ed's career spanned nine years: 1964–1968 with the Cardinals, 1969–1972 as a member of the San Diego Padres, and part of the 1972 season with the Chicago White Sox. He played third base for 404 contests and roamed the outfield for an additional twenty games while compiling a career batting average of .238. He could display some punch with the bat at times, swatting 25 homers over 671 at bats for the Padres in 1969 and 1970. His highest batting average came in 1970, when he hit .285.

Meanwhile, his son Scott, whose middle name is Edward in honor of his paternal grandfather, entered the 2002 season with six years' experience, having broken into the majors in 1996. He attended Morris High School, where he was a league MVP and an All-State baseball player. After graduating in 1990, he went on to major in finance at the University of Illinois.

Scott, who now plays in a garage band called Sand Fox, began his career with the Oakland Athletics, as their sixth-round selection in the 1993 free-agent draft, and had had a short stint in the majors by 1996. By then he had proved himself to be an outstanding glove, having led his league in various defensive departments in the minors in 1994, 1995, and 1996.

The following season he showed some signs of clout as he collected 28 doubles, 4 triples, and 14 homers—not bad at all for a young infielder. More important, he again led the league in a defensive category—this time topping all American League second basemen with his sparkling .990 fielding percentage.

Born in 1972, the 6'2", 225-pound switch-hitter surpassed his father's career home-run total of 39, as well as his runs driven in total (174), by his fifth year. By then he had moved on to the Anaheim Angels, going there in 2000 as a free agent.

Speaking with the Spiezios is a pleasure. Scott, well spoken, answered questions smoothly and professionally, typifying his baseball background. His father reeled off stories easily, affably, and with intense fatherly pride in his voice.

When he was asked if he felt that baseball did indeed help him bond with his son Scott, Ed Spiezio replied, "Yes, I do. The hours and hours and hours spent together going through practice, hitting and fielding practice—any kind of practice you can imagine, almost on a daily basis for years—made baseball the one sport we were really serious about, but I spent time with him on other sports as well. We'd sometimes spend three, four hours a day on baseball, so being together definitely helped us bond."

Ed first realized that Scott might have a chance to be a successful athlete when his son was in a crib. Scott weighed in at more than nine pounds at birth and was always pretty big for his age.

As Ed said, baseball truly was the one sport they were serious about. And, boy, were they serious. So it was not so very long after Scott's birth that Ed started him on the road to success, doing so from about "the time he could walk." He had tiny plastic balls that he'd throw to Scott, and his son smacked them with authority early on.

Scott was pleased that his training began early. He said their really serious routine "started when I was probably 3, as far as practicing every day. He took an old give-away bat that he had—I think it was Julian Javier's of the Cardinals—and drilled holes in it—it was a wooden bat—so that I could swing it. It looked like a woodpecker got a hold of it. That was before they had aluminum bats, and it was the next step up from a Wiffle bat.

"So we started in my front yard and I'd hit tennis balls. He'd throw them to me, and I was a switch-hitter right off the bat. I'd hit [thousands of] tennis balls. When I started getting old enough to hit the neighbors' houses, we moved to the backyard. We had two pitching mounds in the backyard and he'd throw tennis balls again. We probably had like 400 tennis balls in tennis-ball hoppers. He'd throw them and we'd play games, and when we were done we'd go pick them up and hit them again."

Ed wished his father had used such concepts to help him improve. "When I was a kid, my dad spent a lot of time with me," he said. "He hit me ground balls, but at that time he wasn't aware of [techniques such as] using tennis balls. So, when I was young, I would remember the [hard] ball bouncing up and hitting me, and it hurt. With Scott, I just hit him tennis balls, which gave much quicker hops, unbelievably quicker hops. I felt if he could catch them, he could catch any ball, plus if he got hit, it wouldn't hurt him. I think that's what really helped him a lot.

"I used to hit rockets at him with tennis balls, and he would come up with them. I also have daughters who were really super tennis players. I would hit serves at them, and they returned the serves, where Scott would catch them when he was small.

"It all paid off, as it usually does. If you put hard work into things and if you're a little bit lucky, things do work out," Ed said.

That hard work continued as Scott got older and outgrew his yard. "After that we'd go down to the high-school field and take ground balls until the groundskeeper chased us off," Ed said. After a while they got to know the Spiezios, and father and son became a fixture around the field.

In fact, at times the training was a family affair. "My mom would come out and she'd turn double plays with me," Scott recalled. "My sisters, Deborah and Suzanne, would play tennis and we'd kind of work it in to where they'd be working on their serves or their ground strokes and I'd be working on my hands on the other side [of the net], catching—trying to catch them off short hops and long hops. And we'd play games like that where I'd throw the ball back and they'd hit it back and I'd have to catch it again."

Even when the seasons changed, the Spiezios weren't deterred from their rigorous workouts. Ed developed drills for his son, relying on his knowledge as a former player, employing an acumen that a collegiate coach would envy.

"I lived in Chicago, so when the winter came we had stations set up in the basement, where I could hit off a balance beam," Scott said. "We had a ball on a string that I'd hit while standing on the balance beam. We also had a kind of like carpet padding wrapped around one of the poles, and I'd hit that to develop power. I had a tee set up [to hit off] where I'd hit into a blanket, and I'd take ground balls off the wall. Sometimes I'd even use a golf ball or a racquetball. It was a cement basement, [so the balls] would be a little bit livelier."

He continued the litany of drills. "I'd hit in front of a mirror down there just to see how my mechanics were. Also, we'd go down to the high school and they had a cage that they'd let us use, usually on the weekends. So we'd hit down there until I got in high school, and once I got in high school I could use it whenever I wanted. There were a lot of things to keep me occupied."

Scott said that since his father was well known in town, that opened doors (including those at the high school) for him. However, he added, it didn't hurt that "they knew that I was going to be coming there pretty soon, and they wanted to help me out. Really, the high school coaches were unbelievable, wanting to win and working hard. We'd practice harder than anybody. They had stations set up in high school, too."

Even when Scott strayed from the subject of his father's influence, it was only momentarily, and merely to point out that his father was as diligent as he was. He added, "For me, my dad was a real hard worker. He'd come off work and go straight to practice with me, then he'd go out golfing for an hour. He was always doing something, and then he'd practice with my sisters on their tennis. One of them actually got a scholarship to a real nice university in Illinois for tennis and academics."

In addition to having Scott hit tennis balls, Ed created a new ball for his son. He would take a regulation baseball, remove the cover and the ball's guts, then insert socks instead. Sewing it back up produced a sockball that, unlike a tennis ball, could be made to curve. "It would come up to the plate like a pancake sometimes," Ed said. "But that was OK, because you achieved the curveball that you wanted and it would be hard to hit it on the screws. When you did, you really felt great."

One other advantage that a sockball had over a tennis ball was the matter of self-preservation. As Scott grew older, he became so adept at drilling the ball that a line shot back to the mound would truly hurt his father. It got to the point where Ed bought—and found—protection behind an "L" screen. It was the type used to shield batting-practice pitchers in the majors. Believe it or not, getting hit by a tennis ball is no fun. "It hurts. It'd leave a nice welt on you," Ed said.

Still, Ed didn't mind much, and he said the batting practice with tennis balls was done "on almost a daily basis." He added, "It was good for his timing and his hand-eye coordination. I also could do things like throw change-ups, I could spin a ball up there, but it wouldn't be an effective curveball, and I could hit spots pretty well even though I wasn't a pitcher."

Ed's ability to throw to different locations worked well for Scott. When he wanted to work on, say, pitches on "the inside corner, up," he recalled, "I could work on it like a machine [for Scott to hit]. Then we'd go to inside, down; and up and away, then low and away. Then I would play game conditions with him. I'd move the ball around so that he would get the feeling of what a pitcher was trying to do to him."

With that in mind, Ed would try to emulate the thought process of a big-league hitter, exposing Scott to a peek at the majors way in advance of when he'd actually enter that world. Ed also played in the kinds of game conditions that were comparable to what every little kid ever did when he lived out a fantasy on, say, a basketball court. As Ed put it, "I'd take the last second shot, down by two, and we'd win it on a three-pointer. Well, I'd play those same conditions with Scott. Two down, you're up, with a chance to win the ball game with a guy on third base—gotta drive him in."

During the 2000 season, Scott faced such situations in real life. He hit three "walk-off" hits, two homers and a game-winning single. A reporter interviewed Scott about his theatrical flair, aware that Ed had once hit a dramatic game-winning home run off Steve Carlton. Scott said his big hits made him think "about when I was in the backyard playing with my dad and there were two outs in the ninth inning and I was up and hit a home run—that's what came back to me."

Ed was pleased to hear his son say that, and not only for nostalgic reasons. He said that Scott was really employing a trick that he himself has known about for years, visualization. "People are starting to talk about [that technique for success] now. Once your mind sees [you attain something], sometimes you can do it.

"You hear about a player like Bill Russell dreaming something, then doing it on the basketball court. I used to do that when I was in Little League and things would happen, but I didn't know why. You don't realize how powerful your mind is."

Now, it apparently works for his son and for players like Atlanta Braves pitcher John Smoltz, who used a psychologist to help him train his mind for success pretty much along the lines of the training and thinking Ed espouses. Ed definitely believes the mental game is of the utmost importance, saying, "It's the only way to play the game—that *is* the game to me, the game in the mind, so powerful and important."

There was always logic behind Ed's techniques, dating as far back as when he had different mounds in the backyard. His reasoning was simple: he wanted to re-create the conditions Scott would face in different leagues as he grew up. One mound was 45 feet from the plate for Little League; another was 54, to simulate Pony League conditions. When Scott needed a third one, the major-league regulation 60 feet, 6 inches, they used the high-school field. Ed insisted that it was important for Scott to play under realistic game conditions whenever feasible.

Some fathers who played in the majors were on the road so often that they couldn't coach their sons, but Ed was through with baseball by the time his son began to play in youth leagues. "He coached me pretty much through Little League, probably till I was 11," Scott said. "I think I started at 7. All the way to 11, he pretty much was my [only] coach. Then after that he was always helping.

"He wasn't the coach, but he'd come out and help with B.P. or help in the infield—that kind of stuff. Once I reached probably about the age of 15, he kind of left things to the coaches, let them take over." But throughout it all, Scott said, his dad was, of course, his No. 1 fan.

Unlike many Little Leaguers who went on to the majors, Scott can't recall winning a baseball championship as a kid. Even with the excellent coach he had in Ed, Scott said, "I don't think we ever did win a title."

And, unlike some fanatic youngsters, Scott didn't seem to mind. Winning was important, but winning a title wasn't a big deal to him. He said quite simply of his youth on many a baseball diamond, "It was a real good time."

It was also a fine time to learn. Ed imparted more inside baseball to his son than a crew of youth coaches could manage. Those insights, coupled with Scott's natural ability, led to success. Scott recalled, "When we were playing when we were 7 years old, there was me and this other kid that were pretty good, and the other guys on the team were decent, but not that great. I played short and he played first. Anything basically to the left-field side of second base I covered, and anything to the right-field side he covered, and he covered home, too.

"I remember a play to center field. I think I passed our center fielder, and I beat him to the ball, threw it home to the kid who was playing first at home and we got the guy out. They called him safe because we were both out of position.

"So, yeah, my dad just taught us to be aggressive, to just track down everything and try to be in every play. We were probably too aggressive at first. I mean, when it came around to where the other kids were a little bit better, we were always in position."

He also felt that his dad taught him to out-hustle everyone else on the diamond, and that lesson has carried over to the majors.

Ed took Scott to a youth baseball game once and had him hit live pitching rather than hitting off a tee like the other kids, since Scott was already at an advanced stage. Ed pitched to his son that game and, instead of lobbing the ball underhand, threw overhand. It didn't matter to the young star, as he walloped four prodigious homers, tying the record for the most homers ever hit in a major-league game—even if it didn't qualify as a big-league record.

Ed said that the other kids couldn't even reach the fence, or, if they were lucky, they might hit one on the ground that would roll to the fence, but Scott was launching "high, towering" shots over the fence.

A couple of friends of Ed who were bankers approached him and teased Scott that he was already good enough to make it to the major leagues. Although they were joking, their comment turned out to be prophetic, and it was one prediction that Ed didn't find shocking—he *believed*.

Ed helped that prophecy become a sort of self-fulfilling one by continuing to train Scott in the basics of the game. He'd have his son lay down as many as 150 bunts before allowing him to start the rest of his practice session. This helped Scott watch the ball all the way to his bat. Then, and only then, was it time to swing away.

Often, when a father handles his son's training and spurs him on to the professional ranks, writers accuse the father of being the equivalent of a stage mother. For example, bold headlines and sensational stories in national publications blared out how Marques Johnson's father set up chairs in his driveway and virtually forced his son to dribble a basketball while weaving through the chairs for countless hours. The sportswriters almost likened it to a Basketball Bataan Death Dribble.

An article in a prestigious national publication also reported that Gregg Jefferies had a training program set up by his father that was almost obsessive in its range and intensity. All this makes for wonderful, albeit exaggerated, storytelling. But both Johnson and Jefferies told me (in interviews) that the stories were way overblown. Both boys loved the games they played and, they said their training was fun, not a task.

Likewise, Ed lovingly established his elaborate training "regimen" for Scott. While he and Scott spent aeons working on the game, they were savoring every moment of their time together. Scott is the first to point out that he was not forced to go through all the baseball drills that he did; he had fun.

"He enjoyed all of it," Ed said. "You hear stories about [people like] Brooke Shields's mother, who kept pushing and pushing. When you talk to them [their children] later on, they realize if they didn't have someone who cared that much and had that much passion, they probably wouldn't have made it.

"I think Scott is starting to realize now that all the time we put in together is really paying off. He's able to do things now that he wouldn't [otherwise] be able to do. I mean, all his buddies have college degrees, but they're making nowhere near the money he is, and he loves the game.

"As you build a kid's interest in the game, and if it's done correctly, where you don't overdo it and they enjoy it—you make him feel successful, that works. He started feeling successful when he got into Little League at 8 years old. When people would see him, they'd say, 'There goes Scott Spiezio.' When a kid hears that, it makes him feel good about himself.

"As his success and confidence builds, he feels more and more of that. And then you get to the point where you feel, 'Hey, I can make it to the big leagues.' People think you're crazy, but you do it."

Ed said he was reminded of how his father used to go around saying that Ed was "going to be a big leaguer. 'Oh, sure, Ed, we know,' they'd say. And then I knew my son would be [a major leaguer], and he knew it. If you believe that passionately about it, and you have a few breaks here and there, stay healthy, things can happen—you can get there. I did it, and it can happen to other people, too," he concluded.

In fact, in many respects Ed was ahead of his times with his attitude and his drills. While it's true that Jefferies and his father put in a grueling training program that was said to include swinging a bat underwater in a pool hundreds of times left-handed, then right-handed, Ed said he actually started training along these lines himself "probably over fifty-two years ago, or so."

Ed then said with a laugh, "It was a long way ahead of Jefferies. He was ahead of my son as far as being older than my son. He hit the major leagues sooner, and when the article [about his training came out], it just rang all kinds of bells. It was like, 'Oh, my God, he did what I was doing.' "

Perhaps it's not so surprising that people have imitated some of the Spiezio techniques, because Ed said he presented his drills at clinics. "I had put this stuff out there," he said, "and it's coming around now." With all his great ideas, people have even suggested that he write a book on training youths for baseball.

If he did, Ed said, he would probably include one idea from the Jefferies family. "Gregg's dad took it a little step further by putting numbers on the tennis balls he'd throw to his son so he'd have to concentrate on the number that went by [trying to pick that up as he hit]. That's really a great idea for focus and concentration."

So great that in 2001 the Cleveland Indians bought a new pitching machine that propels numbered tennis balls of various colors at speeds upwards of 150 miles an hour at players in an effort to train their eyes to pick up the color and the numbers. If they succeed, the logic goes, they will easily be able to pick up and follow pitches thrown at around half that speed.

Meanwhile, as a child Scott always felt that his father was special. Naturally, when any child becomes aware that his father is engaged in a respected, almost venerated, field of work, a sense of pride often sets in. Scott said, "I think I bragged a lot to people about that and, you know, I think it was pretty impressive to me."

But while Scott knew that his dad's playing big-league ball was special, he also took it for granted. He said that although it was impressive to have his dad make it to the majors, "at the same time I really didn't understand it. So I just figured, Yeah, I'm going to do it, too. It was no big deal. It was neat that he was a big-league player, but I really didn't understand it probably until I got here."

Meanwhile, Scott related an often-told family story about the end of his father's baseball career. "He actually retired, I guess you could say, on my birthday. My first birthday. I was born on September 21, 1972, and he retired at the end of the year in 1972. But what he tells me is that he was with the White Sox and by the time I was born they were out of the playoffs. They had been in the race up until late September, and I guess Chuck Tanner was the manager and he allowed my dad to go home for my birth and there were only two games after that, so basically he retired the day I was born."

Still, Ed's connection with baseball was far from over. He then had time to take his son to games. In fact, probably the first time Scott got to go to a big-league game where his father was on the field was when Ed took him to an Old-Timers' game.

It was quite a day for the young Scott, as he got to meet St. Louis Cardinals legend Stan Musial. Although Musial had retired the year before Ed began his career in the majors with the Cardinals, he was still affiliated with the team in various capacities. Unfortunately, Scott, who was about 10 at the time, was too young to fully appreciate his meeting with the Hall of Famer.

Another Cardinals great from the past, eighteen-year veteran of big-league play Walker Cooper, grabbed Scott and placed him on his knee. Moments later, yet another St. Louis legend, Red Schoendienst, strolled by and greeted Scott.

Scott said he was impressed, though, "the big thing that I remember is the two or three times we went to Old-Timers' games where he [Ed] played. They had the '64 Cardinals, versus whoever, the Yankees or the '68 Tigers versus the Cardinals, and we'd go to those games. We went to one at Detroit

[Tiger] Stadium, and I got to meet some of his ex-teammates and some of the new players that were there.

"The game was right before the regular season game," he continued. "So I got to meet guys like Alan Trammell and guys like that. It was a thrill for me, because I'd get to go out on the field and shag balls back and forth. Most of the kids in my situation did that when they were growing up, but being born after he retired I didn't get to do that until the Old-Timers' series [of games] came out."

So, early on Scott was exposed to the baseball scene, and, again, most experts feel that never hurts the development of youngsters who are on their road to the bigs. In truth, though, as a child Scott got to go to some big-league games, but it wasn't as if he lived at ballparks. "We didn't go to a lot of games," he said, "but we'd go to a couple of Cub games."

Most of the games he saw were the ones he participated in, including one of the great memories of his childhood. As a youth, one of Scott's earliest "trials" to test his ability occurred in the Junior Olympics. When Scott showed up on the first day of those Olympics, he wasn't sure he belonged, wasn't sure he was good enough to play against such an elite group.

He told his dad, "These guys are pretty good. I'm not sure if I can compete." Then, according to Ed, "After a day or two it was like, 'I not only know I can compete, I'm just as good or better than most of these kids.' It happened very, very quickly."

When Scott was trying out for the Junior Olympics, he ran into a ton of standout athletes, including Lakers center Shaquille O'Neal and a boy destined to capture the Heisman Trophy in 2000, Chris Weinke. Back then, Weinke played first base on Scott's team after having carried the Olympic torch in the Opening Ceremonies.

Also at the Junior Olympics were future big leaguers Shawn Green and Jay Powell. Teams from all over the country showed up. In baseball, the West team was favored to win due to the influence of so many California players, but Scott's cold-weather team from the Midwest won it all to haul in the gold medal. Throughout the events, Ed was on hand to cheer his son on.

Ed said a similar success story for Scott had happened earlier when he pulled Scott from the summer program in their small hometown of Morris, Illinois, taking him to Joliet, a much bigger town. In fact, Ed, himself a Joliet native, said, "Twenty-some major leaguers came from there, so it was pretty much a hot spot. I brought him there for Pony League; after reaching the age of 12 years in Morris, there wasn't really a lot here for him in this town. So I put him in the same program that I was in at Joliet, and he made the All-Star team managed by the same person who managed me thirty years before. That's tradition for you." Needless to say, Scott more than held his own in Joliet.

Time passed, and Scott continued to evolve as a player. Then came time for him to sign his first professional contract. Scott said that his father was helpful in other facets of baseball beyond training.

"He was a [union] player-rep with the Padres. You really didn't have agents back then, but now it's so much more sophisticated you almost need an agent coming out of college. We did have—I guess you would call them advisers until you signed—we did have an agent working for us. Although my dad did have a lot of input with the decisions we made."

Scott continued, "I mean, he basically told me when they first offered me a contract that I had to go back to school. I went out for the [school] team and played for about three weeks before they [the A's] gave me a better offer that I accepted. But I was going to go back to school if they didn't come up [with the money], and he wanted to kind of steer me in that direction."

Times have changed dramatically since the days Ed roamed the infield. When he was asked if his dad ever teases him about the discrepancies between their salaries, Scott said, "Oh yeah, he always said that I'd make more money than him, and he was right. He said that, basically [in his day], if they had an agent or they tried to negotiate, they'd get blackballed out of the game.

"That is probably what happened to him. You know he was 31 when he left the game. In today's day and age, that is when you really are getting into your prime as far as [being] a hitter."

One would think that with his knowledge and experience of the game, Ed could have been a fine utility hitter a lot longer. Scott certainly agrees with that, saying, "Yeah, but at the time the money wasn't there. He had a furniture store. He thought, Hey, I'm not going to mess with these owners anymore. I'm going to make my own money and run my own business. He still has that furniture store. He doesn't work there that much, but he still owns it."

Since Ed had served as a player-rep, he had gained some insights into the business end of the game, and he was able to pass that invaluable information on to his son. For example, he told Scott the history of the schism between labor and management in baseball. Unlike some naïve young players, Scott knew early on that the game of baseball is hardly just a game. It is, in fact, a cold, hard business.

Owners are as reluctant to part with their money as a frugal shopper armed with a stack of coupons. Ed pointed out that there has always been acrimony between players and owners which, at times, bordered on the absurd.

Ed often had to approach Padres part owner and general manager Buzzie Bavasi over disputes. Those experiences schooled him in how management could be. Ed would often stick up for a young player who felt he was being cheated out of sums of money as paltry as $50 for, say, moving expenses. Even though the money was due to him according to his contract, the cash didn't come easy.

Ed said Bavasi's management style could easily have been, "Let's keep our players happy. After all, he does have it coming to him." Instead, according to Ed, Bavasi would balk, squawk, and even threaten him. "He would get on me: 'Spiezio, I'm going to send you to Timbuktu.' And I'd be thinking, Buzzie, it says in the contract if you're going to bring this guy in from the minor leagues, you have to pay to bring his family here.

"At that time, he'd fight over 50 to 100 bucks. I mean, it's incredible the numbers we're talking—to me it's hard to comprehend what I had to do to get a player some extra money. It was my job to say, 'Hey, you owe the guy the money.'

"I didn't realize there was such as place as Timbuktu, but there is. If I did, I'd have been more afraid," Ed said. Of course, Bavasi was referring to shipping Ed to the low minors. "I didn't realize how far he wanted to send me," Ed continued, laughing. "In my day the money meant a lot. You're talking about twenty years where the minimum salary was stuck at $6,000. Today you're talking $200,000."

Nevertheless, that is how the game was in the 1960s and 1970s, with the players' association not having much leverage. Now the well-informed Scott, aware of the behind-the-scenes machinations of the past, can fully appreciate how far pioneers such as his father helped push players' rights.

Twenty-one years after his retirement, Ed's suitcase began to resemble that of a world traveler, with decals splattered all over. Only in Ed's case the destinations were spots like Medford and Modesto, as he followed Scott, who had just signed his first contract, on his long but steady trek through the minors.

Ed was justifiably proud when Scott broke into the professional ranks. As Scott tells it, "My first year I only played for about two months. I signed late, around June 30, 1993. So I played July in a small town called Medford, Oregon. That was rookie ball. And then they moved me up to Modesto, California, for the last month. I don't think he made it out that year. But the next year, in Modesto, he came out and saw some of my games. Then again, in Double-A he came to a lot of my games, then in Triple-A I was in Canada and he came a couple of times up there as well. Then he was there for the first game I played in the big leagues. I played in Cleveland, and he flew in from Chicago for that."

The trip was well worth it. "My first hit was off of Chad Ogea," Scott recalled. "It was a line drive to right field, and the next day I went two-for-three off of Orel Hershiser."

In truth, the tale of Scott's first appearance in a big-league uniform is nearly a saga. "I wanted to see his first [big-league] game," Ed said. "It happened so quick, I wondered how I was going to do it, but I kept saying, 'We gotta go. We gotta go.'"

Todd Crose, who had been an assistant baseball coach when Scott played at Morris High School and is now the head coach there, kept pushing, too. Although it took much scurrying, the trip was feasible, so they finally decided to take it.

Hurriedly, Ed and Crose made their way through the streets of Chicago to Midway Airport, where they just managed to "jump on a plane and make it to Cleveland." The difficulty in making the trip was compounded by the fact that Scott was "called up all of a sudden. I almost didn't make it." Further, due to bad weather their flight was delayed, so although they made it to Cleveland, they could well have missed the game that night.

Ironically, after all the difficulty of getting to Scott's debut game, the inclement weather that plagued Ed's travel caused the cancellation of the contest.

However, in the long run he lucked out. He said, "The game got rained out and the next day they had a doubleheader. Then we thought, Oh, no, it's going to get rained out again. But it didn't, and he got to play. So we got to see his first at bat; he hit a rocket down the line—it should've been a double, but the right fielder made an incredible play to stop the ball [holding him to a single]. So I saw him in his first big-league at bat, and he got a hit for me that first game."

That day was the culmination of thousands of hours of work. Ed says he feels proud now when he saunters up to the will-call window at a big-league park to pick up a ticket that his son has left for him. However, the thing he is most delighted about, he said, is "just the pride in knowing he's made it to the majors—people don't realize just how hard it is to make it there."

Ed experienced another one of the perks of having a big-league son a few years ago. Just as Scott received the Javier bat from his father when he was young, when Scott got older he returned the favor. He wound up getting his dad a nice piece of baseball memorabilia, a Mark McGwire autographed ball. Ed had his share of his own souvenirs from select hits and home runs, so other than the McGwire ball, Scott noted, "There is really nothing that he wants. He just wants to see me do well. If I were to give him stuff like that he'd just tell me to hold on to it."

Some parents relish coming into the locker room, but Scott said he thinks his father "doesn't like to see the clubhouse. I know a lot of dads probably have never seen one." Instead, Scott said, "He likes to talk to people that he sees on TV a lot—the coaches or some of my other teammates. He'll say, 'Hey, I was watching the other day, and that was a great play,' or 'That was a great at bat.' He tells them basically he enjoys watching them and stuff like that."

One big-league story that Ed loves to tell concerning family was the time he was in Milwaukee to see Scott play. Ed says he can still picture himself cradling his first grandson, Sam, his daughter's child, in his arms while sitting in the stands. He remembered it as being a freezing-cold day. Sam was bundled up, but Ed couldn't resist peeking at him through the thick, cozy blankets from time to time.

"It was very early in the season, and we brought him to the game. I was sitting behind home plate, holding him. I couldn't believe that I was holding my grandson, who was about two weeks old, and watching my son play a major-league game. There's just a feeling that comes over you. It was such a special moment; I can remember looking up at the sky and saying, 'God, is this heaven?' Chills just come over you.

"Ueck [Milwaukee announcer Bob Uecker] was up there in the booth, and I had played with him, but there's no way to get to him. But later on in the game I went up to a guard and said, 'I'd like to speak to Bob Uecker.' He said, 'Oh, really? So does everybody else.' I said, 'Well, just tell him Ed Spiezio's out here.' "

Although that didn't convince the guard, after Ed told him the story about holding his grandson while watching his son play, the guard was touched. Ed related how the guard said, "You know, I normally wouldn't do this. But that story's so convincing, I'm going to go get Ueck."

Moments later, Ed and Uecker were reminiscing. Then Ed told him the story of how three generations of Spiezios were in attendance and how he felt he'd almost had religious experience, being there with his grandson. "It sent chills up and down him, too," Ed said.

As a side note, Ed lost his sunglasses in the booth. Usually that wouldn't have been a big issue, but the glasses were an expensive (over $200) and sentimental gift from Scott. Although he returned to Milwaukee County Stadium the next day, searching for the glasses, he had no luck. Then, said Ed, "A year later I'm watching TV and there's Ueck with my sunglasses. He probably wondered where the hell they came from."

Like many fathers, Ed doesn't always agree totally with front-office and managerial philosophies. Scott broke in with the Oakland A's, an organization that, Ed said, was "very disciplined—they wanted all their players to take pitches, but I wanted Scott to be more aggressive, to swing the bat. I told him a few things I'd like to see him do at the plate."

Torn between two authority figures, Scott was hesitant but listened to his father and went on a tear. Owing to his torrid streak, he was shortly called up to the parent club, which had to have made him feel that his father had Robert Young–like parental wisdom (although it's doubtful that the actor famous for his paternal role in *Father Knows Best* could have hit his own weight in the majors).

Ed can not only relate to his son but empathize with him as well. During a visit to California in August of 2000 to watch Scott, Ed observed the Yankees and Angels play a three-game set. At one point, he turned to his wife and said, "You know who has the best hands on either ball club? Scott."

Then, about ten minutes later, Ed spied [coach] Alfredo Griffin "going over to Scott at shortstop during pregame. Later, after the game, I said to Scott, 'What did he have to say to you?' Scott said, 'You'll never believe it. He told me I hand the best hands on the ball club.' It was unbelievable."

Coincidence aside, Ed bristled a bit, saying, "Why would he tell you that when he, in spring training, said that you can't play second base. Scott said, 'I don't know, Dad. It's unbelievable—here's a guy who said I can't do it and then he comes over and tells me that. I told him, "I not only know that, I had the best hands in Oakland." ' When you see it, you can't miss it," Ed concluded.

During that same series, Ed dropped by to shoot the breeze with Yankees Joe Torre and Don Zimmer. Ed spoke of how frustrating it was that the Angels hadn't pegged Scott into a fitting position with the club. He commented on how difficult "it is to find your niche with a ball club—to find a spot where you can play regularly, where you fit." He continued, "As I was talking about that, Scott Brosius, who used to locker next to Scott, came into the dugout and he was a perfect example of what I was saying. He had just left Oakland, where he played several positions. All of a sudden, he goes with the Yankees and he's a perfect fit at third base." This illustrates how a parent, even with his son already entrenched in the majors, is always hoping for more, for the best for his son.

Ed also related how Scott went to the Angels as a free agent, departing from Oakland because "he felt that he was going to be their second baseman." When he wasn't given that job, Scott became "extremely frustrated," as did his caring father, of course. Ed said Scott "could've gone anywhere, but he actually took less money to go there because they were the ones who promised him that he would be their second baseman."

After making the promise, the Angels looked Scott over, and, as if they had never seen him before (and they certainly *had,* as Scott had just played with the A's, in the same division as the Angels), they said they felt he was too big. Ed said, "They didn't want to have [first baseman] Mo Vaughn and Scott on that side of the infield—their pitching wasn't that great that year, so one of the consultants for the team said, 'With Mo over there, and our pitching the way it is, we don't feel that we can put Scott over there, too, because we'd have two big guys on that side of the infield.'

"This was at the beginning of spring training, and they hadn't seen Scott [a lot]. They just saw his size and said he couldn't do it [play second]. I told them to look at the stats he's got, just look at them, and let him play there. For them to come up to him five or six months later and say he's got great hands, they should have known that. I told them, 'Don't think about if he can or can't, just put him there. See what he can do.' "

Like any good parent, Ed went to bat for his son, but even though he was a former big leaguer, nobody listened. Once Oakland saw the light and gave him a chance, however, they quickly realized that Scott could play fine defense at second, and moved him over from his first position at third base. "They liked that he had a third baseman's arm at second base," Ed said.

Ed is quick to praise his son's defense, saying, "I wasn't anywhere near as good a fielder as he is. I had great hands, but I didn't work at it as much as him. Because of that, I worked him much harder."

Ed is also proud of his son's versatility, pointing out that in 2000 Scott "played six different positions" if you count the designated hitter spot. "He played two positions in the outfield—left and right—third, second, and first base, but I *know* third base is his best position—he's an outstanding third baseman, as good as anybody in the big leagues. People don't realize that because he doesn't play there that much."

But, Ed noted, his son isn't just a glove expert. "He has the ability to not only hit, he hits with power from both sides," he said. He added that while he and Scott may have trained along the same lines, Scott "has his own stance. I wanted him to do certain things, then as he got bigger and stronger, I let him do things his way. Sometimes I think maybe I should have forced him to hit the way I did because I like the way I hit, but you have to develop whatever comes natural to you."

Ed loves to see his son take his cuts, but now, with Scott on the West Coast and Ed still in his native state of Illinois, it's somewhat difficult to get together. However, Ed says, he's with his son every chance he gets. One spring, for example, he was able to spend the entire exhibition season with Scott.

Other years, Ed says, "I go down to see him for at least part of spring training. I get to see him when he comes to Chicago, too. When Milwaukee was in the American League I got to see him more."

Recently, Ed also kept up with his son's progress via television and telephone. "Most of the time it's satellite, because he's back in Chicago," Scott said. "He does talk to me on the phone and tries to find out other things that are going on. If he sees something with my hitting, he'll let me know. He came out once this year [in 2000] and he's going to come out for two days when New York is here. He comes out two or three times a year."

Ed was also very glad that his own father had a chance to see Scott play in high school. Unfortunately, he passed away before Scott progressed further up the ladder and on into the professional ranks. Ed's father, who was also named Ed, was on hand, however, to watch Ed's career, including the three main highlights—each and every one of the World Series the Cardinals were involved in during Ed's era.

That included the 1964 Series win over the New York Yankees, in which Ed saw no playing time, the 1967 World Series against the Boston Red Sox, and the heartbreaking Series loss to the Detroit Tigers in 1968, which, like the 1964 and the 1967 Series, was a seven-game set.

One other wish Ed has for his son is that he'll get a World Series ring. Ed said that he owns "two World Series rings and one pennant ring when we had Detroit in the bag and that one got away."

Incidentally, Ed's first ring came with relative ease during his rookie year. He was just coming off an appearance in the College World Series in 1963. He began the 1964 season in the minor leagues playing for Harry "the Hat" Walker, as a cleanup hitter, despite the fact that he wasn't an extremely big man. However, shortly after, when he hit over .400 at Tulsa in Double-A ball, they skipped him over Triple-A ball with a call-up to the majors; then came that coveted ring.

So he went from the 1963 NAIA College World Series, where, in fact, he was the MVP the year before, to *the* World Series just a year later. "It was awesome to look across the way and see Mickey Mantle, Roger Maris," he said. "Those were my heroes. I was in a daze just being there; it was *the* Yankees, they had dominated for years. It was amazing just to be on the field with them."

It seems apparent that Scott's paternal grandfather was a big help in supplying a strong bloodline for the family. He played a great deal of semi-pro baseball and was an excellent boxer. At the tender age of 15, Ed's father not only competed against a 26-year-old but defeated him. To this day, local newspapers in Ed's hometown of Joliet, Illinois, will print "On This Date" items such as "65 YEARS AGO 15-YEAR-OLD WON BOUT."

So Ed feels that the Spiezio line of baseball players actually begins with his father. He also credits his father with the origin of the family's attitude that big-league success was attainable. "He started it all," Ed said, "especially the idea that it could be done."

His father knew how difficult it is, and how much of a dream it is, to make it to the majors, but he also had faith in Ed. "I picked up on that idea for Scott," said Ed, who not only worked with his son, drilling him into making it to the majors but almost willed him into making it, too.

Another generation of Spiezios has arrived. Scott, who now has a son of his own, a toddler named Tyler, reflected on what the future holds in store. "My dad really didn't push me," he said. "He was always available. And basically he said, 'You are going to succeed in something, so I'm going to help you do something. So pick what you want to do. If it's schoolwork, we're going to get the best tutors. If it's golf, we're going to get you all the lessons. If it's baseball, well, then, we're just going to practice until you're tough enough to make it.'

"Whatever my son chooses to do, I'm going to be there to help Tyler practice—probably guide him to work as hard as I did and to work as hard as my dad did and his dad did."

Scott believes that despite his father's love of baseball and his father's pride in his success, he is prouder of Scott "as a person than as a player. I know that he really enjoys the fact that I'm in the big leagues and all our hard work paid off." But, he said, his father is also quite proud "that I've got a great family. A great family and a baby boy."

Clearly then, it seems safe to say that Scott (and, for that matter, all of Ed's family) provides Ed with his main sources of pride. Focusing for the moment on Scott, Ed said, "Scott is very special. People tell me, 'You must have done something right.' "And, of course, they're right.

Ed said, "You can't believe how many people wrote to me, and people don't write much nowadays. They'd say, 'What a fabulous kid you have.' Everybody who has been around him loves him."

One example of these admirers is the scout who signed Scott to a professional contract. The scout, a father of four, told Ed, "I hope to heck that I would be lucky enough to have my children turn out like yours." Such compliments about Scott are hardly rare.

Ed also got numerous letters from people in a city where Scott had played minor-league baseball, telling him how special his son is. One of Scott's college teachers stopped in to see Ed one day "out of the blue." Ed said, "She told me, 'I knew your son was from this town, and when I saw your store I just had to stop and I had to tell you what a wonderful son you have.'

"I was at a wake, and the lady whose husband had died pulled me over to the side. You can imagine what her thoughts were, but she said, 'I just had to tell you this—you have a wonderful son. He's a wonderful baseball player, but I'm going to tell you something—he's a much greater person.' At a time of crisis, she pulls me aside and she tells me what a great person he is. He's just a great kid, considerate.

"He comes back home because of the people that he grew up with. They actually love him—not like, love him. He's that type of kid—it's really nice that I can say that about him."

In early 2001, Ed said, his son got a call from a man he'd stayed with in Oregon who had a problem with serious headaches. The only hospital that could help him was in Chicago. Scott found out about this, and he called the man, picked him up at his hotel, and brought him home to stay with the Spiezios. Ed obviously raised his son to be a good man on and off the field.

It is apparent that as upstanding men *and* as players who worked hard to enable themselves to forge their way into the majors, hard work paid off for the Spiezios.

Chapter Eleven: The Speiers

Both Chris and Justin Speier grew up in Alameda, California. Justin said he lived "right in the Bay Area. I was born there, but we've lived in Arizona the last sixteen, seventeen years. So I grew up mostly in Arizona." He now resides in Paradise Valley, Arizona. For the record, he was born on November 6, 1973, in Walnut Creek, California, and is the oldest of six children: three brothers, Luke, Cole, and Travis; and two sisters, Erika and Brittany.

In the majors, he has grown up in several teams' systems. It started for him when the Chicago Cubs tabbed him their fifty-fifth pick in the June draft of 1995. They threw him in one big-league game and traded the 6'4", 205-pound right-handed pitcher to the Florida Marlins in 1998, with whom he appeared in eighteen outings. The following season saw him appear in nineteen games with the Atlanta Braves.

In 2000, after being claimed off outright waivers, he got his first big-league victory, and posted a fine 5–2 ledger with an excellent ERA of 3.29 over a career-high 47 stints for the Cleveland Indians. It's been said that a pitcher who can strike out two batters for every walk surrendered is doing an outstanding job; Speier managed that feat in 2000, with 69 strikeouts versus 28 walks issued.

At any rate, his first win came on June 18, in Detroit's Comerica Park, when he worked 3⅔ innings, fanning a personal high seven batters. Used as a middle reliever, he struck out more than one batter per inning in 2000, a fantastic accomplishment, with his 69 strikeouts stretching over just 68⅓ innings of work. In key situations he has excelled; opponents hit a mere .152 against him with two outs and runners in scoring position.

Charlie Manuel really got to know Justin when he managed him, beginning in 2000. "Justin's dad was in the other league, and I used to get to see him sometime in spring training, but I didn't really know him real well," Manuel said. "But Justin is quite a competitor. He's one of these guys that you want on your team; he's a battler, a fighter. He's real aggressive, and he has an outstanding personality."

Proof of this assertion came in the early days of the 2001 season, when the Indians needed a contingency plan in case their two healthy catchers went down. Justin, a former catcher, volunteered to go from the pitchers' rubber to behind the plate if necessary. "I asked Justin if he could do some catching for us, and he said, 'Yeah, I'll do it,' " Manuel recalled. Such a move would have been virtually unheard-of, as pitchers are a precious commodity and catching is such a perilous position. Still, it wasn't surprising to learn that Speier was up for it.

In 2001 he faltered a bit early in the season and was sent from the Indians to the New York Mets, who said they liked his arm yet shortly after acquiring him them put him on waivers. He was then picked up by the Colorado Rockies.

Meanwhile, his father, Chris, lasted nineteen years in the majors, covering a span of 2,260 games, which in itself is a great accomplishment. In August of 2000, Justin, then 26 years old, commented, "If I want to play as long as my dad did, I'll have to keep pitching until I'm 45."

Chris rose to the majors after spending just one year in the minors at the Double-A level in 1970. Initially, he had been drafted by the old Washington Senators but chose to attend college. So he left his Alameda, California, high school and went to the University of California at Santa Barbara.

He was, in fact, a fine shortstop (who, at times, showed that he could play any infield position) for the Giants, the Expos, where he is a member of their Hall of Fame, the Cardinals, Twins, Cubs, and finally, again, the Giants. He hit .246, including .290 as a pinch hitter, with 302 career doubles and 112 homers. The two-time All-Star hit for the cycle twice, had a five-hit game once, and had a single-game high of eight runs driven in.

His career fielding percentage stood at .971, and that figure, entering the 2001 season, ranked among the twenty-five greatest fielding percentages by a shortstop in the annals of the game. In addition, he took part in 1,121 double plays. In 1981 he hit .400 for the Expos in the Divisional Playoff Series, and in the 1971 League Championship Series he hit .357 for the Giants.

Chris was the Arizona third-base coach for the 2001 season, coaching not far from his residence in Scottsdale. He had managed in the Diamondbacks system for four years, winning a Class-A championship and the Manager of the Year Award in 1997, before departing in 1999. He then began coaching at the big-league level for Milwaukee. Thus he has enjoyed success beyond his playing days and is highly thought of in the majors.

Justin said baseball helped him bond with his father, but he also noted, "I knew that the job presented a situation where he was gone for three months out of the [season's] six months because he was on the road. But there's a give-and-take, because you really got to look at it like five months out of the year I got to spend the whole off-season with him.

"It was a great experience, because I had a love for the game and I got to learn a lot from him and from his teammates and coaches, too. It was great for me, being a baseball player as a kid."

Having a big leaguer for a father didn't cause Justin to preen on the playground or the local diamonds. He said he didn't get treated in any special manner, "because most of the kids my age really didn't know who my dad was because of the generation—when my dad was playing most of my friends were a lot younger. So they didn't know who he was, and I didn't really mention it. It wasn't a big deal to me. He was just my dad."

In other words, while he was proud of his father, he never felt that he had to gloat about his accomplishments. It was enough just to have Chris for a dad. Perhaps because of that attitude, Justin says he never felt any pressure to live up to the family name. "My dad never really set any expectations for me in the baseball aspect," he said. "He was just real supportive of whatever I wanted to do, whether it was to play baseball or do anything."

As the son of a baseball player, Justin grew up, according to Chris, "in a few places, but he was born in California [around San Francisco, where Chris played] and stayed there up until 1977. So he was about 3 or 4 years old when we moved up to Montreal, Canada, where we spent seven years.

"He was like any typical young boy in regards to sports—he loved to play everything," Chris continued. "The one thing about growing up in Canada, he missed out on football and basketball. He continued to play baseball because of my involvement in that.

"He got a tremendous introduction to downhill skiing and ice hockey. It was a different upbringing than [the way] I was brought up, but it definitely widened his horizons," Chris said.

As for Chris's background, he noted that he was always active in sports, but which sport simply depended on whatever season was in. "If it was football season, I was playing football; if it was basketball, I was playing basketball; and if it was baseball, I was playing baseball."

By way of contrast he said, "Up there [in Canada], you have two seasons, and it's basically hockey season and then you have a week off and then it's hockey season." He laughed about that, but basically he was stating the truth.

Despite the other sports, it was clear that baseball was largely responsible for the father-son bonding in the Speier family. "Oh, definitely," Chris said. "It gave us a lot of common ground. Those quiet times when you're trying to get through to somebody—certain ideas, it's a common ground that I've used many times in our discussions about life scenarios. 'It's like this, Justin, when you're on the mound and such and such happens, all you got to do is step back and look around and see guys behind you. You don't have to take the whole world on your shoulders.'

"I mean, I've used different analogies in regards to baseball that have helped us because he's gone through it, he's lived it, and he can experience those things—he *understands* it. Also, it's a common ground that he can use to start a conversation."

Another special perk Justin enjoyed, thanks to his father, was trips to spring training. "We went every year," he said. That also allowed him to add to his baseball memorabilia collection. "I collected cards and some autographs. I think my mom has all my cards and stuff. We'll pass them down to my kids when I have some kids someday."

As a kid, Justin didn't really have a favorite player. "It was funny," said his father, "because Justin worked at the ballparks quite a bit where I played. And a lot of times he worked on the visitors' side, so he had a chance to interact with a lot of the opposing teams. Of course, he loved Mike Schmidt and Pete Rose, all the major stars who came in, but he never really said there's this one guy that I really like. He really enjoyed having the camaraderie with all of them."

Justin remembered his days with his dad back then. "He quit when I was 15; I batboyed the last three years of his career. I helped out in the clubhouse. I'd bang out spikes, run errands, and help out with the laundry," he recalled. Then, his voice taking on the enthusiasm of a fond memory, he said, "It was great. Oh, yeah. It was fun, because if you have a love for the game you get to be around the best in the game. You got free gloves and great advice from his managers and coaches. Roger Craig helped me out, and Bill Fahey."

While Justin did collect baseball cards, Chris said he didn't help him in that department. "He worked in the clubhouse and he'd get broken bats, pictures, and things from the guys, but he did that [collecting] all on his own. He wasn't big on stats. I think he wanted to collect [memorabilia], because he said, 'You know what? These might be valuable someday. They might help me pay for my college education,' and some of it did."

As for playing baseball as a child, Chris felt, Justin would have been better off in the United States. "For Justin to get into a real competitive baseball [league] at that young age, which was not that important, there *wasn't* a lot of competitive baseball," he said. "They had Little League—they had all that. I'm just saying the competition level was not as strong as it had been in the States."

By the time Justin was ready for high school, the Speiers had moved to Phoenix, Arizona. "He played high-school baseball there. His development came much later in his life. He was a catcher and he did a good job behind the plate, had a strong arm as a youngster, but his hitting was just so-so. As he got a little bit bigger, he got stronger, but it never got to the point where there were a lot of people who stood back and went, 'Oh, wow, this guy's something special.' "

When, then, did Chris begin to feel that his son might have a crack at the majors? "Well," he said, mulling the question over, "to be honest, I didn't know if he did, just because he was a catcher. I knew that he had pitched a little bit in college. I mean, just once in a while. He had some success, but I knew that in his heart he didn't want to be a pitcher; he wanted to be an everyday player. I didn't know if his bat would carry him that far.

"I thought that his catching skills could get him that opportunity to play pro baseball. Now, however far he got on that development side would have told, but he never got that opportunity. When he signed, it was adamant. When the Cubs drafted him, they said, 'We want you to be a pitcher.' He made the decision in his heart, and that was probably the hardest decision he had to make, because he had to give up playing every day.

"Once he made that decision, boy, he had a lot of success early—he did a great job. I was very, very surprised. What I saw early in him when I finally got a chance to see him pitch—he had very good stuff," he said.

Chris related how he came to play shortstop. When he was in high school, he said, "I was not a big kid, I was fairly small. I was 5'10", 155–160 pounds, so I had the physical abilities that a shortstop had to have. I had a strong arm and I had good hands; I was a decent hitter—I mean, I didn't crush the ball, I didn't hit a lot of home runs.

"But there were people who saw me, and there were scouts that saw me when I was 16 that were interested, then again at 17 and, of course, 18, when I graduated from high school. But there wasn't that 'This guy's going to be a stud.' " The bottom line is, of course, both father and son *did* make it to the majors, albeit at different positions.

Justin spoke of how some players wind up at the same position as their fathers, then he explained how he came to be a pitcher. "Every kid when they grow up, they want to play the game as much as they can. So I was a catcher and I was a shortstop. I caught in high school and in college, but I knew eventually I would end up on the mound, because I had a strong arm. I just wanted to go with the position that I'd probably find the most success at. Thank God it worked out to where I was able to get on the mound, have a good arm, and have some success."

Chris said he never really tried consciously to preach to Justin, laying down an overabundance of lessons about life as his son moved toward the majors. "That was one thing I was a little shy of. I never wanted to push any of my children into a direction that they were not comfortable with. And as a father I think you teach them the basic things and you fine-tune little things in regards to the baseball side."

So when Justin was growing up his father was very supportive without being overly intrusive, but he did want to get across at least a few messages about life, and some concerning independence. Justin said, "Even though he was in the big leagues, he was real strict as far as what he wanted us to do. We had to work, get a job. If you wanted a car, we had to buy our own car and pay for our own insurance. So, as far as that's concerned, he wanted us to learn the value of money."

"I think the main thing that I always tried to portray to my children, including Justin, was you want to love what you do, no matter what it is," Chris said. "If you're going to do that one thing, you need to put full effort into it.

"But I also stressed that the athletics and those types of things were secondary to his primary growth at that time, and that was the academic side and a spiritual side on his part. The main thing was God gives everyone different talents, and I wanted to take any pressure off of him by continuing to mention that just because you're my son, I don't expect you to follow in my foot-steps or anything like that.

"So, I almost went the opposite direction in regards to their sports—I was very supportive, but I didn't become a full-time teacher."

But make no mistake about it, he did help and teach Justin a great deal about the game. It's just that Chris didn't weigh baseball above everything else in life, as some parents might be guilty of doing. Even now, he says he will give some tips to his son "occasionally if I see something on a tape, or I might ask him what his thought process was on certain people [batters]. I'm not a pitcher; I don't know all the mechanics about it—I leave that up to his pitching coach. I wouldn't venture to go into that realm.

"I think [I give tips] more so maybe on the psychological side. He's beginning to understand what it takes—you can get to the big leagues, but what do you need to do to stay there? It's more about that."

Even though Chris was never a pitcher, I asked in our interview, couldn't he, as a former hitter, show his son how batters think? Wouldn't that benefit a pitcher—to get into the mind of a hitter and see what he thinks on certain pitch counts? Chris replied, "I didn't get into that with him."

He had a reason for this: the way the game was played in his day is somewhat different from how hitters today approach the game. "So many hitters right now have changed in a lot of their philosophies, and every hitter is different," Chris said. "[I could] say, 'It's three-one [count], I'm sitting middle-in [looking for a pitch in that location]. I want a fastball that I can turn on.' But there are a lot of guys who say, 'You know what? I like the ball middle-away. I'm looking for a ball out over the plate.' So I didn't want to go there with Justin—he's learning.

"As a pitcher, it's tough. You go out there and you make forty quality pitches and all of a sudden you make a mistake on one and it costs you, and it costs you big. That's got to be very frustrating. From that side, I think I've always tried to be very optimistic and upbeat with him: 'Keep your head up. You're going to get the opportunity.' But, you know what? He's been so great about that; he understands it already, and he's, 'Hey, give me the ball. I want to go back out there.' "

With that in mind, Chris predicted that Justin would be around for some time in the majors. "Oh, yeah. I think he's only going to get better. The one thing he has is he's usually had pretty good command with his fastball. That's very, very important—to be able to locate that. Now your other pitches play off of that. Both his other pitches, his slider and his split finger, especially the split, are getting better." Chris said Justin has developed an off-speed split finger, so he can "throw it when he's behind in the count. That'll be his ticket right there."

He envisions Justin remaining a relief pitcher throughout his career. "Number one, he's very durable. He's got that arm that his father was blessed with, that I can throw every day and have very little problem with it. In the relieving corps, that's a plus—to pump that guy out there two, three days in a row and you don't have to give him those [more customary] two days off."

Despite Chris's contention that he didn't give a preponderance of advice to his son, Justin liked what he heard. He said of his father, "He gives a lot of advice as far as the mental aspect of the game goes—like maintaining an even keel regardless of if you do good that day or if don't do good that day. You've got 162 games, so you can't get too high or too low in this game. He gives more advice as far as enduring the season."

Over the years his relationship with Justin changed. "We had a very tumultuous time when he was a teenager growing up," Chris said. "We had *real* difficult times, just the father-son thing. And now, when I think about our relationship, it is all that I've always wanted in a relationship with a son and more so. Right now we have such a deep respect for each other, and an openness that I've always longed for. I think it's because of both of our growths as people. It's a wonderful, wonderful relationship that we have. I think fathers all want that type of relationship, and I'm just blessed that I now have that with him."

One difficult moment Chris said he "just had to share [for the book]" took place when Justin was in those terrible teen years. "We were out of town, and he was left at the house to take care of the home. We said, 'Hey, absolutely no parties here—no parties whatsoever.'

"When I drove up in the driveway [upon returning from the trip], a lawn chair from the backyard was sitting atop a tree. I said, 'Hmmm?' His story was, of course, everybody found out his parents were going to be out of town so they all just came over anyway, and he couldn't stop them. He paid dearly for that one." It was one of those moments that doesn't seem so bad now but was of biblical proportions back then: the parting of the seas; the levitation of the chair.

Another trying moment, but quite different from the lawn-chair incident, occurred in 2000, when Chris was coaching with Milwaukee and the Brewers faced Cleveland, with Justin on the mound. Interestingly, Justin didn't find the meeting too uncomfortable, not nearly as much as Chris did. "I pitched two games against them," Justin recalled. "I got a base hit to right field, so that was pretty cool."

Justin said it was also "cool getting to see him during the baseball year because that doesn't really happen that often." Normally the Indians, as members of the American League, wouldn't face the National League Brewers, but because of interleague play the Speiers had their reunion.

"More importantly," Justin continued, "it was fun pitching against his team, and it was also good to see him those three days. We went out to dinner and hung out."

Still, it wasn't all fun and games, especially for the father. Playing against family members can be awkward, or worse. Chris's version of the close encounter with his son varies a great deal from Justin's point of view.

"It was terrible, a very terrible feeling," Chris recalled. I remember the night it happened, and he's got the bases loaded with two outs and he's facing one of our hitters. He strikes out the guy, not allowing any runs, and I almost wanted to yell, "Yes!" at third base [where he was coaching].

"*Almost* wanted to but couldn't, because you're caught in that position where you want your team to do well, but here's your son out here; if our team does well, that means they're batting him around a little bit.

"I just told him, 'That was really tough.' But it's funny, because as he came off the mound he gave me a little smile and a wink. It was a situation I don't think I would like to be in a lot. I really wouldn't."

The reason going up against his father was easier for Justin was due to the fact that his father was a coach and not, say, an opposing player or the manager of the enemy. Justin's emotions weren't torn, since he was pulling 100 percent for his Indians. "You want to beat those guys, so as a player you just go out—it's just a normal setting. We had played my dad's team before, so it's not a big deal. For him it was probably a little bit difficult, though."

Nevertheless, Justin's hit against his dad's team *was* a big deal, and a happy result for both father and son. Upon reaching first base, Justin said, "I looked in his dugout and said, 'Thanks for all the B.P. you threw me all those years.'"

While he had seen his son pitch in high school and in college, it was from the stands, not from the opposite dugout. Chris added, "I didn't get a chance to see him [often] in the minors because I was working the same time he was."

Justin recollected that the very first time his father saw him play in a professional game was another time their teams faced each other. "It was when I was in Triple-A and I pitched against his Triple-A team—he was the manager of that team. He was with the Tucson Sidewinders, and I was with the Iowa Cubs. I pitched against his team twice. It went good; I came in for an inning both times. It was definitely nice for him to see me.

"I gave up a run one time, and he's always been real supportive and real positive as far as my outings are concerned."

Chris added, "I did run across him once before this time [the Brewers-Indians contest], though. He was with Chicago and I was with the Diamond-backs, and we played each other. He did pitch against us once, but it was in a situation where I think they had a six-run lead and he came in and did well, but, again, it was not a very comfortable position to be in."

Chris also got to see his son when Justin was with the Cubs and Chris was with Arizona during spring training, since both teams hold their exhibi-tion seasons in the state of Arizona, in the Cactus League. "I don't think we ran into each other pitching-wise, though," he said.

Even back in Justin's high-school outings, Chris said his feelings when watching his son were typical of most dads—happiness and excitement, punc-tuated mainly by nervousness and anxiety. He always tried to stay "quiet and calm, and let him play," he said. "I've been involved in so many Little Leagues, and I've watched the parents get that too-involved scenario and put too much pressure on their kids—that was one thing I really wanted to take away from him; it didn't matter what he did so long as he was playing hard and doing what he had to do."

One would expect Little League parents and coaches to pester Chris, asking him for advice and tips, since he had big-league experience. However, Chris said, "most of the time they left me alone. There were always guys who would talk about different hitting and throwing techniques and 'Would you work with my son?' I would accommodate them if I had the time."

When it comes to watching Justin now, Chris said his main source of information and video clips is ESPN and the ballpark's out-of-town score-board. "I check the scoreboard because I know his uniform number and I can see if he's in there or not," he said. "And then there's the box scores the next day." In addition, the two Speiers are in touch over the phone a great deal.

While Justin was growing up, Chris was available more than enough to help guide his development. "Oh, definitely, he'd go out and throw me batting practice all the time," Justin said. "I remember towards the end of his career we'd go in early [to the ballpark] and he'd throw me batting practice every day. He'd throw and I'd hit left-handed; he'd throw and I'd hit right-handed. It was pretty special."

His help didn't end there, as Justin still appreciates Chris's occasional tips. "He knows a lot about the game," Justin said. "He knows a lot about pitching, he knows a lot about pitchers, and he knows what hitters do. So he gives me advice on how to go about facing hitters sometimes. He looks in the paper to see how I do; he keeps track on how I'm doing."

Justin addressed other advantages of being Chris Speier's son, including genetics. Coming from good stock, he felt, is a definite plus. "My dad had a strong arm when he was coming up," he said. "He threw the ball across the diamond like Shawon Dunston did when he was young—he had that kind of arm. So I think there's a lot of truth to [hereditary factors]; I got his good arm."

Then, with a laugh, he explained that the hitting chromosone that was present in his father was missing in him—that genetic condition led to his ultimate career choice: "I couldn't hit the curveball like he could, so I ended up on the mound."

However, he pointed out that heredity can't explain everything. He doesn't totally espouse the heredity versus environment argument. Instead, he argues for heredity *and* environment, saying, "It's a little bit of both aspects. If a kid's around the game a lot and he loves the game and plays it all the time, you can build [assets such as] arm strength that way, too. I have a strong arm, yet I played baseball year-round. Maybe I increased my strength that way, too.

"There's my other brothers and sisters, who don't have that strong arm. It's the luck of the draw, too. They're athletic, and my one brother, Cole, does have a strong arm—he's a pretty good ballplayer. He's 16 years old and he's going to be a junior this year. He pitches and plays shortstop. When he gets older he might have a chance—we'll see what happens. But my other two brothers have interests in other things. My whole family has an interest for the game because my dad's still in it and I'm in it, but I don't think all my brothers and sisters have a *love* for the game. Baseball plays an important role in our family. Maybe it all comes down to if you really have an interest in something, you can get it done," he concluded.

Science aside, while Justin's exposure to the world of baseball gave him a head start, he reiterated the fact that his father never steered him toward that sphere of life. "He said, 'If you want to play baseball; if you love the game, hey, I'll help you with it.' So I love the game, and he helped. Ever since I can remember, I've been playing."

Given that he's the son of a diligent worker, it was hardly surprising to hear Justin's thoughts on team play. For example, he believes a player sometimes has to suck it up and play hurt. He said, "You see guys who go out there, real professional guys, and play with little, nagging injuries. No one's ever 100 percent.

"My dad played [at] 100 percent maybe three times in his whole career, and he played nineteen years. So that's just one of those things—you just gotta go out. You're never going to be 100 percent, you just gotta give it 100 percent."

Justin is one of many sons who believe "my dad is more proud of me just as a person, more so than the baseball aspect. When we talk on the phone, we talk more about how our families are doing and how all my brothers and sisters are doing more than baseball. We talk about baseball also, but more about life than anything."

As the oldest child in the family, Justin said that he can remember seeing his father on a big-league diamond. "Probably when I was three," he said. "When I was about 1 year old, my dad was playing with the Giants. I don't remember then, but I remember more vividly when he was in Montreal. I'd go into the ballpark with him then, and when he was with the Cubs I'd go in."

When it comes to looking back as an adult and succinctly capturing what his father is all about, as well as the feelings he has for him, Justin unabashedly stated, "My dad's a great man. And he was both a great mentor and a great father for me. When he played the game of baseball, he went about it hard. He came from the old-school way of playing, and he instilled that in my game, too."

Others agree with Justin. "It looks like [Chris] did a pretty good job with Justin," Clarence Jones said. "He comes in and he goes right at the hitter. He's got a pretty good split [finger fastball]. You can't say too many bad things about Justin."

More praise came during spring training of 2001 from Justin's manager, Charlie Manuel. "He's a gutty kid," the Indians skipper said, "and he'll take the ball every day." Those attributes are highly appreciated at the professional level.

No matter what happens with Justin's career, Chris knows that a career isn't as important as family. All things considered, Chris compared his biggest personal baseball thrill to the wonders of having a son. "Well, there's no comparison," he said proudly. "Having a son by far surpasses anything I have ever done on the field, that's for sure. I get so many more great feelings of pride with all my children, with whatever they accomplish. I'm sure there's a little 'specialness' once in a while that I'm very proud of what he's accomplished in his life and what he's gone through. To be in the position that he's in right now has been a tremendous achievement. Not because of his baseball ability but because of his manhood. That's the thing that I'm most proud about."

He thought back to the first time he saw Justin as a baby, and said, "I was scared to death. I thought he was going to be born on the Bay Bridge. It was real late at night, and I remember my—at this time my ex-wife, his mother—just screaming, telling me to pull over, that she was going to have the baby. It was a life-changing event."

Ken Griffey Sr. with his Donora High School teammates

Photo courtesy of the 1969 Donora High School Yearbook

Ken Griffey Sr. and Ken Griffey Jr. in the Reds' dugout, 2001

Photo courtesy of the Cincinnati Reds

Bobby and Barry Bonds

Photo courtesy of the San Francisco Giants

Adam Kennedy, age 5

Photo courtesy of Tom Kennedy

Tom and Adam Kennedy, 1995

Photo courtesy of Tom Kennedy

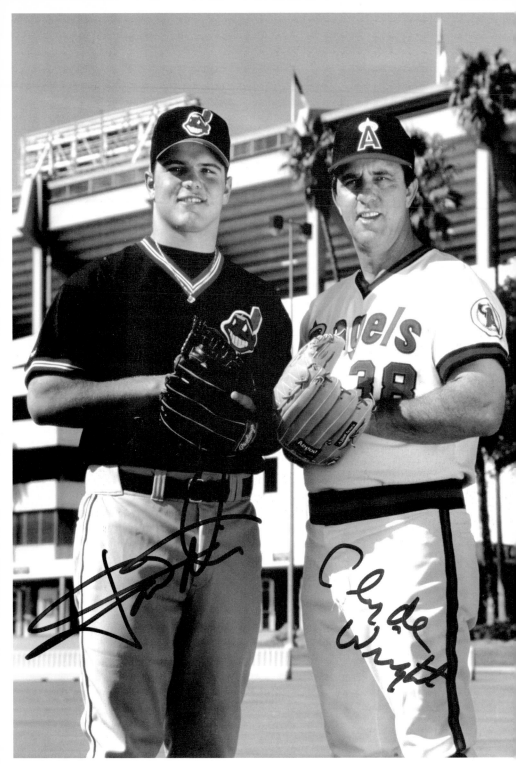

Clyde and Jaret Wright

Photo courtesy of Clyde Wright

Tom and Ben Grieve at New York Mets father/son game, Shea Stadium, 1978

Photo courtesy of Kathleen Grieve

The general manager and the batboy, Tom and Ben Grieve, 1988

Photo courtesy of Kathleen Grieve

Scott Spiezio at the plate

Photo courtesy of the Anaheim Angels

Scott Spiezio in the field

Photo courtesy of the Anaheim Angels

Todd Stottlemyre on the mound

Photo courtesy of the Arizona Diamondbacks

Marcus Giles

Photo courtesy of the Atlanta Braves

Wayne and Scott Stewart, 1990

Photo courtesy of Wayne Stewart

The author and his boys, 1998

Photo courtesy of Wayne Stewart

Chapter Twelve: The Wrights

Clyde Wright was born in Jefferson City, Tennessee. His father was not particularly athletic, nor did he encourage Clyde to play baseball. "My dad ran the farm when I grew up, and he saw me play one game in the big leagues when my brothers drove him to Baltimore," Clyde said. "I pitched against the Orioles, and Boog Powell hit a line drive that hit me in the [protective] cup. My dad tried to get me to quit and go home before I got hurt. I said, 'I can't do that, Dad.' I'd been gone from home two or three years, but he still didn't want anything to happen to his son, just like I don't want anything to happen to my kid."

Still, he said, his father was proud of him, as he surely was of "my other five brothers, and they didn't play baseball."

Although Clyde was born down on the farm, where his family raised everything from wheat to corn to tobacco, he moved to California when he became a member of the Angels. He and his wife, Vicki, decided to stay there to raise their family, which includes big-league pitcher Jaret and another son, Derek, who was 16 in 2001, at the time of this interview, nine years younger than Jaret.

Derek "couldn't care less if a baseball falls in his lap or not," Clyde said. "He tried it a couple of times in Little League and he didn't like it. He decided when he was 13 that he didn't like it, so I said, 'Well, fine. You don't *have* to play, son. I'm not going to push you to play.' But he's got some of the finest skateboards that's ever been bought.

"This year he told me and Mom, 'I think I want to go out for track.' That's fine, so he's on the track team and enjoying that." Now Clyde has found himself going from the diamond to the track, where he'll watch his younger son take part in the triple jump and the mile relay.

Clyde has two daughters between Jaret and Derek. The girls are Stacey, who "graduated from B.Y.U., and Devon who plays water polo at Orange Coast College. She was the MVP of her league in high school for three straight years," Clyde said. "That's the toughest sport I think I've ever seen." Clyde feels that way partly because, he said, he hates the water and can't swim well, so he knew she wasn't following in his wake. Meanwhile, Stacey ran track and played volleyball in high school. He says he's just as happy for his girls when they compete as he is for Jaret.

Clyde decided to use his baseball knowledge to open a business, and he now runs a pitching school, which he began around 1980. And make no mistake, he knows what he's talking about. After all, here's a man who, among other accomplishments, owns a no-hitter. Clyde was also very pleased with "the year that I did win twenty-two games." His lowest ERA of 2.82 was also posted the year he won 22. The next two seasons Clyde displayed great consistency, winning 34 games with ERAs of 2.99 and 2.98. In five of his ten seasons in the majors, his win total was in the double digits.

Despite those numbers, it was understandable to hear him listing his no-hitter as "the highlight of my career." He had a story about his no-hitter that he wanted to share. "When I threw the no-hitter against Oakland in 1970, [A's owner] Charlie Finley sent me a watch and put a little note with it: 'Congratulations. You pitched a fine game.' That's how I remember Charlie Finley; and for that damned orange ball [a Finley innovation], because I gave up seven runs one day experimenting with that thing [in spring training].

"It was terrible. I think Catfish Hunter pitched in that game, and he didn't like it, either. The ball was too slick. They said they wanted the hitters to see the ball better. If they saw it any better, the pitchers wouldn't have a job," he concluded.

Clyde, never a hard thrower, uses his homespun humor well. He spoke of the incident in spring training of 2001 when a Randy Johnson pitch struck and killed a bird, whose flight took it into a path directly in front of home plate. "And the feathers just flew," Clyde said. "I'm glad it wasn't me that hit the bird. The bird would probably have got up and gone to first base."

Longtime coach Art Kusnyer confirmed Clyde's contention. "I played with Clyde with the Angels," he said. "I was talking with him just before his boy signed, and he said that his son Jaret got all the fastballs because Clyde was a soft-tossing-type guy."

Despite all his glory, Clyde declared, "Another highlight of my career that makes people say, 'You're crazy,' was when I got to sit in Yankee Stadium by the dugout one Saturday afternoon when they had an Old-Timers' day when I was with the Angels. And they introduced [Joe] DiMaggio last. And I'm telling you, that place went nuts. I had goose bumps about the size of golf balls on my arm.

"I was checking it over with the manager [Bobby Winkles] of the Angels. I said, 'You got goose bumps?' He said, 'Yeah. I got goose bumps, too.' I got to see all those guys; you read about them all the time. I kept up with them as a kid. And I got to play against [Mickey] Mantle, I got to play against [Roger] Maris, [Al] Kaline, [Harmon] Killebrew. You know, they just weren't ordinary ballplayers—they were damn good."

In short, he was overjoyed to have played in one of baseball's golden eras, but he appreciated other great periods as well. "The thing that people don't understand is we had it nice when we played. We played the game hard, but the group before us in the 1950s, holy Toledo. How'd you like to go into Cleveland and face Bob Feller, Early Wynn, Mike Garcia, and Bob Lemon. Hell, that's oh-for-the-weekend. Then, you got to take the train up to New York to run into Vic Raschi, Ed Lopat, and that group."

He also spends a lot of time keeping up with the game that he loves so much. "I'm a baseball nut," he said. "I watch it on TV, and I watch the old-timers when they're on, when they have them on that classic sports channel—Stan Musial and Willie Mays and all those guys.

"And I played against Mays and some of them in spring training. When I wasn't pitching, I'd sit on the bench and I'd say, 'Boy, I'd like to see him hit the ball in the gap. I just want to see him run.' But it was amazing some of the things he could do." Even if the gap shot hurt his team, it was only spring training, so even an active player like Wright couldn't help being a fan on occasion.

His son Jaret was born in Anaheim, two days before the year 1975 came to an end. He stands 6'2" and weighs in at 230 pounds. He now resides in Newport Beach, California. In high school he posted an 8–2 slate in his senior year to go with a fine 2.83 ERA. Striking out 111 batters in 82 innings, he was his league's MVP and was voted the L.A. High School Player of the Year by the *Orange County Register* and the *Los Angeles Times.* Unlike his father, a southpaw, Jaret, who finished fourth in the 1997 voting for the Rookie of the Year, is a right-handed pitcher.

Jaret's shoulder problems gave him many troubling moments. In August of 2000, he had surgery to repair a torn labrum and a frayed rotator cuff. Instead of breaking camp in 2001 for a trip north to Cleveland, he had to stay behind in Florida to work on a comeback. In late April, he got a chance to work out in Cleveland. When he returned to the familiar clubhouse, he quipped, "It's good to see me here."

However, it was a temporary stay, since he was merely going through a session with the Indians' pitching coach, Dick Pole. Jaret's next stop was Buffalo for a thirty-day injury-rehab assignment with the Indians' Triple-A affiliate.

Still, he said he could see some positives concerning his plight and his career. He said that he finally knows what it takes to survive as a big-league pitcher. That insight came at the expense of a two-year bout with shoulder problems, limiting him to thirty-five starts over that span of time.

He observed, "I've found a real good perspective on playing and what it takes. Before, it was a little easier for me with my arm. I could throw and battle through a lot of things because of my arm. But now, after surgery, if you don't put the time in, you're going to go down. That's not what I want to have happen."

Determined, the strong-armed righty said, "It's like you have a near-death experience, and just being able to get a cup of coffee is something you cherish. It's been very frustrating. I'm just happy to be throwing again, and it's re-energized me to come back. You have to feel confident that they fixed it and you're on the road to coming back."

On May 19, 2001, he worked himself back into the majors, getting a start against Anaheim, right in his old neighborhood. He told *USA Today/Baseball Weekly,* "I felt great. It felt like my first start ever. I was standing on the mound trying to take it all in." He was able to last five innings, throwing ninety-eight pitches in a no decision. His velocity was in the 92–94-miles-per-hour range on his best fastballs.

He said he wasn't sure if making his first start in his hometown was a positive or a negative. "I don't know if it was harder, but it added something to it. The pressure is there, whenever you're pitching, especially the first time after surgery."

All his hard work paid off in a victory on May 30, 2001, his first since May 11, 2000. "It feels really good," he said. "That's why you put in all that work. You want to help your team win, keep them in the game. So getting that first win is satisfying."

Unfortunately, he apparently wasn't fully recovered. After going 2–2 with an ERA of 6.52, he was returned to Buffalo for further work and evaluation. It was ironic that in 1997 he marched through minor-league stops in Akron and Buffalo up to the majors, because in 2001 his rehab took him through those same cities before his return to the bigs.

If the man Mike Hargrove once called "a very young Roger Clemens" succeeds with a repaired shoulder and a new outlook, he may attain a goal his dad had for him, truly learning how to pitch. Some hurlers are actually throwers more so than pitchers. Jaret, experts feel, may still have the ability to be something special.

Charlie Manuel took over the reins of the Cleveland Indians in 2000, inheriting quite a few players who were the sons of big leaguers, including the Alomars, David Segui, Justin Speier, and Jaret Wright. He said of the Wrights, "I've known them for a long time. Their makeup is something a lot similar— both of them are kind of loud, a little cocky, but very friendly kind of people.

"Clyde is a big competitor; Jaret has learned how to pitch in the major leagues. He's been here two or three years, but, at the same time, he's been hurt the last couple of years, so basically he's just learning how to pitch in the majors."

Entering the 2001 season, some writers were saying Wright, the tenth man selected in the '94 June draft, had reached his peak of fame four years earlier in the 1997 World Series. There the rookie right-handed pitcher was given the nod to start the Series-deciding seventh game. This was a youngster, then only 21, who hadn't even been on the Cleveland Indians' forty-man roster that spring. He had clawed his way all the way up from the low minors to the World Series in one year. In fact, entering the seventh game, his lifetime big-league victory total of eight ranked the lowest of any man who ever started the final game of a Series.

His stats back then merited respect, though, as he went 8–3 in sixteen starts before going 3–0 in postseason play during his rookie season. That year he became one of just six rookies to win three games in a single postseason. When the Indians faced the New York Yankees that year, Jaret became the youngest starting pitcher in Division Series history, and he even won the deciding game of the series, sending the Indians on into the ALCS.

One of his postseason wins was a victory in his first World Series start, Game Four versus the Florida Marlins. In that Series, Jaret became the second-youngest pitcher ever to start the deciding game of a World Series. For that matter, he was just the seventh rookie ever to get the starting nod for the seventh game.

Maybe all the hype hurt Jaret. Cleveland manager Charlie Manuel thought so, because " . . . it raised everyone's expectations so much. He was not a finished product at the time. When he pitched in the postseason that year nobody had seen him. For a short period of time, Jaret got by pitching the way he did, but then he had to change and learn how to pitch different ways to fool hitters."

Just before Jaret returned to Cleveland after surgery and rehab, Manuel continued his observations. "I think he has matured a lot since then," he said. "The injury has helped him mature. His attitude has definitely changed. I think he's ready to go."

Clarence Jones was the hitting coach for the Indians in 2000 when he jokingly compared the Wrights, saying, "Well, they're both a little 'off,' but most of the pitchers are like that. Jaret throws a lot harder than his dad."

Joe Nossek, an astute observer of the game, said of Clyde, "I was with Clyde in Milwaukee at the tail end of his career and know [him] quite well and [have] always enjoyed [him]. He's a great competitor, and Jaret has the same qualities—you see the same things in the father as you do in the son. I don't think it's coincidence. It's inbred, I think."

While he can't help noticing that Jaret throws much harder, Joe said, "Clyde was aggressive, too. Jaret has a reputation of knocking people down, but Clyde wasn't afraid to, either, and that's part of pitching. If you're going to do it, though, you don't want to be hitting people in the head. You want to be under control."

Joe believes Clyde may even have earned a reputation for throwing in when he had to, like Jaret, but in his era throwing tight was expected, not un-usual. "When a guy hit a home run back then, the next guy up was the guy who got drilled, not the guy who hit it, and they thought nothing of it," he said. "It's completely different [now]."

Finally, Cleveland coach Ted Uhlaender pointed out several obvious differences between the two Wright pitchers. "One's right-handed [Jaret], one's left-handed, and they have completely different personalities. The way they throw [is also different]; Clyde wasn't a power pitcher and Jaret is."

Clyde said Jaret was a "normal" boy growing up. "Sometimes he'd lis-ten, sometimes he wouldn't. He grew up going through grammar school and high school playing sports. To me he was just a typical high-school kid."

Maybe so, but Clyde had to admit that he was atypical when it came to baseball prowess. "In his junior year—he had an awful lot of talent when he started throwing the ball really hard," the proud papa said. Up until then, he *could* play the game "better than the average player," certainly, but it was then that he really found his fastball. "He was throwing it ninety-plus.

"I started thinking, After he gets out of high school we're going to let the air out of that football. We're not going to play football,' " he said, laughing. He recalled that that was when he first began to believe his son could indeed "make it in the majors."

Clyde couldn't recall Jaret's having statistics like an ERA of under, say, 1.00, in high school, but he did recall that he did well pitching, "and he was a pretty good hitter, too.

"He had a lot of natural talent. I've seen a lot more kids that had a lot of natural talent, but they just don't work at it and it kind of goes by the way-side," said Clyde, who felt that his son had the determination to take his talent where he is today. "He could have gone to the minor leagues and not worked as hard as he did—it's tough to ride that damn bus and wake up at 6:00 in the morning and you're still on that bus."

While baseball was always a big part of their lives, Clyde said, "My son never saw me play baseball in the big leagues. I was retired. He saw me play when he was a year old, over in Japan, so he can't remember that." In all, Clyde spent three seasons, 1976–1978, in Japan, so Jaret was only 3 years old when the Wrights returned to the United States.

It wouldn't be too many years, though, before Jaret showed an interest in baseball and in pitching. "As far as bonding with him, I have a pitching school here and he would come to it," Clyde said. "Half the time he listened, half the time he didn't listen. You know, the hardest thing to do is try to teach your own kid.

"I've had some pretty good kids come out of here [his school]. Jaret came out of here, and Ted Powers was here and Eric Ireland and Mike Sweeney, the first baseman for Kansas City, he was here all the time. Robbie Nen was here, too; quite a few guys."

There is one lesson Clyde tries to pass on to budding pitchers more than any other. "Throw the ball over the plate," he said emphatically, stressing control and no free passes to first base, which almost inevitably haunt pitchers. "I tell them, 'Look, if you're afraid, let me ask you, Why did they make the bat? They made the bat to hit the ball, but only one guy can bat at a time, right? Doubleday gave you nine guys to fight that one. Let him hit it.'

"How's this for a stat? When I threw the no-hitter, how many strike-outs do you think I had?" He paused, then provided the surprising answer. "How about *one*? Twenty-six guys hit the ball—we caught it twenty-six times; I only struck out one guy.

"I passed on to Jaret what I was taught in baseball. Then, when he got to play pro ball, he called me one day and he said, 'Dad, they're telling me the same things that you told me.' I said, 'No joke. I only played thirteen years. Don't you think some of it rubbed off?' "

Clyde said that he always tried to teach Jaret about baseball and life. "The thing that I really like about my son—he's got a good heart. He's not afraid to help somebody, and he knows where he is [in life]. When he gets a check every two weeks, he knows he's not just an average guy working. He knows he's a big-league player, but that it's not going to last forever. He understands all of that.

"A lot of times people think just because he's our son who is playing in the major leagues, and I played in the major leagues, that if he *didn't* play there we wouldn't love him as much. Well, that's dumb. If he's out digging ditches, you're going to love your kid just as much as if he's out making $10 to 15 million a year," he said, pointing out that love "doesn't change."

He also pointed out how difficult it is to teach certain baseball concepts, such as control. "It's like when you try to tell somebody to pitch inside. The kids [such as his son] throw hard, so it's a lot tougher for them to pitch inside, because if they throw the ball 95, 96 miles an hour, and they miss by three or four inches, somebody's going to get knocked down [or worse]. But a guy that throws it 85, he throws it the same place and the hitter can get out of the way of the pitch—they have more time [to react].

"But I didn't push him and, I tell you, he learned most of it on his own. When he had the operation this winter [prior to 2001], I've never seen a kid work that hard to get back into shape to try it again."

Although he admired his son's tenacity, watching him struggle to gain his old form also frustrated and saddened Clyde. "Oh, sure, because I don't like to see any player get hurt," said Clyde, before adding, with his tongue mostly in cheek, "unless he was the guy in front of me on the pitching staff that was going to send me back to the minor leagues—then I didn't care what happened to him. I didn't want him to die or anything, but if he got his leg broke or his big toe broke, I didn't care. I sure didn't want to go back to the minor leagues." Joking aside, his son did, in fact, have to go back to the minors at the start of 2001, and again shortly after his first victory, when he had seemingly recovered, to rehab for his shoulder. That was a concern for Clyde.

Again, on a serious note, he added that the feeling of futility and empathy often brought on by someone's injuries "magnifies when it happens to your kid. Sure, I hated to see him get hurt, because I know the amount of talent that he has. He's still got a lot of talent.

"It's like the other day, I went to Florida and watched him pitch down there [in March of 2001], and he got it up to 92, 93 again. Guys are telling me down there, 'Well, he only got it to 92, 93.' I said, 'Good God Almighty, I tried for thirteen years, trying to get it to 90.' What's wrong with 92 if you learn to pitch . . . you can be just as successful as you can pitching 95, 96."

Apparently, coming back from surgery taught Jaret that there's nothing wrong with that approach. "When I first came up," he said, "I tried to throw everything as hard as I could. [Now] I'm trying to make good pitches down in the strike zone."

His manager, Manuel, commented, "I think Jaret is starting to grow up. He's a little bit older, and I think he's getting wiser. I've seen big changes in the last two years. He talks about his breaking ball and change-up now. No longer just talks about his fastball."

Admittedly, speed is a great asset, and Clyde noted, "I think he threw some pitches at one time—98, 99." Joe Torre even said, "There's no question he was an overpowering pitcher back then [circa 1997]. He had a little bit of the intimidation thing."

That said, Clyde pointed out that men like Warren Spahn didn't throw as hard as Jaret, adding, and "he was outstanding, wasn't he? Unbelievable. People forget that [Bob] Gibson never threw that hard—like in the high 90s— either, but I watched a special on him and the year that he had the 1.12 earned run average. He started thirty-four games and had twenty-eight complete games." So if Jaret gets his speed back to where it had been, great. If not, his career doesn't have to be over.

In fact, even though Jaret was hitting 95 mph during his comeback, and he knew he had lost some speed, he still found a positive in the experience. "I think," said Jaret, "when I hurt myself I was in the process of learning how to pitch in the big leagues. Coming back is a really slow process. You have to really hit your spots and move the ball around a lot more, because your velocity isn't the same as when you went on the D.L. [disabled list]. So having to have better command has really helped."

He also felt that his change-up, which was a minor weapon of his in the past, had become a pitch he felt comfortable with—a pitch that can help him win again in the majors. Thus he was pretty much echoing the words of his wise father. So although Jaret didn't always listen to his dad's advice when he was a kid, he seems to be an apt pupil now.

In addition to the pain of seeing his offspring try to rehab, Clyde also said, "It's when they lose—it eats you up inside." He said it's never easy to see a member of his family compete and lose. "When I'd watch Jaret pitch and he'd get hit around and lose, I can't help him. It's just like my daughter playing water polo—I can't help her. It's just like the one playing volleyball in high school—I can't help her. The parents are supposed to be there to help their kids, but there are just some things you're useless at. You just sit there and take it.

"The hardest thing about being a dad for a professional athlete is to sit there and watch it on TV and hear all the negative things. You want to hear the good. I don't care if you're a sportswriter or whoever, you want to hear good stuff about your kid, but the thing about the negative [that is troublesome occurs] especially when you're sitting there knowing they're [the comments] not true."

Even though Clyde knows that harsh critiques from the media come with the territory, having tasted a few nasty morsels himself, he still finds it hard to swallow. "It hurts a lot worse when they're talking about my son. When I played, I was the first one to know if I was horseshit or not. I would tell them, 'I don't need to pick up the paper and read it, I know it as quick as they take me out of the game.'

"Sometimes you would win a ball game, maybe 7–6, but you didn't pitch that good, and you *knew* it. You just got lucky and won. Then there's sometimes you get beat, 2–1, but you feel better then, because you did your job. The other game, 7–6, you didn't do your job. You got the win in one and a loss in the other one, but there are different feelings."

He said that in the 7–6 example he'd find himself going home asking himself, "Wait a minute, what the hell did I do wrong? What's going on?" At that point, he'd analyze the game, thinking things through.

Jaret, he feels, probably hasn't reached that level of the pitching game. "Not at this point," he said. "He's starting to get there." One must give young pitchers some leeway, though, as there is a plethora of facets to learn when it comes to pitching.

"When I faced batters," Clyde said, "I would go [in his mind] one, two, three pitches ahead to try and get the out. When I played, it was set in my head that if I could get the batter out on four or five pitches, I would be happy.

"But the thing about it that you've got to understand is this: with guys that throw hard, the batters generally foul off a lot more pitches, just nick them, so you're going to throw more pitches in the ball game," he said.

Then, by way of comparison, he spoke of how economical Greg Maddux of Atlanta is with his pitches and how surgeonlike he is with his pitch location. He may not possess a blazing fastball, Clyde pointed out, but he wins. He also likened his approach to that of Bob Feller, who preferred to save his arm and not throw tons of pitches when that could be avoided. All of these lessons should come to Jaret in time.

As Clyde put it, "When you become a complete pitcher, then it's a lot of fun; when you can trick a guy. If he's looking for a fastball, you throw him a change-up—you just go the opposite way. Then one time he's sitting there thinking, Well, he's not going to throw me a fastball, *then* you throw a little fastball on him. It's just cat and mouse, and it's fun to try to outfox a hitter."

Clyde said he first began to toss such tidbits of knowledge to Jaret "around the time he was in Little League, when I'd tell him to pick his leg up and use his legs because his legs are a lot stronger than his arm. So you use the legs to take the brunt of all the pounding."

Clyde also spoke of how he and his son both loved the game, sharing baseball as their common ground. As a matter of fact, he said that Jaret had always been in love with baseball "and surfing—oh, Lord, he loves to surf."

However, when it came to bonding with his son, both in the past and now, baseball remains a key to their relationship (with golf coming into play, too). "That's what we talk about," Clyde said. "He can talk about surfing, but I don't know one thing about that."

As for baseball from days gone by, Clyde used to tell Jaret tales of when he himself pitched. He joked that if someone overheard those stories, "I was probably the greatest player that ever played for the Angels, because every year I'd just keep getting a little bit better after I retired. I just added a little bit more on [to his stories to his son]."

When it comes to sheer velocity, Jaret has absolutely no need to embellish when he discusses his skill with his dad. Clyde is well aware that their pitching styles are different. The most salient point, he said "was about 20 miles an hour different. I have no idea how that happened. People always ask me, 'How do kids throw harder?' I tell them, 'Well, if I knew, I sure as hell wouldn't be running this pitching school. I'd hire myself out to all thirty major-league teams and tell them.' If we knew, we'd have a ton of money.

"You can see a 6'6" guy that breaks his neck trying to get it to 90-plus. Then you see some little guy that's about 5'8" or 5'9", that can throw it 95 with no effort at all. It just doesn't make any sense," he said, his voice rising with in-credulity, even while conjuring up the image of Houston Astros closer Billy Wagner. Wagner is listed at 5'11", 180 pounds, but that's probably being gener-ous; still, his fastball has been clocked at 101 mph on at least one occasion.

Another stylistic point about baseball, which Clyde could discuss with his son, concerns how things were in his time versus the state of the game today. He said, using hyperbole liberally, "We've got a pitcher for everything now. We've got one to pitch to the left-hander if he's not had a bad night. We've got a right-hander to come in to a right-hander, but if he's over 240 pounds we bring in another one. It's unbelievable."

Even though Jaret may not find today's trend so weird, being a baseball contemporary, Clyde did say that he could relate to his son better on most is-sues than a father who hadn't played the game. "Sure, sure I can. I *know* what it's like." For example, he said that while it's difficult for a player to go through the physical aspects of the game, "you can kinda put up with that, go through the work, and do it." As a former player, he knows how grueling it can be to get into shape and to prepare an arm to perform an unnatural act of physics.

"But I'm telling you," he interjected, "when you stay out [due to in-jury, for example] and you're sitting on your butt for five or six months and can't do anything—I mean, you can't go play golf, you can't do *anything* physi-cal, the mental part is what really kills you."

So when it comes to relating to Jaret's having to sit on the baseball shelf, Clyde feels for his son. He compared such an athlete to a caged tiger, yearning to get out and to be active. "I know when I was playing, if I missed a turn, oh, I'd just get ill—bite somebody's head off," he said.

" 'What do you mean, they're telling me I can't pitch?' They [coaches] would say, 'It's better for you this way, right?' "To which he'd reply, "Well, who are you? What makes you smarter than me? It's my body, my arm." This sce-nario makes one happy not to have been a pitching coach back then.

Clyde was more fortunate than Jaret in that, he said, "I was lucky to never have any operations, so everything turned out pretty good." He also feels that his son has an attitude of wanting to come back, wanting desperately to pitch. "I know he wants to pitch. The first time they let him throw in a game, he had to drive about an hour and a half [to work in a rehab situation]. When I was talking to him he said, 'I don't care if it's a softball game, I just wanted to get back out there.' " Like his father, Jaret is, says Dad, "a competitor."

Perhaps that attitude was never more evident than when Jaret was on the hill in the World Series. And *that* is something Clyde never got to do, work in a Fall Classic. So how do Clyde's accomplishments, such as the no-hitter, compare with a Series appearance?

Would he swap one for the other? "In a damn minute," Clyde nearly shouted, "I tell him, 'Son, you don't realize this, but I'm ticked off. You know I played thirteen years and never even got to a playoff game. Here you are at 21 starting the seventh game of the World Series.' "

Naturally, Clyde was there that night. Also in attendance was golf legend Jack Nicklaus. "They showed big Jack up on the screen," Clyde said. "I kid all the time. I say, 'Big Jack came to see my son pitch.' But he's from Florida— hell, he was pulling for the Marlins. I knew that, but I say it anyway."

He also says his son did a fine job. "He had it going pretty good for about seven innings. Then they took him out after he gave up the home run to Bobby Bonilla on a straight change and the ball was up. I can tell the pitches. He was ahead, 2–1 when he came out, then they scored a couple of runs and Cleveland gets beat, 3–2. He got a no decision and they lose the World Series."

Philosophically, Clyde also said, "Even though it hurt for me and my son, I was still happy for the Florida manager, Jim Leyland, a classy guy. If it couldn't have been my son and Cleveland, what the hell's wrong with Leyland? Nothing. There's some guys you see who manage in the big leagues and you hope they never win a game. It's just like when I played—there's some guys you respected, some guys you didn't."

Jaret and Clyde get together even when the Indians aren't in the World Series. "I go down to see him now and then; I like to go down and spend a week in Cleveland," Clyde said. "When they come to Oakland, we might fly up there and watch him and when he comes to Anaheim, we watch him.

"But, you know, he's got his friends—he's 25, he's not 16 or 17 anymore. When you get older, the distance gets a little more apart. I'm not talking about as far as father and son goes but as far as seeing each other."

Aside from Jaret's Series appearance, another memorable time Clyde saw him pitch was at his initial outing in professional baseball for Burlington. "He opened up in 'A' ball, and my wife and I flew down there without him knowing it. We sat outside the gate because we knew where the players parked, and we knew what kind of car he had. So when he came walking down and it looked like he had on his game face—he was getting all serious—we jumped out from behind the car and he said, 'What are you doing here?' We gave him a pretty good surprise.

"We also saw him pitch his first game in the big leagues against Minnesota. The ironic thing is *I* pitched my first game against Minnesota, but about thirty years apart," said Clyde, who has flown thousands of miles to Cleveland to see Jaret. Even if his son had done poorly, it would have been well worth the trip, but, Clyde recalled, "He won. He gave up a few runs, but he won. Got it out of the way, and that was super.

"All our family was there, and we went out to eat. He took us out to dinner and he paid, believe it or not," said Clyde, who added, to show that he was just teasing, that Jaret "takes care of his sisters and his brother; he's a pretty good kid."

As Jaret grows older, Clyde finds that their relationship is becoming more one of equals. "When I talk to him now, it's not like a dad talking to him, it's like baseball players talking. When he was 16 or 17, I was his dad; now we talk baseball and it is on a different level. I'm not his dad, in a sense; I'm the guy that played pro baseball."

It seems that the two Wright pitchers have come to appreciate each other more and more as their lives go on. Clyde said that lately, when it comes to commenting on his feelings for his son, "Every time I see him on TV, I look up and I say, 'Damn, that's *my* kid pitching on TV!' I try to put myself in the same position as a [Mel] Stottlemyre or a Dick Nen, with his son pitching. I just wonder if they have the same feelings when they flip on the TV and they see their kids.

"I remember the first time I saw him on TV I said, 'I can't believe this.' I got nervous, and I still get nervous when I see him today. And I don't think it's going to change if he plays fifteen years and I turn it on fifteen years from now and I see him out there. I'm still going to get nervous for him."

Even with the multitude of butterflies dancing and fluttering in his stomach like so many knuckleballs, Clyde says it's a great feeling to see Jaret on the mound. "It's an outstanding feeling, super."

Looking back, Clyde noted that, while his son may be a big-league player now, he "always see[s] the little kid that came to me one day while playing Little League and asked me, 'Dad, why did the other manager walk me with the bases loaded, why wouldn't he let me hit the ball? I throw it over to *his* son and let him hit it.' Now, that's a tough one [to answer for a child]."

When he was asked if, now that Jaret has grown older, he has begun to appreciate how difficult it truly is to earn a living in the majors, Clyde replied, "I think all the kids that play in the big leagues now appreciate what their dads went through when they were playing. It's not easy. It's not easy to be there every day, 162 games a year, plus spring training. It's not easy to have baseball take up so much of your time.

"You really don't have that much time to do anything else. But the thing about it is it only lasts ten or twelve years. Sometimes a lot less than that," said Clyde, who feels that's yet another lesson he's gotten across to his son.

One interesting sight that Clyde saw took place on August 27, 1997, when the Indians visited Anaheim. It was Jim Thome's birthday, and to honor the popular star his teammates pulled the hem of their pants up to knee level, à la Thome. Cleveland's offense that night went berserk, with Matt Williams tying a big-league record with six runs driven in during an inning. The Indians scored more runs in that inning than they had during any other inning all season, and the wearing of the pants hoisted high became a tradition for some time afterward.

The beneficiary of the run onslaught was Jaret Wright, who grew up about five minutes away from Anaheim Stadium. Clyde was glad to see his son get such solid support, and delighted to see him record another victory.

Clyde said that when it comes to parenting sometimes the children can teach the father a lesson. "The only mistake I made as a parent was I didn't go to my daughter's water polo banquet one year," he said. "It won't happen again. She understood why I wasn't there, but I felt terrible."

One aspect of being a baseball father that never changes, Clyde said, is the feeling he gets when Jaret is on the mound. "I still get nervous," he said. "I don't think that's going to change." Still, with the nervousness comes a positive. He spoke of the wonderful feeling he also gets when he watches his son. That feeling of pride is one he would never trade for anything.

Chapter Thirteen: The Grieves

During his career, Tom Grieve was an outfielder and designated hitter, spending eight years in the major leagues. The bulk of that time was spent with the Texas Rangers, but he also appeared in the uniforms of the Washington Senators (which shifted to Texas in 1972), the New York Mets, and the St. Louis Cardinals, with whom he wrapped up his career in 1979. He was the Rangers Player of the Year in 1976, the year of his career highs in homers (20) and runs batted in (81).

He owns 65 lifetime homers, 254 runs driven in, and a career batting average of .249 over a 670-game career (nine seasons). Born in Pittsfield, Massachusetts, where he was a standout high-school player, he stood 6'2" and weighed in at 190 pounds during his playing days.

Later, after working his way up the Rangers front-office ladder, he became the general manager for the team and currently serves as one of its announcers. In all, he was the team's vice president and G.M. from 1984 through 1994, and had spent almost thirty-one of his thirty-two years in professional baseball with the Senators-Rangers franchise. He entered the 2001 season with six years' experience in the television booth.

His son Ben was born in Arlington, Texas, in 1976. He bats lefty and throws righty. Ben, an articulate young man, stands 6'4" and weighs in at 220. He has played for the Oakland A's and later the Tampa Bay Devil Rays, after being involved in a three-way trade during the off-season prior to 2001.

Soft-spoken and sincere, he comes off as a very nice person because, in fact, he is. Although Ben looks almost baby-faced, once he's in the batter's box he's quite intense. A fine hitter, he enjoyed his first 100-RBI season in 2000 (with 104), to go with his 40 doubles and 27 home runs, one shy of his personal season high. In 1998, he made the All-Star team in just his first full season.

He has been a star since childhood and was a high-school All-American selection by *Baseball America* in his senior year, when he hit a staggering .486 for James W. Martin High School in Arlington. He was the Minor League Player of the Year, as named by *Sporting News* in 1997, the same season he was the Most Valuable Player in the Southern League (at Huntsville). One year later, he captured the American League's Rookie of the Year Award.

Like many players who had a father playing in the big leagues, Ben was too young to remember his father as a player. By the time he got old enough to appreciate that, his father had retired. Still, he's proud of his heritage, to be sure, as he's not the first child in the family to excel in athletics.

Before becoming a scout for the Detroit Tigers in the Texas area, Tom's other son, Tim, four years older than Ben, pitched in both the Kansas City Royals and the Arizona Diamondbacks organizations.

Ben's sister, Katie, two years his junior, is also an athlete. She was a fine volleyball player at Arlington Martin High School and at Auburn University.

The Grieves made baseball history when they became the first father-son combination ever to be selected in the first round of the free-agent draft. Tom was picked by the Senators in 1966, while Ben was the second player in the entire country to be selected in the June 1994 draft.

Like so many boys, and not merely the ones who make it to the big-league level, Ben said baseball clearly helped him bond with his father. "Yeah, definitely," he recalled. "Just playing catch with him and before dinner, that was a good time to talk. It's better than just sitting around watching TV. You get to talk about guys on the team, what he was doing—stuff like that; he kept us informed."

Tom agreed, saying there was no doubt that, more than anything, baseball helped him relate to his boys. "Absolutely, with all our kids. We also have a daughter, Katie, and I found that the times when our conversations stretched the furthest were while playing catch or, in my daughter's case, kicking a soccer ball or bumping a volleyball. Whatever it might have been, they seemed to let their guard down. We did it so often and so much, pitching batting practice to them, going to the park, throwing—it was the one activity that we all had in common that we did the most. So I don't think there's much doubt about that.

"Now it's probably golfing, where you're in the same golf cart, you're walking the golf course together for four hours. But back then, there's no doubt that baseball-related activities were the way our whole family bonded."

In addition, Tom declared that baseball had helped him bond with his own father. "My dad was never a player who played more than high-school baseball or anything like that, but he loved baseball," he said. "He was a big fan of the Braves, and Warren Spahn was his favorite player. We played catch day after day, and I'd wait for him to come home from work at 5:00 to play catch. I think that some of our best conversations were probably while playing catch.

"I liked the Yankees and Mickey Mantle, and we'd argue over who were the better players, who had the best team. He'd talk about the players and there was no doubt that was what sparked my interest in baseball—that introduction to the game. And I think that's all he intended; he had no idea whatsoever that it would lead to anything—even playing in high school.

"We had a neighborhood full of kids my age who all seemed to like baseball the same way, and we all played Little League. A lot of us went on and played high school together. Fortunately for me, I had the talent to go further than that, but I think the introduction to it with my father had a lot to do with that.

"We lived in Pittsfield, Massachusetts, so we were about equal distance between Boston and New York, and he would take us to a Sunday doubleheader once a year, usually in Boston, sometimes in New York. In addition to the Braves, he liked the Red Sox and Ted Williams. I liked the Yankees and Mickey Mantle, so it was usually a Red Sox–Yankees game. I have plenty of memories of those games. Mantle went oh-for-four every time, and Ted Williams seemed to get three or four hits every time."

So, Tom said, going to those games at an early age got him involved in baseball and made him want to become a ballplayer. Therefore when he became a father, he "started tossing baseballs when Ben was, probably, 2½ or 3 years old. People say, 'Did you force your son?' or, 'Did you push your son?' I encouraged him in that direction, but I would never have pushed him or encouraged him to continue to do it—in Tim's case, the same way—if it wasn't something they loved. In most cases, they were begging *me* to 'Let's go play,' or 'Let's play catch,' or 'Come pitch me batting practice.'

"When I saw they had that desire and that love to do it, then I certainly encouraged them and was available any time I possibly could be. But, yeah, I introduced it to them in much the same way my father introduced it to me. Got them a glove, played catch with them when they were little, tossed balls to them. And when they showed an inclination and a love for it, then I gave them all the opportunity to do it as much as they could."

Since left-handed hitters have several advantages in baseball, Tom was glad to see Ben starting to hit that way. "It's funny," he said. "It's the only thing anyone in our family, or extended family, that I know of does left-handed. He just picked up a bat the first time it was time to hit the ball and it was left-handed. He golfs right-handed, shoots a basketball right-handed, throws right-handed, and hits left-handed."

Tom compared his stance and style at the plate with his son's and felt they weren't alike. "I think we probably look alike as far as facial features go, but he's much taller. He's 6'5", I'm 6'1" and he's a left-hand hitter, I'm a right-hand hitter. The way that we play and do things I don't think has much resemblance at all."

He even felt that they were different when it came to their philosophy of batting and their approach to hitting. "I think we're probably different in that regard, too. I was a little more high-strung and emotional; he's very reserved—the kind of player that you can't really tell whether he's gone oh-for-four or four-for-four. I've never seen him throw a bat, I've never seen him throw a helmet, I've never seen him raise a fist. I've seen him smile a couple of times when he couldn't help it.

"But when I was a younger player I would throw helmets and kick fences. That's not something I'm advocating, that's just the emotion I had. It became much more under control as I got older, but I think his whole personality is probably much different than mine. I would say he's stoic. He *feels* everything, he just doesn't display it."

One very emotional period of Ben's life had to be when, Tom said, "He had the opportunity to be a Ranger batboy when he was probably, 10, 11, 12, 13 years old, and I think one of the things he came away with from watching the players was his style of not being too high and too low. Seeing the games every day, he's seen guys who had that attitude and guys that didn't, but that's something he seems to have come away with."

Tom said he didn't appoint his sons as batboys for any ulterior motives, such as giving them a taste of major-league baseball. "No," he began. "I would never even suggest to them that they wanted to be a batboy if they didn't love baseball and love being around it, and, most of all, that they respect the game, respect the players, respect the umpires, and do their job in a professional way.

"They wanted to do it, and most of the batboys back then were the sons of players or front-office people. Back then you could be a batboy when you were 10 or 11 years old. Since that time, in one of the most ridiculous edicts I've ever seen, [some] agency determined that it's a violation of the state of Texas labor laws to work at night if you're under 16 years old, which, I think, was originally intended for the sweatshops but has been brought down to also include being a batboy even if your father is at the game and you're going home after the game with your father. It's a $10,000 fine, but back then you could be young.

"They wanted to be batboys, and it's been my observation that the younger kids are probably better than the older kids. If for no other reason, because they don't have their head in the stands, they don't have girlfriends, they're not worried about what they look like in their uniform, and they hustle at all times.

"Ben hustled more as a batboy than he did as a Little League player, and it wasn't that he never hustled [as a player], it was just he was on top of everything. He took the job seriously. He'd race out to get the balls to the umpires, and they were never late; they knew exactly what their job was and they loved to do it. So, in answer to the question, there was no ulterior motive other than it was probably taking advantage of an incredible opportunity to give one's kids a thrill of a lifetime.

"There was no thought that either kid might be a major-league player at the time. It was just the thought that they loved baseball, and what memory could possibly be better than spending the afternoons and evenings with big-league players at a big-league ballpark?" Tom said.

So the boys asked him if they could handle the chores and Tom, as the G.M., could see to it that their desires were fulfilled. "Ben was a batboy for, probably, three years, maybe [when he was] 11, 12, and 13 or 10, 11, and 12, right around in there; Tim probably for two or three years." Tim, five years older than Ben, was about 17 or so when he last served as a batboy, around the late 1980s, according to Tom, who began his stint as a general manager in 1984.

Ben and Tim shared duties with other youngsters, especially since, their dad recalled, "there were days when they had Little League games and couldn't do it. There was a kind of pool of batboys. In fact, one of our favorite pictures is a Ranger team picture that includes both boys as batboys."

Of all the perks that came with being a batboy, Tom says what his children loved most was the practical jokes they observed, even when they "were the brunt of jokes played on them by the players. They liked coming home and talking about that kind of stuff."

As might be expected, Ben agreed that one of the high points of his youth was "when he [Tom] was the G.M. and I got a chance to be the batboy with my brother [Tim]. Being around the clubhouse was probably the one thing I enjoyed the most, and getting to do the stuff batboys do," Ben said.

Even though for most of his life Ben had the chance to be associated with and "hang around" players, he still felt "it was a pretty big deal. No matter who you are," he said, "when you're at a young age you like to be able to brag to your friends about all the guys you get to see and hang out with in the clubhouse."

Probably out of respect for his father (or perhaps just because they were a great group of guys), Ben said all the players were very nice to him. "I liked all of them," he recalled. "Steve Buechele was real nice to me; Gino Petralli was the catcher with them and was real nice, and Mike Stanley was another one."

Stanley, who wound up as a teammate of Ben's in Oakland, said he remembers the young Ben Grieve working in the Rangers' clubhouse. "It's been tremendous following a ten-year kid who was my batboy when I first came up. To see him now, flourishing and 'creating' into a great major-league baseball player, has been fascinating and fun to watch."

Stanley also remembers Ben taking batting practice "albeit," he said, "I think it was with an aluminum bat, but he used to hit in old Texas Stadium and put them out—pretty impressive." No doubt about it. After all, many youngsters could tee the ball up while standing on the grass behind second base, use a corked bat, and still fall short of the warning track.

While there was no single incident that stood out as a pleasant childhood memory from that period of his life, Ben said the pleasure came from "just the everyday things—there's a lot of stuff that goes on in the clubhouse behind closed doors that most people don't get to see. Being around the big-league life was probably the main [positive] thing."

Most players whose father also played in the big leagues say they feel that just being around players and the clubhouse scene really does help prepare them for their ascension to the majors. Exposure to their dad and his colleagues helped men like Ben learn how to act, what to expect, and even what not to do. In short, it helps players to become comfortable, to be able to relax, and to be able to handle the demands of being a major-league player. On the other hand, players who begin their career in awe of their arrival in the bigs might act insecurely and therefore play tentatively.

Thus it's hardly surprising to learn that Ben believes his father's influence was enormous. "He definitely got me going. Obviously he knows a lot about baseball, being a player and a general manager. I'd say he had a lot to do with it [Ben's career]. That's probably the main reason why I'm where I am at now—it's who he was."

When the boys were young, Ben said that Tom spent a lot of time teaching them the fundamentals of baseball. "If I was struggling, he's a big-league player, so if anyone's going to pick up something you're doing wrong, then it's going to be him.

"And, being around the Rangers, their coaches would help me out. My dad would set it up so I could go hit with the big-league hitting instructor and pitch with a big-league pitching instructor. Stuff like that is pretty invaluable," concluded the articulate outfielder. Without a doubt, then, having a father like Tom Grieve truly helps.

Whether Ben learned to have class from his dad alone, or from his dad and his batboy days, he learned his lesson well. Never a showboat or a hothead, Ben's refusal to raise a fist was quite evident during the 2000 season, when one incident clearly pointed out the type of man he is.

He faced the Cleveland Indians and their hard-throwing ace Bartolo Colon on August 23, one day after there had been bad blood between the two teams. Facing Colon, Ben knew he had to stay loose, as only moments earlier his teammate at the time, Tim Hudson, had brushed back David Segui, leading to a confrontation. When Ben stepped up to the plate, retaliation was in the air. One writer said two things saved Ben from serious injury—his "young reflexes and the knowledge of what was coming."

Ben, having lots of baseball savvy, said, "I was ready to duck. That's the only way I could have gotten out of the way." Colon reared back and whaled two fastballs directly at Ben's head, coming within inches of striking him.

At that point, Ben later said, "I figured I could either charge the mound or get back in the batter's box." He paused, then added, "I'm not the type of guy to run out after the pitcher."

Tom said, "When I played, I was hit several times, and sometimes when I thought it was on purpose; I never charged the mound. I think charging the mound is a little bit of a *SportsCenter* phenomenon and a macho thing. If you don't charge the mound, you look weak, and if you do charge the mound, everybody sees what a macho guy you are on *SportsCenter* that night.

"But I think Ben's right, you have a choice. Some guys don't make that choice; they take one step and start yelling and, hopefully it's going to be broken up, but you do have a choice: you either drop the bat and sprint to the mound or you drop the bat and go to first base. I have a lot more respect for the guys who drop the bat and go to first base."

Tom agreed that the macho approach is fueled, at least in part, by a peer-pressure mentality at times and is perpetuated by the exposure given to brawls by the media. Maybe so, but he dislikes that scenario nevertheless. "Every time I see a guy get drilled, drop the bat, and go to first base, I feel good," he said. "Number one, you avoid a five-minute delay of the game; number two, it's not good for the kids watching the game to see the fight; number three, it just shows respect for the game that you go to first base and you don't *have* to display this attitude of fighting back."

Tom agrees that Ben's attitude is not only the correct approach to the game but shows a lot of class and dignity. That style can be likened to a comment once made by legendary pro football coach Paul Brown. He felt that when a player makes a good play or even scores a touchdown, there is no need to flaunt oneself with a self-serving display of theatrics. "When you get to the end zone, act like you've been there before," he said. Ben neither charges mounds nor, for that matter, does he engage in histrionics when he homers. He doesn't need to. He's "been there" before.

Tom said several of the men who were the best he ever saw at remaining stoical even when plunked by a pitch were Will Clark and Don Baylor, the all-time leader in getting hit by pitches. "Clark's been hit a number of times, and a lot of times when it was on purpose," he said. "He dropped the bat and went to first base. And Baylor [did the same], never rubbed it [where he was struck]." Then, he added with a laugh, "Ron Hunt would do it on purpose."

It's hard to determine exactly where, when, and how Ben got his positive attitude about the game. "I think what Ben learned from me would be very difficult to pinpoint," Tom said. "I think more or less he had been around me so much from the time that he was 4 or 5 to even now—I throw batting practice to him in the wintertime. And I was the general manager of the Rangers for ten years during that time he was a batboy. I coached several of his youth-league teams. And we drove to the games, we drove home from the ballpark, we sat on the bench during batting practice—so I guess what I'm saying is whatever he's learned from me, it would be hard to say, 'My dad taught me not to do this' or 'My dad taught me to do this.' It's just kind of assimilation of thoughts over a long period of time." (He compared it to the process of osmosis.)

"He's a very bright kid and he, I think, took in the things, not just from me but from Bobby Valentine, from the players—he used to love Ruben Sierra and Steve Buechele and a lot of the Ranger players, and he would listen to them. You wouldn't think he was listening. He doesn't look like he's listening, but he's taking in the things that seem to work for him. His style, his attitude, the way he does things, what he believes in baseball, I think in a large regard has to do with what he's picked up over the years.

"I think he's probably picked up the idea of being a patient hitter, swinging at good pitches—although I think he's going to get better at that as time goes on, since he hasn't gotten to where he needs to be yet. But he's probably picked that up from watching games with me and listening to other players. There are a lot of players who don't care if they walk; their philosophy is 'Swing the bat at all costs.'

"We used to watch the game with my whole family, and other people as well, in a box at the ball game. As the game's going on, you get frustrated, you get happy, you make comments about players. And kids want to please their fathers [so] he probably picked up on things I like and things I didn't like, and probably tried to do some of it."

"If you asked Ben to try to come up with what I had told him more often than not, I think the message I tried to deliver to him is: respect the game, to be always prepared to work as hard as you possibly can, and never take anything for granted. Then, do your best on a daily basis to have fun and make it a game.

"A relatively simple message, but, nevertheless, I think in the off-season you have to work out. If this is your profession, then you have to give it 100 percent of your attention and don't take it for granted. Work hard and be early at the ballpark and late to leave—that kind of a work ethic. Then, at the same time, to not live or die with every at bat, to not feel that it's the end of the world if you go oh-for-four or the top of the world if you go four-for-four.

"Take advantage of it, to enjoy it—it's not going to last forever. It's an incredible time that so many people would trade their profession for—to have one at bat in the big leagues—so don't take this incredible opportunity that you have as a big-league ballplayer for granted. I've never sat down and said those exact words to him, but over a long period of time I think that is probably the message that I delivered to him."

Tom feels that Ben has done a fine job with his life. "The things that make me feel the best about Ben are not anything related to his performance as a baseball player," he said. "I'm very happy for all that and I'm very proud of all the things that's he's accomplished, and hopefully what he'll go on to accomplish, but the things that make me feel the best are when people come up to me and compliment him on the kind of person he is.

"When you will say, 'He gave me a great interview,' and say how cordial he was, that makes me feel better than someone coming up to me saying what a great swing and what a nice game he had. When friends from back home say, 'I went to see Ben play. He came over, took time from batting practice, and was so nice to my kids. He spent ten minutes talking to me, signed my autograph—what a wonderful young boy you have.' *That* makes me feel way better than anything to do with his performance.

"So the thing that makes me feel best about him as a dad is the kind of young man that he's grown up to be, rather than the player he is." Tom added that, as good a player as Ben is, he thinks he's actually a better man.

Ben, too, said he has always had the feeling that his father is more proud of him as a man than as a player. "He wouldn't care if I was playing baseball or not," Ben said. "He's proud of me whatever I'm doing. You know, my brother and sister don't play baseball—that doesn't mean he likes me any more than he likes them."

Although Tom has been busy during baseball seasons with his own obligations, Ben said he always made it a point to make time to see him play. "He came up and saw me play in my first year in the minor leagues in Medford, Oregon," Ben recalled. "My brother was pitching for the opposing team—he had just got drafted, too. So my dad got to see us both play against each other in both of our first professional years."

Looking back, Tom elaborated, "The first time I saw him play in the pros was in the Rookie League up in Medford. In fact, the unique thing about that was my oldest son, Tim, graduated from T.C.U. and was drafted by Kansas City the same year—1994—that Ben was drafted by the A's. They each had a rookie-league team in the Northwest League, and Tim was in Eugene, Oregon. Their first series of the year was against each other.

"My wife went out for that series, and Ben had had a couple of games under his belt; Tim hadn't pitched yet. In about the fifth or sixth inning of the game Tim's manager brought him in to pitch, to face Ben. So Tim's first pitch as a pro was to Ben, with my wife in the stands not knowing who to root for. I didn't see that, but I saw both of them play against each other in that league a few weeks later.

"Tim has described it as he felt uncomfortable because he's always rooted for Ben to do well, and here he was out there trying to pitch. Believe me, the competitive juices were such that Ben, I'm sure, was trying to hit a home run and Tim was trying to strike him out. At the time, Tim was probably a little more advanced than Ben was, and was kind of a finesse pitcher with a really good split-finger pitch. Ben had never seen that pitch before. They faced each other five or six times that year. Tim struck him out four times [including their first encounter], and I think Ben had a single and a fly out—something like that."

Had it not been for a "couple of injuries," Tim, who did play in the minors for a few years, might have made the Grieves a three-player family. As it turned out, he had to stop playing in the 1990s. Like his father, though, he was able to stay in the game. "Now he's scouting for the Tigers in the state of Texas," Ben said.

Tom recalled Ben's first big-league contest. "I watched his first game in my broadcast booth on a feed off a TV screen. I think he was three-for-four and had three doubles and five RBIs against the Giants."

The first time he saw Ben live in a big-league uniform was when he faced the Rangers. "It was when he was called up for the month of September. We played them in September, and it was in one of those three games. I know he hit a home run in one of the games and had three hits in another game, so I had the opportunity to see him do well the times I saw him that year.

"Early in his career, he had extraordinary success against the Rangers. The first time he came back to play here in Texas, he hit two home runs in a game against the Rangers, and I was always with the Rangers at those times."

Through it all, Tom said that describing his relationship with Ben couldn't be done in a short space of time. "I think we have a close relationship. I don't call him to ask him how he's hitting or to really discuss baseball on any technical level. It's more as a dad, and the things I'm more concerned about are 'How are you eating? Who are your friends? Who's your roommate? Are you getting your rest? Are you working out?' I mean, the well-being kind of things that a father worries about with his son more so than calling him to analyze his swing or things like that. We don't do that."

Perhaps another reason Tom doesn't interfere with Ben's sweet swing is that Ben possesses such good form at the plate. Some fathers will see their son on television, think they notice a mechanical problem, and promptly call him with tips. So what if Tom spotted a flaw in Ben's game? Then what? Tom replied, "Two years ago, in his second season, he got off to a start where he was something like 13-for-120, I think; he got off to a terrible start. And, as there is in any players' season, [there are] ups and downs, times when you're not going good, and I do tend to call him more when he's not going as well as he would like, but not to tell him what to do, just to let him know that his perfor-mance—and I don't say these words to him—but just to let him know his performance on the field has nothing to do with our relationship as a father and a son, and to show support. 'Hey, basically hang in there, keep working hard, and you're a good player and you're going to bounce out of it.' That kind of message more than, 'Hey, I saw that you're trying to pull the ball; hit the ball the other way.'

"Now, occasionally he might bring something up and it's worked into a conversation, but I don't tend to call him. I feel that the coaches he has are competent, they're working on certain things, and it can be sometimes danger-ous to deliver a slightly mixed message. There's a lot of different ways to hit a baseball and lot of different ideas. When you've got too many thoughts going through your mind, you can overprocess things. So I think the simpler you can keep it, the better off you are, so I try not to get into that."

Conversely, does Ben ever give his father information that Tom could use to enhance his broadcasts? "No, I very seldom do that, because in no way do I want to betray the confidence of the clubhouse," Tom replied. "He tells me a lot of things with the understanding, although he doesn't say, 'Hey, Dad, this is off the record,' [because] he knows that I know what I can repeat and what I can't repeat. Believe me, I've got a year's worth of choice things that I could say on the air, but if I start doing that it's going to be pretty obvious where I got it from.

"Sometimes I don't say things because people *might* attribute it to him, even though it didn't come from him. To me, that relationship that he has with his teammates is much more important than anything I could say on the air."

However, if Ben tells his father something that is far from being of a confidential nature, say, for example, that a certain pitcher has a nasty slider that he loves to use on certain counts, Tom *will* relate that to his audience. "Oh, yeah, and I might say, 'Do you mind if I say that?' 'No, I don't mind.' Things like that. After he got a couple of hits and had dinner with us, I might say, 'He really enjoys his mother's home cooking; it seems to help him on the field'—some-thing corny like that."

When Ben was young and Tom discussed baseball over the dinner table, he knew, he said, that his son wouldn't be indiscreet. "Sure," said Tom. "I felt comfortable talking to both my kids about anything I was doing. I wasn't the kind of dad that brought work home and we discussed everything to do with my job on every day, but there were times when I would talk about play-ers that disappointed me, players who were lazy, players who weren't living up to expectations, players that were making too much money, players who I ad-mired, things that I didn't like about my job, other general managers—I would talk about all these things, and it never concerned me one single bit that they would go out and betray that kind of confidence.

"Much like I know what I can talk about on the air that has to do with him, they knew the things that they could talk about. The other thing is, both of them saw a lot of this on their own when they were batboys.

"The thing I always liked about them was they didn't come home and squeal on the players to me, either. They didn't say, 'Hey, I saw such and such in the clubhouse eating a hot dog and drinking a Coke in the fourth inning,' or, 'I saw such and such talk back to [Manager] Bobby Valentine.' And I never asked those kinds of questions because I didn't want them ever to feel that they should betray what they see in a clubhouse. Even if they never became players—I didn't know they'd be players at the time, but that, to me, is an opportunity that you don't want to destroy by being a little tattletale on the players. But I think they learned a lot."

Ben backed what his father said. True to his baseball background, Ben always knew what he could tell his friends and what he couldn't tell them. "I would never give away any secrets," he stated.

During the baseball season, the Grieves try to get together whenever possible. "When he comes here to play as a visiting player, he has stayed with us so he eats all his meals here, and occasionally we'll go out if my wife's not cooking," Tom said. "Now, the fact that he's got a home here in the area, he'll probably stay there."

Likewise, if Tom visits Tampa Bay he's sure to hook up with his son. In the off-season before 2001, he said, "I'm planning to go down for spring training, see some games, and get together. When we [his Texas broadcasting crew] would go to Oakland, occasionally my wife would come. We would eat with him—not every lunch and every dinner, because I respect his schedule, and I don't want him to deviate from the schedule that he has unless it's comfortable for him to do it.

"Ben is a real homebody," Tom said. "He loves coming back to our house. He's married now, and has a house of his own, but up until last year he spent the winters here and we do a lot of things together. We golf together, as I mentioned, and when he works out he wants me to come in and throw to him. We watch sporting events together. He loves his mother's food. He loves to be around the house. It's a close, loving father-son relationship."

Tom also feels that in addition to being a father and a son, he and Ben are also friends. "We like to go to movies together, and he's got a fantasy football-league team that we talk about. A lot of things that fathers do with their sons, we do together."

Even when they're apart, Tom can easily check on his son's progress. Each day in the press box, members of the media are laden down with copious notes, statistics, and results from the previous day's contests from around both leagues. Tom finds himself searching through the thick packets to see how his son has fared.

"I don't think there's a day goes by that my wife and I, and it's a little easier now—we have the DirecTV baseball package, so we get to see a lot of games. It will be a little different this year, with the three-hour time change from Oakland to Tampa Bay [his new team in 2001]. We saw a lot of late games in Oakland. So my wife's summer—mine revolves around my job announcing— but her day revolves around whether Ben's game is on TV and what time it comes on. She watches every inning of every game.

"My partner has a computer, and on it in the upper right-hand corner he puts in the pitch-by-pitch for every one of Ben's games, so as we're announcing the game I can look at the corner of his computer and see pitch-by-pitch what happens in his game. We watch the box score, watch the statistics, and in that regard I don't think I'm different, or my wife is different, from any other family. I would suspect that every major-league baseball player's family that has the capability to do that does the same thing. I don't think it's unique, but we do that."

Tom said the fact that his son has already surmounted some of his own career totals in offensive departments such as home runs has been a great source of pride. "There's absolutely no rivalry in our family between my wife and I and our children. We hope that everything that happens in their lives is better than anything that happened in our lives. It would be hard for that to be the case, but that's what we wish for our kids.

"I think, based on where Ben was drafted and the expectations that the A's have had on Ben until the time when he was traded, that if everything on the field *didn't* surpass what I had done, they would have been very disappointed with his selection. So, yeah, I looked at him and assumed that in a very short period of time whatever I did would be easily surpassed by him."

Joe Nossek, a veteran baseball player and coach, compared the Grieves. "Ben's done real well," he said. "His father was a good player who had a couple of good years, and Ben looks to be a much better hitter and has had a couple of good years already. His dad, I think, ran a little better and maybe had a better arm, but Ben looks like a real accomplished hitter from what we've seen up to this point."

Meanwhile, Tom said that he hasn't spoken to many other fathers of big-league sons about their shared experiences but, he said, "I'm pretty friendly with Buddy Bell. Jeff Burroughs's son was just [recently] a No. 1 draft choice. I've met Bobby Bonds and talked with him, but I don't think I've had these discussions.

"I had the discussion what it's like to have a son with other people. In fact, frequently people are interested to hear that perspective, but with other ballplayers the assumption is everybody feels the same way—I know how the other dads feel. I really don't talk to them much, as I do fans, friends, and people like that."

So what does he tell them? "My feeling watching him play now, the feeling that you have inside, the pride, the apprehension, the emotional roller coaster with oh-for-fours and three-for-fours is really no different than when he was a Little Leaguer. It's very similar to what any parent feels for a child whether it's a sporting event, whether it's a spelling bee, whether it's a dance rehearsal. You have anticipation and the hope that everything is going to go well. All those feelings, I think, are pretty much very similar to the feelings that any parent has—any caring, loving parent has for one of their children.

"The fact that he's a major-league player is something that's a great source of pride, but I don't find myself just sitting there going, Wow, he's a major-league player. You wake up thinking, How is my son doing today? Not, How is this big-league player doing?

"I'm very happy that he's getting this opportunity, but mostly because it's what he always wanted to do and there are very few people who really get to, day by day, live their childhood dream in a successful way, and he's doing that. For that, my wife and I are very grateful.

"I'd like to think that we would have the same feelings about him no matter what he was doing if he was enjoying it and doing as well as he is in his profession."

When Ben does call it quits, he could perhaps become an announcer or a G.M., making the Grieves a unique father-son combo from the field as well as in the booth or front office, but Tom doesn't see that happening. Tom did say, "I'd love that if that's what he wanted to do, but it's not any hidden desire that I have at all. I guess you can't rule anything out, but when I was 25 I was much more outgoing than Ben, and the things that I've done off the field are things that, at this time, I don't envision Ben ever wanting to do.

"I think that one of the biggest differences between players in my generation and the current generation, of successful players, anyway, is the huge disparity between the salaries that we've earned. When I got done playing, I *had* to have another profession, because I had to live. I had to earn a living. Many of these players are going to retire between the age of 30 and 40 with so much money, they won't have to work if they don't want to.

"So, I don't know, when Ben's done playing, and hopefully that will be fifteen or twenty years down the road, that a day-to-day grind, such as a general manager goes through, would be something that he'd even want to do. If he chose to do those things, I'd be thrilled to watch him stay in the game and see him do it, but I don't anticipate that would be something he'd want to do."

Ben might shy away from a G.M. job because he has seen, firsthand, what a trying occupation it can be. Just as a father anguishes when his son plays poorly and delights in his fine performance on the field, Ben could relate to his father's ups and downs as a general manager. He said the job was both enjoyable for his dad and pressure-packed. "His job he has now as a TV announcer, I think he likes it a little more because of the lack of pressure, and he's still able to go to the games and enjoy them. But now he doesn't have to come home with a sick feeling after they lose. But he likes both—I think if he had his choice, he'd be doing what he's doing now."

While players are generally measured by what statistics they put up, general managers are gauged by the trades they make. That holds true even though everyone knows most general managers will score some knockouts, and, by the very nature of the game, get fleeced. (At least, that's the way the media will portray a swap that backfires.)

Ben summed it up by saying, "He had a couple of good ones and a couple of bad ones. I think he traded a few mediocre guys [Mitch Williams was the only name player in a package deal] for [Rafael] Palmeiro [and Jamie Moyer] when Palmeiro was with the Cubs. He made a similar trade the same year and got Julio Franco, who turned out [to do well and make it] a pretty good trade.

"Then, the one bad one, I guess, is Sammy Sosa for Harold Baines and Fred Manrique. That one probably sticks out in everybody's minds the most," he said with a grin at the obvious understatement.

Of course, Tom did not have to field all the culpability for that ill-fated transaction. It was under an interesting Texas regime back then, in that the trade was made when another member of a pretty famous father-son duo was in charge of the Rangers. That man was the co-managing general partner George W. Bush, who makes up one-half of a rare presidential father-son combo. Later, Bush could joke, "I signed off on that wonderful transaction: Sammy Sosa for Harold Baines."

Not only will July 29, 1989, stand out as a day of infamy for the Sosa trade but it was somewhat exacerbated by the fact that Texas also tossed in two more players. They were Scott Fletcher and Wilson Alvarez, a left-handed pitcher who would throw a no-hitter for his new team in his first start—which was also only his second big-league start. While Baines continued to be a solid producer, Sosa exploded. Just four years after being traded to the Chicago White Sox from Texas, Sosa crashed 33 home runs and joined the exclusive 30 home runs/30 stolen bases club. His 66 homers in 1998, followed by 63 more in 1999, also caused eyes to pop everywhere in the baseball community.

Being a general manager was beneficial for Tom, though, when it came to helping his son with contract negotiations. "All I did was assist him, counsel him in the year leading up to the draft, when it was obvious he was going to be a high draft choice." He said he helped Ben with "what to say, who to talk to, when to work out for guys. Then the draft, the whole signing bonus, occurred during a fifteen-minute conversation with Sandy Alderson, who was the general manager for the A's. And my being a general manager seems to have facilitated the whole thing.

"Once that was over, then I kind of bowed out of that area of it, and Ben has an agent just like many of the players do," Tom said. "In fact, I got a call from the commissioner's office when it was reported I was serving as his agent that it was a conflict of interest.

"I said, 'Well, somebody reported that I was his agent. I'm his father, and I'm assisting him through an important part of his life. It has nothing to do with my affiliation with a major-league team [Tom was the Texas G.M. at that point]. I'm not being paid, there's no signed contract, and I would suggest that you call the Oakland A's and find out if they would rather have one of the high-powered agents negotiate this contract, or let me do it for him. If they suggest they don't want me involved, believe me, I'll step out and you can deal with Alan Hendricks, Jeff Moorad, or Scott Boras and the signing bonus is going to be bigger than the one that I negotiate, it's going to take longer, and it's going to be much more painful for everybody involved. Now if you want that to be the case, then go ahead.'

Their reaction, Tom continued, was one of " 'No, no, no, we just had to make a call. That's basically the extent of it.' As a father, and I don't mean this in a negative way towards other fathers, but as a *well-informed* father, who knew what fair was, and knew all the protocols, [that] probably made it a little bit easier for Ben, because it was something he never had to worry about."

Ben agreed that his dad's experience as a general manager was clearly beneficial when it came time to signing his professional contract. "He did my contract before I had an agent," Ben said. "He was helpful then, and he's helpful in anything I need, even the contract I just now signed [in 2000]. He was keeping me informed about what he thought about it. He's a smart guy."

By way of contrast, Tom pointed out that there are fathers who come into negotiations with irrational requests because they don't understand how the baseball system operates. He also said that he believes baseball fathers and dads are "all different. Some take a step back and let the major-league teams do the coaching, do the instruction, and are supportive in a positive way as parents. Others are much more involved, and I would feel more comfortable not mentioning names, but Pat Corrales, who managed the Cleveland Indians and was a coach with the Rangers and now he's a coach with the Braves, told me about a time when one of the dads was asked to leave the clubhouse in spring training because he was getting completely in the way of the coaching that was going on with his son. He was viewed as a nuisance and a disruptive influence.

"So I think parents of major-league players probably run the gamut that would be expected of parents of any child. They're all very well-intentioned. You probably see it written about more in tennis with the female tennis players and the dads there, but there are big-league dads that are like that as well."

Tom doesn't fit into the meddling category of father. Not only does he come across as a class act, players and management all agree, but he *is* a wonderful man.

As Ben once said, "I'm always having people come up to me and tell me how much they like him and how much they respect him—like umpires, guys on other teams that have played with him, and coaches. So, from what I've heard, he must have been a great guy when he was the G.M., and he still is."

People make the same glowing comments about Ben. Art Howe, who managed Ben in 2000, said, "I knew him when he was a batboy in Texas. He was just a real quiet kid, unassuming, and he's still the same kid. You don't know whether he's gone five-for-five or zero-for-five. He comes to the ballpark ready to do his job, very professional. I think he learned that from being around the game his whole life. Just a fine man and a credit to the game. He's going to be a heckuva hitter, and he *is* a pretty darn good one already, but he's going to be an outstanding one someday."

Chapter Fourteen: The Oleruds

Interestingly, Dr. John E. Olerud, father of two-time All-Star John G. Olerud, graciously did his interview for this book about a week after what was believed to be Seattle's second-worst earthquake jolted the city. At the time, he was in his car, which his son had recently purchased for him, headed for the airport, where he was to fly to the annual meeting of the American Academy of Dermatology. When he felt the initial tremor, his first thought was that something was wrong with the car's suspension system. When he saw the control tower at the airport, he realized the problem was more serious. Luckily, although his flight was canceled, the quake didn't affect the Oleruds much at all.

Like Bobby Brown, a Seattle native (as are the Oleruds), and Doc Medich, John Olerud's father played professional baseball and also became a doctor. For that matter, by way of yet another comparison, one could toss in the name of Casey Stengel, who gave up the idea of becoming a dentist in order to play baseball. (Legend has it that dentist chairs weren't set up for left-handers, freeing him to become a baseball star.)

Brown was a player for eight seasons, making it to the World Series four times, before he opted to become a doctor. And then, from 1984 to 1994, he returned to the game as the president of the American League. Medich enjoyed an eleven-year career, winning 124 contests. Coincidentally, Medich grew up in Aliquippa, Pennsylvania, the home of another member of a father-son baseball combo, Tito Francona. Meanwhile, Dr. Olerud was a successful minor-league catcher who played the game from 1965 to 1971.

Earlier, he was his baseball team's Most Valuable Player twice at Washington State University, and is a member of the Cougars Hall of Fame. He also won All-American honors in 1965 and advanced to the highest level of the minors, Triple-A, with the California Angels, the St. Louis Cardinals, and the Montreal Expos.

In the minors, he played behind men who went on to achieve varying degrees of big-league fame. There was "Buck Rodgers in the Angels organization, and Tom Egan," he recalled. "With the Cardinals, Joe Torre was catching in the big leagues [clearly blocking Olerud's shot at the majors], and Ted Simmons caught at Triple-A the year that I was there, but he only stayed about a month and I caught the rest of the summer there at Tulsa, with Warren Spahn as the manager." That was the summer he was elected the Tulsa Oilers' Most Popular Player by their fans.

Now, not only is he the head of the dermatology division at the University of Washington, where he got his M.D., but he has also managed to publish rather than perish. He has written grants and papers and is highly respected as a member of the staff at the university, where he does both administrative work and research.

John has a relative on his father's side of the family who also played big-league ball, Dale Sveum. "My dad's mother was a Sveum," said Dr. Olerud. "My son John and Dale are second cousins." Sveum, who mainly played on the left side of the infield, was in the majors with seven teams from 1986 to 1999. As recently as 2001, he was a minor-league manager with the Altoona Curve.

His bloodlines strong, John became only the sixteenth man since the start of baseball's amateur draft in 1965 to make his professional debut in the majors. Of those players, only four never spent a day in the minors; John is one of those four.

In 1993, as a member of the Toronto Blue Jays, he flirted with the coveted (and equally elusive) .400 plateau for most of the season. He finished with a lusty .363, helped in part by a twenty-six-game hitting streak, to lead the American League in hitting (he also topped the circuit that season with his sterling total of 54 doubles). Further, in that breakthrough season, he led his league with his 33 intentional walks drawn (still tied for the most ever for a year in American League play) and his .473 on base percentage. He was an All-Star that year, and again in 2001.

John should also be proud of winning the 1993 Hutch Award, because that annual trophy goes to the major leaguer who best exemplifies the character, fighting spirit, and competitive desire of the late Fred Hutchinson. And that's not all. Olerud shares the National League record for the most consecutive times that a player reached base safely. From September 16th through the 22nd in 1998, he got on base 15 times in a row on 6 singles, a double, 2 homers, and 6 walks drawn.

In 2000, he won his first Gold Glove Award for his slick defense at first base. Going into the 2001 campaign, he was a lifetime .299 hitter. Further, his postseason stats are stellar, with a .304 average in League Championship Series action and .385 in Division Series play.

Born in 1968 in Seattle, John, a left-hander, broke into the majors back in 1989 with Toronto and spent time with the New York Mets before returning to his hometown as a Mariner in 2000. With the exception of his stints in Toronto and New York, John has been a sort of homebody. After spending his high-school days at Interlake in Bellevue, Washington, he attended Washington State (the same school his father and mother attended), where he was voted *Baseball America*'s NCAA Player of the Year from 1987 to 1988. Back then he *did* hit over .400, at .464 (in fact, he hit .434 for his entire college career), while also pitching, posting an untainted 15–0 record (2.49 ERA, with 113 strikeouts in just over 120 innings).

With that background, he was pleased to go back to the state of Washington with the Mariners as a free agent. Dr. Olerud agreed that his son was delighted to return to home soil. "He thinks he made a good decision coming back to Seattle, but it was not a real easy decision," said Dr. Olerud "You might think it was sort of a slam dunk for him to make that decision, but he really enjoyed his time in New York and really liked the people. I think he's very happy that he's in Seattle now."

John Olerud is the antithesis of the surly, spoiled, modern baseball player. He is generous with his time, polite, and highly cooperative with the media. During his drive for a .400 season, he still took the time to answer countless questions patiently, even though most of them had to have been unbearably monotonous.

He remained modest even when under the scrutiny that potential .400 hitters inevitably attract. He said of his drive for that magical plateau, "I think someone can hit .400, but it would have to be someone who's a good contact hitter and can run. I'm not that kind of guy."

He almost seemed more concerned about the fact that all the media attention was taking away some of the time he normally spent signing the many autograph request he receives in the mail. "I've been getting a lot more fan mail," he said shortly after his Toronto team-record hitting streak came to a halt. "And a lot of people are sending cards in and that sort of thing. I'm trying to handle it, and the last couple of years I have been able to do it. It's a lot of work. It doesn't sound like much work, but the more mail you get, the more difficult it is to get through it all. I'm getting way behind in the fan mail, so I've got to get going on that."

Because Dr. Olerud played minor-league baseball, you might say that baseball paid his way through medical school. "In those days," he recalled, "you didn't need quite as much to pay for medical school and they weren't paying as much for bonuses as they do today, but I got out of medical school without any debt, primarily because of the signing bonus I got and the salaries I got during the summer."

Olerud explained how he balanced the worlds of medicine and sport: "I would go two quarters a year to medical school after the first year. And one year I did some studying during the season. I would just make a complete change from medical school, intense academic work, to baseball, which was intense physical work."

But that delicate balance eventually became strained. "The med school here at the University of Washington was very accommodating to my special needs," he explained. "One of the professors was a former All-American baseball player, and I even had things worked out to where I could have done my internship on a split-year basis, but the baseball people were less accommodating of the fact that I was a medical student, and they wanted me to go to winter ball." Doing that and staying in med school was impossible.

At one point, when he was with the St. Louis Cardinals, coming off a good season at the Triple-A level, he said, he was told by team officials that he was not "a good long-term prospect because I was finishing medical school the next year, even though I was still doing a good job. So they sold me to the Montreal Expos. When I went to spring training with them, after being an everyday catcher the year before, they told me I'd be going to the minors, splitting the catching, platooned with another guy from Double-A the year before. He was 21 and I was 28, so it seemed like the writing was on the wall. So the baseball people seemed to have more problems with the fact that I was a medical student than the medical people did with the fact that I was a ballplayer."

In all, he was with the Angels for five years, the Cards for one year, and the Expos to wrap things up. When some minor leaguers were getting September call-ups to the majors, he would be enrolling in med school again, even though, he said, "I had a few years that probably would have warranted a September call-up. But that's just the way things were structured."

Although Dr. Olerud never made it to the majors, he said, "I would go to major-league spring training fairly often, because I was a catcher and they always needed extra catchers. There were a couple years where I was on the forty-man roster with the California Angels. That was my closest brush with the big leagues."

In retrospect, he said it was a good move to get on with his life, leaving baseball behind. Then he grinned. "I think in the grand scheme of things, after I've had a chance to look back over the years, I think I'm probably a better doctor than I was a ballplayer," he said.

When his internship was scheduled, he decided to devote himself to medicine full-time and give up his baseball dream. Another factor that led him to retire from the diamond was the low pay; with scant income (the most he ever made in the minors was $8,000, which he couldn't help comparing with what he'd earn as a doctor) and a daughter, Erica, as well as a son to support, he knew it was time to quit. Little did he know that his big-league dream would live on through his son, who, at the time, was only about 4 years old.

Any father is bound to have a flood of memories about his child, and Dr. Olerud is no exception. "One of the things I recollect back on is when I was still playing—I guess one spring in Florida, when John was a 3-year-old—he was hitting with a Wiffle-ball bat down on the beach, drawing a pretty good crowd around," he said. "People were pretty impressed about how this little guy could hit. That was one of the first times it occurred to me that he was outside the ordinary in his interest in baseball and his ability. As a youngster, he always really enjoyed playing ball and loved to hit.

"His heroes were baseball players. Until about a year or so ago, when my wife redecorated our basement, he still had posters of George Brett and Don Mattingly on his wall downstairs—those were his heroes.

"I don't remember him having cards and stats as much as having posters. He got things signed from the Mariners players when he was a Pepsi Junior Mariner, but he'd also read baseball books. That was clearly one of the things that he enjoyed a lot," Dr. Olerud said.

So was baseball instrumental in helping the Oleruds bond, or was it secondary? "Oh, yeah, that was really what we did together," Dr. Olerud said. "With my daughter it was more academic things and working on homework together. With John it was really the sports things that we did together. He just got such a kick out of baseball that I'm sure that for somebody who really loves the game and who has a son who gets a kick out of it, that's the most fun."

Dr. Olerud said another interesting story about his son's level of interest in the game and the people who played the game was the fact that "when he was being recruited by different colleges one was Stanford. One of the things he had to do for his admission application was to write an essay. The question was 'If you could spend a day with anyone in history, who would it be?' I'm sure they were looking for names like Winston Churchill and other important historic figures, but John wrote his essay about George Brett. I'm sure they kinda wondered when they saw that.

"Along the same lines, when John first played against Brett, John got a base hit and George was playing first base," he continued. "John was just awestruck to be in the same place as George Brett. And then George says, 'How's it going, John?' And John wasn't quite sure how to answer him, whether it should be 'George' or 'Mr. Brett.' "

Obviously, John had come a long way from the little boy who, according to his mother, Lynda, spent more time running around the park than actually watching the games when his dad was a player. It almost goes without saying, but Dr. Olerud wanted it known that "I'm incredibly proud of John, and probably more proud of him as a person than as a ballplayer. He's a very positive role model for kids, and I think he works hard—he gives you everything he has, every day, and he does it in a quiet way that doesn't call a lot of attention to himself. I just think he's an extraordinarily good person, and he's had remarkable achievements as a ballplayer, too. But I'd say that's secondary in terms of what makes a dad proud."

Amazingly, John nearly didn't get his chance to make it to the big leagues, because he had a harrowing brush with death. It all began on January 11, 1989. John had just finished an early-morning workout as a member of the Washington State University baseball team. Suddenly, he keeled over in the field house. Rushed to a doctor, he was diagnosed with a subarachnoid hemorrhage; he was bleeding from a blood vessel at the base of his brain.

Dr. Olerud recalled how it all began: "John had called me the night before and had a cold, not feeling very well. Then I got a call the next day from a physician friend at the student health service about nine in the morning that John had collapsed during a timed mile run and had a grand mal seizure. I got on the next plane going over there and by noon I was in Pullman.

"I went over to be with him and [was with him in] Spokane [at the hospital where John was flown] and just stayed there with him for, like, two weeks. I was in fear. If there was any avoidable mistake or a decision to be made and they needed to get a hold of somebody in a hurry, I didn't want them to have to come looking for me or calling for me. I stayed with him in his room most of the time he was in that hospital in Spokane."

John's medical problem was a brutal ordeal for his parents, especially for his father, who, being a doctor, realized the dangers and ramifications of his son's condition. He said the most intense part of their troubles lasted at least several weeks.

"My wife went straight over to Pullman and slept on a mattress beside his bed until he came back to Seattle," Dr. Olerud said. "It was a very, very frightening thing. The mortality rate for an aneurysm that bleeds a second time is about 70 percent." That was one statistic the doctor withheld from his already petrified wife, but it was, nevertheless, a very sobering realization.

Getting back to the first day of John's condition, Dr. Olerud said, "At the time I talked to the doctor, John still wasn't with it very much. He didn't know where he was or what had happened. Then John and I took a helicopter to Spokane—medevacked him over there to a medical complex.

"At the time, the question was had he had a cardiac event? His heart rate was so slow, it was in the twenties when they brought him in—that can happen when you have an aneurysm.

"They thought it might have been like [basketball star] Hank Gathers, who died of a heart problem, so that was one of the possibilities. Another one was that since he'd had a bad cold, we worried that he might have meningitis or a brain tumor. An aneurysm was clearly in that same possible scenario.

"He threw up during the whole trip to Spokane in the helicopter. Every time he threw up, I was worried that he'd have another seizure and that would be the end of it, but they got him off the helicopter right away. They took him in for a CAT scan, and it turned out there was no brain tumor," he said.

The nightmare was far from over, though. "They got him to a bed upstairs and a neurologist saw him," Dr. Olerud continued. "They did a spinal tap, and his spinal fluid looked like strawberry pop—it was bright red. The pressure was three or four times normal. It was clear that he had bled, so then they started looking for the aneurysm, but they didn't find it.

"It turns out that about 15 percent of the time when you have a subarachnoid hemorrhage, you don't find an aneurysm. If that's the case and the person survives for six months, their subsequent likelihood of bleeding again goes back to the general-population statistics. So we were hoping that he'd fall in that category.

"After two weeks of bed rest, they let him go back to Pullman. My wife went along with him and, like any worried mom, she wound up sleeping on the floor beside his bed and driving him to class because he was on seizure medicine and couldn't drive.

"About three or four weeks after his hemorrhage, his neurologist let him go back to light workouts. Then the Cougars were ready to start the season, and he was cleared to start running again and play.

"About that time, I asked that his [medical] studies be sent to Seattle to be evaluated here because the last thing you'd want is for him to have another episode of bleeding and find out you'd overlooked something. So we had Dr. Richard Winn evaluate his studies. He's probably the best-known aneurysm surgeon in North America.

"We had to call John, who was ready to play the first games of the year, and tell him, 'You need to come back to Seattle for another arteriogram.' That's where you put a catheter in your groin and run it all the way above your heart and then squirt dye into the blood vessels of your brain. Not exactly something you look forward to, but John agreed, drove home, and, sure enough, the new studies showed the aneurysm very clearly.

"He had it fixed with about six hours of surgery. It was very scary, because people die of aneurysms or become crippled as a result of aneurysms that have bled. It's not real common to walk away from aneurysm surgery and have a career as a professional baseball player. That really was a miracle for John— that he was able to do that without [ramifications], other than losing twenty, thirty pounds of weight and a lot of strength.

"I think six weeks after his aneurysm was clipped, he was back playing baseball for the Cougars. Once you get a clip on the aneurysm, it's fixed. He's got a metal clip that sort of looks like the kind of hair pins that women use on their hair; it pinches open and is nonmagnetic.

"They did take a window of bone out the skull to get access to the aneurysm that had to be wired back in. That's why he wears that helmet all the time [even when playing defense], to protect against any stray ball. He's got wires in his skull in that area, where you see a dent in the side of his head.

"When the Blue Jays looked at John as a postoperative person, they talked to their own neurosurgeons, too; he was a better risk than people who've had their shoulders or knees operated on. He'd had a problem and it was fixed," he said.

If John ever took a direct blow "over where he'd had the bone taken out, he might get a skull fracture," Dr. Olerud continued. "But Dr. Winn didn't even think he had to wear the protective helmet in the field. That was just something John and I agreed to do as a sort of 'belt and suspenders' kind of thing. But he's probably more at risk riding in a car than being hit with a baseball with his helmet on."

Remarkably, John underwent surgery for the removal of an aneurysm at the base of his brain on February 27. Almost exactly six months after the operation, he was playing big-league baseball. Despite the seriousness of his condition, and with the support and help of doctors, and, of course, family, he has gone on to accomplish the dream of a lifetime.

Just as Dr. Olerud anguished through John's health problem, he reveled in his glory, a highlight of which was John's 1993 drive to reach the elusive .400 plateau. "It's always a lot of fun when he's having success," Dr. Olerud said. "We were really enjoying it. In our family, baseball has been very important. It really meant something to us that he was playing in the big leagues.

"When Pat Gillick was trying to sign him, he had a chance to go straight to the big leagues and play on a team that was contending for a pennant. There are guys like Ernie Banks who played their whole career and went to the Hall of Fame and never played on a pennant contender.

"The sense of baseball history really meant something to our family. So the fact that he was having that kind of a year really did put goose bumps on me. To hear people like Ted Williams [the last major leaguer to hit .400] critiquing his swing—it was an awesome experience. He did a good job, and handled the pressure and all the tension very well."

Dr. Olerud recalled another George Brett/John Olerud anecdote: "I think it was the year that John had toyed with .400 and Brett was kind of winding his career down a little bit, and George, I'm sure, had heard or read stories about how John had sort of idolized him as a younger person. Anyway, George was struggling a little bit and John was having one of those wild, crazy good years, and John's playing first base when Brett drives a single to right field. As he rounds first, he's over there and he taps John on the shoulder and he says, 'I hit that one just like John Olerud.' "

One honor John received that is unrelated to his skill as a hitter was the Hutch Award. Dr. Olerud explained, "They had just decided that they would move the Hutch Award [center] back to Seattle because Fred Hutchinson [for whom the award is named] grew up in the Seattle area and his brother Bill built the center—a very important part of the landscape here now for cancer treatment.

"John was the first person to win the award here in Seattle. The award is given to an individual who exemplifies the fighting spirit of Fred Hutchinson, to come back from adversity. So they considered John's aneurysm as the factor that he had overcome to get to where he was. Obviously, the list of people who have won the award is very impressive and continues to be very impressive, so it's a great honor."

His hitting ability aside, John would still be special. Although fans are also aware of his defensive skills, many aren't aware that he was, in fact, a fine pitching prospect. "I pitched growing up all the way through college, and I played first base as well," John said.

When Dr. Olerud was asked if his son was good enough to pitch in the minor leagues, he replied, "I think John could have probably pitched higher than just the minors. I think he could've been a major-league pitcher. We were told that the way they had him scouted—*Baseball America,* I think, had him picked as the No. 1 position player in the draft, and the fifteenth or sixteenth pitcher. He was 15–0 in his sophomore year, the year that he won the College Player of the Year Award.

"He's one of those guys who really was a student of the game. He was a Tommy John kind of pitcher, with a reasonable fastball that he had very good control of and a great straight change-up. We didn't let him throw a curveball until his growth centers were closed as a senior in high school. So he had to throw a good change-up."

Dr. Olerud didn't want his son to fall victim to what happens to many Little Leaguers who hurt their elbows "as a result of a lot of twisting motion at the growth centers while you're still growing. My belief is that Little Leaguers throw curveballs with the main advantage being a change of speed," he said. "But John went all the way up to his senior year without throwing any breaking ball other than a change-up. He was very effective with that off-speed pitch. The change-up, even in college, was his second-best pitch.

"Then he started throwing a slider and a curveball, but he also had a terrific move to first. We had a friend who had just a great move, and we worked on that a lot with John when he was younger. He'd pick off three or four guys a game routinely—that was often true even in college as well. It was like they'd have to hit a double to get to second. Three singles and you might not score. Unless you just guessed with him, you were not going to steal second base."

Further support for Dr. Olerud's contention that John could have made it as a pitcher came from John's only stints facing professional hitters. In winter ball, John worked a total of "I think ten scoreless innings, that was all that he pitched," his father said. "That was the first winter when he went to camp with the Blue Jays." Dr. Olerud's assessment was that his son "was not the kind of guy who could overpower you or just go out there without preparing. He always prepared very well when he was pitching. He'd start throwing in November, when most guys were playing basketball."

The time Dr. Olerud spent with his son was clearly important to him. "The thing that John and I did a lot together was baseball situations," he said. "In those days, the catcher really did call the game and did set the defenses—did all those things. So what I tried to work with John about was when you're pitching, to think like a hitter. And when you're hitting, think like a pitcher.

"A lot of it is just kind of the mental side of the game. And I guess if there's anything that I would take any credit for with John it's just the work that we did on the mental side of the game.

"I think John was one of those guys who was born with great ability, and I threw him a lot of batting practice, but I played long enough to see that there were guys who had more ability than I did, certainly, and John is one of those guys who was just blessed with a lot of ability," he concluded.

"My dad played minor-league baseball," said John Olerud during an interview in the 2000 season, "so when I was real young, something that we did to have fun was go take batting practice with a Wiffle ball. That was something we would do together; then when I got to where I was playing in Little League and that sort of thing, we'd go out and practice. He'd catch me; we'd work on pitching. And we'd take batting practice and work on ground balls and fly balls. It was just spending time together while also having fun."

Although baseball was mainly a joyful pastime for the Oleruds, John said that his dad also had the insight to teach him a thing or two, and games can become even more fun when a youngster knows what he's doing and develops prowess in a given field.

"I think he knew about how the game's played. Being a catcher, he caught pitchers before, so he helped me out with my pitching and pitch selection. With him having had instruction from Bobo Brayton at W.S.U. and minor-league coaches, guys who have played in the big leagues, it definitely helped."

Dr. Olerud's help was invaluable to his son in the past, but even now John has found that he trusts his father's advice so much he still heeds his words. "Definitely," he said. "He's somebody who has been watching me swing the bat since I was little, and he knows my swing pretty well. He doesn't necessarily try to give real detailed stuff, but if he notices something that looks a little out of whack, he'll mention something. But, for the most part, he's kind of an outside observer."

While a few of the fathers interviewed for this book said their memory is a bit hazy when it comes to the birth of their son, Dr. Olerud had no difficulty at all. "I was in the delivery room, and I remember I was just so ecstatic when I saw him," he said. "I was just laughing out loud; it was like somebody who had gone mad. I couldn't stop laughing, I was so exhilarated."

Then, slipping from the proud-papa persona, he looked at his son as a doctor would, clinically. "He had all his fingers and toes." After that leap to the cognitive level, he went back to an emotional center, saying, "It was really a remarkable experience."

When it comes to the names in John's family tree, one can't tell a "player" without a scorecard. Dr. Olerud explained that his grandson is named "Garrett John and John Garrett is [the full name of] my son. He decided to just reverse his name for his son. Kelly [John's wife] has a brother and dad with the first name John. So they thought there would be a little bit of a logjam at the Thanksgiving dinner table with all the Johns if we had another one."

For Dr. Olerud, having the same name as his son has been the source of both confusion and levity. "I remember one time when we were in Toronto there was an island across from where John lived, Center Island," he mused. "Lynda and I went over there one day to ride bikes. When we rented the bikes, we handed this guy my credit card and it says 'John Olerud' on it. He looks at it, looks back at me, and he says, 'You're not John Olerud.' He's thinking I stole John's credit card. Then I said, 'Yes, I am John Olerud—I'm the original John Olerud. And he says, 'Get out of town!' "

Dr. Olerud also has a few tales about his grandson already. "Garrett was born in New York," he said. "I wasn't there for his birth; he's a New Yorker. John has a sort of dry sense of humor, so one of his jokes is he's working on Garrett for some of the New York phrases like 'Fuhgeddaboutit' and 'Gahbudge.'

"Garrett has been the easiest little boy. When he was sixteen days old, he went to the final series down in Atlanta, where the Mets had to win a game or two from the Braves in order to have a shot at the [1998] playoffs. They wound up losing all three, but Garrett was right there on a seat right next to us at the ballpark. He just sailed right through it.

"He's been at ballparks ever since. This last spring training, I was down there a week ago [March of 2001], and Garrett and I went out and watched John hit. Then his dad was going to do something else, and we went over and watched the catchers. He was there for about twenty minutes, just watching them with the pitchers. He was too interested to leave when I'd suggest doing other things. After that he's been getting down in his catching position now everywhere we go. He's right-handed, so I said to John, 'Looks like we may have a catcher here.'"

John's son, Garrett, was born a few years before the turn of the century, so he is a long way from playing baseball, but, says his famous father, "He knows where I work is at the ball game, and he wants to hit the ball. He's got a glove, but that's about it right now. He does come out to the park, too."

Down the road Garrett will determine his own future, because John isn't the type of father who would force baseball on his son. "I think every person is wired differently and has different strengths and weaknesses," he said. "If Garrett is gifted in athletics and he wants to play baseball, that's great, because I can share something with him. If he's interested in art and music, I'm going to be behind him 100 percent, but I just can't help him, because I can't draw, I can't play an instrument, I can't sing. I can't do anything," he said, laughing.

"I want him to go towards his strengths, whatever they may be. So if he does play baseball I think that that might be a little difficult, because people are going to know that he's my kid and they'll expect him to play well and that sort of thing. That could be tough, but it all depends on what he's gifted at."

John was pretty much restating what players from the days of Stan Musial (and earlier) have always said. Musial's son tried to make it in baseball, but he found it difficult for two reasons. First, his skills were nothing in comparison to his legendary father's. Second, Musial said it was unfair of people to expect his son to be another Stan "the Man," but that's exactly what fans and writers did.

Of course, John also realizes that since every generation gets bigger, stronger, and faster, his son might well become a bigger star than he is. "Oh, yeah," he agreed. "He might, but I'm not going to force him into anything that he doesn't want to do, because then that wouldn't be any fun for him. That would be a big struggle. I just want him to have fun at what he does."

With the addition of a sister to the family—Jordan Marie, born late in the 2000 season—Garrett now has a playmate. No doubt Jordan, too, will spend a great deal of time in and around ballparks.

Meanwhile, another parental perk that comes with being a big-league dad taking a trip to spring training is the opportunity that the relaxed atmosphere there gives families to spend time together. "We stay with John and Kelly, so we get a chance to spend some good quality time with them," Dr. Olerud said. "I never get to see as much of the [players'] work as I would like to. I'm one of those people that I, all things being equal, would ride out with John in the morning and just watch people work.

"That's what I've done through the years, but now that I've got a grandson, I wait until Garrett gets up and take him along. There's a lot less focus on watching the kinds of things I would if I was out there by myself, but that's just a different phase in my life—I'm just really enjoying spending time with my grandson now."

All in all, the spring experience is one to be relished. It is also a time when the Oleruds get a chance to eat out together quite a bit. Jokes abound about who will grab the bills in restaurants. "John lets me pick up the tab every once in a while, but most of the time he's all over it," Dr. Olerud said. Of course, there's also always the good-natured "bantering going on" about the money that players get nowadays versus in the "good ol' days."

Despite the repartee, there is no jealousy on Dr. Olerud's part. On the contrary, he says he's delighted that, while he himself was a good player, John went far beyond his own level. "Absolutely," Dr. Olerud said. "It's almost humorous to think that when he was a senior in high school and was deciding where to go to college, the three places that were most in the running were Stanford, Washington State, and Washington, and I played for the coach, Bobo Brayton, who was still at Washington State. So it would've been disappointing for Bobo if John had decided not to go there, but yet I was concerned that I had had really a pretty good career over there and was an All-American—things that might be hard for John to live up to.

"And he goes over there and certainly did not shrink in the shadow of a successful father. He just rewrote the record books over there, both for pitching and for hitting. I think those records will probably stand for a very long time. He was even All-American his sophomore year at two positions, and College Player of the Year. I was very pleased that he was able to do as well as he did. I think all his accomplishments since have very much warmed my heart."

Dr. Olerud feels that he can appreciate what his son has done more than most parents simply because, having played the game, he knows what it takes to endure in the minors and how difficult it is to be a standout, which John certainly is. "You know the hardest part about baseball is the mental side," he said. "For example, you can defeat yourself if you're not able to deal with the mental side of it, and that's the part of the game that I think John does so well. Even the pressure, when he was going through that stretch where he was hitting over .400.

CHAPTER FOURTEEN: THE OLERUDS . 187

"But probably what was harder for him was in the first year, when he was having trouble getting going, and again in his second year he had a slow start. But the thing people are looking for in a young player at that time when you're struggling is how it's affecting you. They look at a guy like John and they know he's eventually going to be a great hitter, but if you're struggling and it's adversely affecting you, then that's when they decide that it's probably better for you to go to the minor leagues and work on things in a less-pressured situation.

"So a lot of [the tribulations of baseball] is working at it—you hustle and if they see it's not affecting you and that you're able to maintain your focus and not get emotionally distraught about it, you're going to be there." And being there is something John has done now for thirteen years, never having spent a day in the minors—a rarity, to be sure.

Dr. Olerud reiterated how he had helped John with the thinking part of baseball from early on. "We'd sit and watch ball games and talk situations," he recalled. "I think he was very well prepared by the time he got to different levels. The other coach who taught John his move to first said that having John on the team was like having another coach—he was always kind of studying and analyzing, making comments that were relevant."

John still remembers the first time his father saw him play in the majors. "He came to visit us up in Toronto, and before that he watched me on TV." He also recalls the first time his dad introduced him to live big-league ball by taking him to a game in Seattle.

"The first game I remember going to was in 1977, with the Mariners when they came [into the league]. I was about 9 years old," John said. During the game, and many more to follow, his father pointed out nuances that he observed, and John absorbed much knowledge.

Dr. Olerud's memories of John's first encounters with big-league baseball as a child differ a bit from John's. He said, "I was there for the first Mariners game, and it would be hard for me to believe that I would be there without him, but I don't have any specific memory of that. But I certainly do remember that he became a Pepsi Junior Mariner and he went to a lot of games."

However, because John was also involved in soccer and basketball, where his father served as a coach, Dr. Olerud said that he now attends "a lot more professional baseball games than we ever did because it's like we were always going to either John's things or coaching Erica's soccer team, my wife and I. We were constantly on the go with the activities, so we didn't get to as many

Mariners games as we do now." Needless to say, Dr. Olerud now watches his favorite team and his favorite player of all time quite a bit.

In fact, throughout John's baseball career—when he was with the Blue Jays and the Mets, and now when he is on the road with the Mariners—his father has always been able to see him frequently. "We've been able to follow him by satellite [television]. We haven't missed too many of the games through the years," he said.

John is well aware of his dad's loyalty. He knows that, like many modern fathers, his dad is able to keep up with him through the world of technology. "He's got a satellite dish, and he tries to catch as many games as he can," John said.

Still, there's nothing quite like seeing one's son in person. John said that his father, who still lives in the Seattle area, not only makes it to home games but also "has come to spring training before, and he's come to road games in New York, Chicago, some of those places, to watch me play."

Of course, Dr. Olerud also holds a season pass at Safeco Field. "I bet we didn't miss more than about four or five games last year," he said of John's first season with Seattle. "I can't stay the whole night, because I get up and play squash at 6:15 in the morning, so we'll stay till the sixth or seventh inning and see maybe three of his at bats, unless it's a weekend or a Friday."

Seeing John play that much, Dr. Olerud vicariously experiences the injuries and slumps with his son. "He's had a remarkably injury-free career," he said. "I think he's never been on the D.L., and he's only missed a week or two for injuries, but, yeah, that's hard. He goes through slumps and struggles, and there are things he's not happy about with his swing. He handles it very, very well—I know it bothers him, but he's able to deal with it. There are other things in his life that are more important than baseball. Baseball is important, but his family and his faith are the most important things in his life."

And what about Dr. Olerud's stint on the field? Did John ever get to see his father play the game? Dr. Olerud said his son did get to see some footage on video. "I think he's seen a little bit, but not a lot—a couple of at bats, but a lot of times I was taking a pitch when they were taking film on it."

John has seen enough, though, to realize that his father's appearance in the batter's box is not like his own. "I tried to teach him some things about how to do hand movements and timing movements—things like that," Dr. Olerud said. "But when I look at videos of myself as a hitter, the swings are very different. I certainly didn't have the pretty swing that he's got."

John worked on baseball and that sweet swing from the time he was, said his father, "just a little guy. He was a little boy when I was playing, and we'd be out in the side yard, playing our little mock-up game. That was what we did for fun. I also coached his teams all the way from the time he was about 7 until he left for college."

On the playing field, Dr. Olerud didn't always coach him per se, John said, but, rather, "he would help out. He'd assist the other coaches." John noted that his father's pointers were appreciated. "The fact that he had played before helped, because he could understand going through the tough times and that sort of thing," he said. "It was great for me that he was able to help me along the way and give me some good instruction."

Dr. Olerud said that he set out not only to teach his son the fundamentals of baseball but also to impart some values to John. "I think honesty and integrity are a couple of things that everybody needs to instill in their kids if they can," he said. "I can think of a number of times when those things were emphasized."

And when it was time to negotiate a professional contract, Dr. Olerud helped out there, too, because back then players couldn't hire an agent if they were in college without losing their amateur status. "John had no intention of signing after his junior year, because he had the aneurysm in January and had the surgery in February," Dr. Olerud explained. "Then he returned to playing in April. He was twenty pounds underweight, and we told everybody before the draft that he was not going to sign. Seattle would've drafted him that year, probably, if he would've been signable.

"Pat Gillick took a chance on him in the third round, hoping that he might be able to convince him to sign if he looked good during the summer. They had a scout follow him all summer long. In fact, Don Welke traveled with him all the way through Alaska and Hawaii and places where the Cougars baseball team played that summer. Eventually, they were able to sign him the last week before school started, but we couldn't hire an agent." So John left college early, had help from his father, and soon broke onto the big-league stage.

When John made it to baseball's center stage, the World Series, he and his father couldn't have been more thrilled. "We were invited into the clubhouse after both of the 1992 and 1993 World Series wins," Dr. Olerud said. "And, of course, we had watched these guys play all year long so we felt like we knew them, even though they hardly knew us, from waiting around for John after ball games. It was fun to get together with these guys who we knew so much about and had watched play so long, like Paul Molitor and Dave Winfield—guys who really were remarkable players, future Hall of Famers." As a rule, however, Dr. Olerud said he doesn't go into clubhouses very much.

Although he wasn't a frequent visitor to John's locker rooms, Dr. Olerud did say that he was impressed with the opulent, plush clubhouse of the Toronto Blue Jays. He couldn't help comparing it with the facilities that he had lockered in as a player. "That was amazing. When John first signed, Pat Gillick took us for a tour through there," he said. At that point, the ex-player became a fan, a tourist. "I've got all kinds of pictures that I took because I was just absolutely dazzled.

"Then John took batting practice there, the first day we saw him in a Blue Jays uniform with the Skydome open and the CN Tower there—it was surrealistic," he said.

Dr. Olerud has never had the urge or the need to boast about who he is. He does say, however, that "people recognize our names, and I kind of get a kick out of that." The kick that he gets isn't an ego trip, though. As he said, "There's a real sense of pride about John's accomplishments."

"Obviously, I don't get to spend as much time with him," Dr. Olerud said. "He's got his own family, and there are lots of demands on his time. We still enjoy one another when we do have time together. He's got a great sense of humor. I love to spend time with him, and I get to do more now with his son here in Seattle. A lot of times, we can kind of help out with the baby-sitting," he continued. "That has really increased the amount of quality time that we get with him."

Looking back, then, Dr. Olerud feels that to share a love of baseball with his son and to see that son wind up playing the game so well is a sort of culmination to a stellar "career" as a father. "I feel very blessed to have been able to watch his development and his career," he said. "I'm glad to see another little guy come along that seems to enjoy balls, too. Maybe Johnny and I might get to coach Garrett along the way together."

While John may be a star baseball player to the public at large, to his father he is, of course, much more. "He grew up to be a really remarkable human being," Dr. Olerud said. "He was a great little kid, too. He was very coachable. He was happy when he'd get up in the morning. He's very lucky his little boy is just like that. He's just sort of baseline happy. He enjoys things in life. He's very patient. I'm one of his biggest fans. I think he's a great human being, in addition to being an excellent ballplayer."

Likewise, John is a fan of his father. "My dad is somebody that I've always looked up to and somebody I've always tried to emulate," he said. "It's hard to compare your dad to other dads, because that's your only experience dealing with dads, but I thought he was great and had a great sense of humor.

"He expected things to be done a certain way, and for me to treat people a certain way. I think his example of watching to see how he dealt with people showed [me how I] should behave or how you should treat people. He always treated me fairly. He's the kind of guy you want to be."

Chapter Fifteen: The Kennedys

Tom Kennedy played baseball in college at U.C. (University of California) Riverside, in his hometown. He said that, baseball-wise, "as far as I got was college. Of course, I played in high school, and then I got a little scholarship to U.C. Riverside, right out here [in the area where he still lives]. We weren't very good, and I wasn't great—I was good enough to play at that level. I had fun and it got me my degree, which was good.

"I always thought if my kids could play some sort of sports through college that would be good because it's a nice avenue, with good camaraderie and you're doing something fun that you like while you're earning a degree. We got [both sons] there, which was one of my goals."

He entered the teaching field and became a high-school baseball coach. Among his most illustrious alumni are Alvin Davis, who went on to play in the majors for the Mariners and the Angels over a span of nine years, and his son, Adam. For one high-school coach to send two players (with a possible third in the near future) to the big leagues is no small accomplishment.

Tom's teams did very well over the years, although he modestly downplayed their performance, saying, "We had some success." When prompted, he elaborated, "In '94, when Adam was a senior, Bryan [his only other child] was a freshman on the varsity. I kind of wanted him to play J.V., and my assistant coach actually talked me into bringing Bryan up. I thought, being Bryan's dad, that wouldn't be right, and it just so happened that that year we did win the

Southern Section CIF [California Interscholastic Federation] Championship." Since California has no state finals for baseball, Tom said, "We went as far as we could." His team, then, was one of the four best in the entire state that season.

Bryan is indeed a very talented baseball player. His father said, regarding Bryan's athletic future, "I don't look at it like [him] having a chance to make it to the bigs. I think he's got a chance to sign [for pro ball] after next year. He'll plug away; he's an outstanding catcher. He's built a little different than Adam. Bryan's about 6'2", about 210. He's a little bigger kid, stockier. So, yeah, I think he has a chance."

Adam Thomas Kennedy was born on January 10, 1976, and grew up in Riverside. He knew from early childhood that his father was running a highly successful baseball program at the local high school. Tom recently called it quits, but not until he had enjoyed quite a run. "He coached for twenty-five years," Adam said during an interview in 2000. He coached my brother in high school, too, and after he left my dad shut it down." Actually, to be exact, Tom said he coached two more years after Bryan's senior season.

Adam, who stands 6'1" and tips the scales at 180, went from J. W. North High School to California State University, Northridge. There he became the school's record holder for career batting average, an astronomical .414; hits, with 337; and runs batted in, at 234. He was a three-time All-American there, and he led all NCAA Division I players in hits as a sophomore (121) and again as a junior (134). That made him the first player ever to lead the nation in hits in successive seasons. Perhaps his sophomore year was his shining season, in that he helped his Matadors win the 1996 NCAA West Regionals with his .565 average there. As a junior, he took first-team All-American honors when he hit .482 with 32 doubles, 26 homers, and 99 RBI.

He began his pro career in the minors with the St. Louis Cardinals as the twentieth player selected in the June draft of 1997. By 1999 he was named the Cards Minor League Player of the Year during a season that saw him play for Memphis (Triple-A ball), in the USA Pan Am games (where he won a Silver Medal), and for the Cardinals (for thirty-three contests late in the year). He even recorded a four-hit game for St. Louis in September. Overall, in the minors, he had hit .300 or very close to it at every stop, with a high of .342.

In late March of 2000, he was traded to the Anaheim Angels, along with pitcher Kent Bottenfield, for star outfielder Jim Edmonds. He led the American League in assists by a second baseman that year with Anaheim. Through that season, he had a .264 lifetime average over 700 big-league at bats, with 10 homers and 88 RBI. In 2000, he scored 82 times and had 53 extra base hits, with 33 coming on doubles and 11 more on triples. In all, it took him just under 300 games in the minors before he broke through to the majors.

People began noticing him shortly thereafter. White Sox coach Joe Nossek likes what he's seen of Adam. In the off-season before 2001, he said, "He had a heck of a year, I thought. He went after it and he did it all year long—showed some consistency, which you like to see. I thought he did a great job for them, and their pitching was injured so they struggled with the pitching but were in it right into September—still had a chance, and he was a big part of that. I was impressed by him, and he could hit left-handed pitching, too." Adam is a left-handed hitter, although as an infielder he, of course, throws righty.

Despite his success, Adam comes across as modest and soft-spoken. His father, Tom, answered questions for this book almost playfully at times, displaying a wonderful sense of humor, as well, to go along with the love and the pride in his voice.

The day Adam Kennedy was born was an incredible experience for his father. "That was amazing," Tom said. "I mean, I got a chance to be in the delivery room. It was around the time when men started to do that. Definitely a life-changing thing. I was an athlete, but I tried to never anticipate that my kids would be athletes, because I wanted to support them in whatever paths they took."

It was almost inevitable that his sons' paths would include a stroll down Baseball Boulevard. That path was one that allowed the Kennedy trio to bond strongly. "Oh, I think quite a bit," said Tom. "It was that common thread. Fortunately, it just worked out that I liked it and they liked it.

"So it was good, although we didn't talk a lot of sports at home. It was like we had a safe zone here, because baseball was such a big part of all of our lives when they were little. We were never overly analytical about it at home."

However, when they got out on a baseball field, Tom made sure that he did teach his sons many insights into the game, such as learning how to hit to the opposite field. "I did that when they were young, not so much as a drill sergeant, but I told them when they were young that it was good to use the whole field, and so forth. They were pretty good at that."

With respect to his father's involvement in his baseball development, Adam said, "He was pretty much my coach my whole life." As such, Adam got a head start over his peers, learning inside baseball and the mental aspects of the game much earlier than most kids did. "I think so, definitely," he said. "I don't know if that's just from being around it so much, like watching so many games, or just instincts, or what—I couldn't tell you, but when I was younger I would always seem to know things like that."

Of course, his dad's input on the fundamentals of the game helped, as did some element of trial and error. "I'm sure I had to make a few mistakes first, which is fine," Adam said.

Since Tom had coached high school ever since Adam was born, the time conflict meant that he couldn't coach his son in youth leagues, but he still played an active role in his son's learning the game. "I purposely chose not to coach him and I was coaching high school any way, so to coach him in Little League or Pony League or anything like that would have been very difficult," he said. "I preferred it that way. I don't think I ever had the deal where 'I knew best' and no one else could coach [him]. I felt getting other coaching—good, bad, or indifferent—other coaching [input] would be beneficial for the kids. I had that philosophy about it, and I think it worked out good."

When Adam attended high school in Riverside, his father finally got to coach him on the diamond. Furthermore, in Tom's off-season, which coincided with Adam's high-school basketball season, he could always be found courtside, cheering his son on.

"I wouldn't play baseball for six months out of the year when I was playing basketball," Adam said. "He would never say, like, 'O.K., you got to get ready for the baseball season.' I was playing basketball, and that's what I was doing. He never made me do anything like that, which was great."

Overall, then, Adam agreed that some of the coaching he got from his father was "not on the field, actual stuff, but at home. He was the first one ever to take me to a baseball field and show me how to do anything. My whole life he's been an influence and showed me the right things and the wrong things. He let me make mistakes on my own, to learn from them. I don't think people realize how important that is as far as letting your kids make their own mistakes—they can learn from them. That helped me out so much."

From early on Adam said his father "always took me out to the high-school field to his practices, to shag balls and mess around." Tom also took

Adam to major-league games when he was young. But, Tom said, "I think he enjoyed going to games and being a fan, but he enjoyed much more being active himself. We didn't go to a lot of games, and he wasn't what I'd call the superfan. He didn't follow it too much. He collected baseball cards and we'd go to shows, and stuff like that, but no, he wasn't real diligent as far as [knowing] players' stats. He would have rather gone into the backyard and played catch or thrown the ball up against the wall 500 times. That sort of thing."

The Kennedys saw a lot of games, though, when one of Tom's former players, Alvin Davis, came to town. When Davis spent a year with the Angels, they would drop in and watch him even more often than before. "As a matter of fact," Tom said, "we have a picture hanging up in the hallway here of Adam and my other son, Bryan, with Alvin—and Adam must be 10 [in that picture]. We followed Alvin's career pretty closely."

So who was the best player Tom ever coached? "There were so many, I can't answer that—there's no [one] best," he said. "Of course, Adam and Bryan are right up there, and Alvin. Alvin reminded me a lot of Adam, in that you knew they were good, but when they were in high school you didn't really predict major leagues. But Alvin had that drive to make it to the bigs."

Tom has a theory that has certainly held true where Adam is concerned. "It seems like those kids who you might predict they'll make it, it's sort of like they're destined not to make it because of the anticipation," he said. "The great Little Leaguer who everybody's ranting and raving about—it's almost like it's a jinx."

He said that, to him, having no hype and having to work hard is actually an easier path to success. "He's got to be good, of course, but if he's sort of struggling to still get to a certain level [it helps]. I think that's been one of Adam's things—he's never felt complacent at any of the levels: college, Single-A, Double-A, Triple-A. Never felt complacent, in that he'd reached his peak. I think now, as a major leaguer, he's still learning quite a bit and he wants to learn." He did concede, though, that his son had always been sort of a natural as far as skills such as great hand-eye coordination were concerned.

Adam picked up the chronology of his career once more. "When I got in high school he became my coach," he said. "It was tough sometimes because of the fact that he expected so much from me, which is understandable. I think any parent would be [like that], but he knew I had the ability to do things right, so he always kept me on my toes."

Surprisingly, Adam wasn't a superstar in high school. "He didn't stand out tremendously in high school because he split his time with basketball, and his basketball team was excellent out here at North High School," Tom said. "I mean, they went to the playoffs every year. They went to the CIF championship, won it [the Southern Section] a couple of times. As a matter of fact, his senior year in basketball the team went undefeated and lost in the finals. He was a guard [at both the shooting and the playmaking spots]. He was tenacious.

"So he was always getting out for baseball a little bit late and [having to] kinda catch up," Tom said. "But basketball was an equal love to baseball when he was in high school."

When Adam traced his baseball origins he, like so many people who went on to stardom, began with the earliest of basics, games such as Wiffle ball. "You name it, we played every game there was out there," he said. "I have a brother, and there were tons of kids in our neighborhood, so there was never a shortage of guys to play [with]."

One of those "guys" was his dad, who joked that they wanted to play so much, "I used to have to hide in the closet from those two guys. They wanted to play forever. I can remember with Adam, in the previous house we lived in before this one, we had a hedge of juniper, real scratchy, that separated our house from the neighbor's house. We would go out there—he was about 4, 5, or 6—and he'd want me to throw the ball so that he would have to jump and 'steal' it, like a home run, going over that hedge. He'd fall into the hedge—can you imagine falling in a juniper hedge? He'd get right back out and want me to do it again. We'd do that forever."

Asked to recount a funny story from Adam's childhood, Tom replied, "He was so competitive, he wasn't that funny." He did say, though, that one pleasant childhood memory was "all summer long we knew that, come one or two o'clock, there was going to be a tennis-ball game or a Wiffle-ball game to be played in the neighborhood."

He said his own father's attitude was one of letting his children "go out and have fun, play, fight with each other"—all of which was a part of growing up. As a teacher, Tom knew that his children would go through the normal stages of development, and that having fun was key.

Not only did Adam go through all the phases but he wound up being quite a talented young man. Eventually, Tom's advice and work with his son came to fruition when Adam progressed from college ball up through the minors and, ultimately, to the majors. "After I left high school I went to college, and I'm sure there was doubt of 'I wonder if he can play at the next level,'" Adam said. "Then I succeeded so much there [college], I don't think that when I got to pro ball he was as nervous or wondering how I would handle it all. I think he was more comfortable with me being able to handle the pressures. Once he saw how I handled everything in college, he figured I'd try to figure out a way how to get it done [in the majors]."

When it was time to actually sign his first professional contract, Adam said his father "was there the whole time, but he was pretty much just like me—he didn't know too much about it; he wasn't going to act like he did. I had an agent for that. He and my dad are real close."

Adam seems to recall that the first time his father saw him play pro ball was in Virginia, when he was playing in the Carolina League. As for Tom's first glimpse of his son in the majors, Adam said that his parents "went to Shea Stadium when I got called up last year [1999]." That required a cross-country trip from Tom's residence in California, but whether the flight should be booked or not was a moot point from the moment the Kennedys learned of Adam's call-up.

What was it like? Tom recalled that the feeling he got then was "probably the same I could tell you about seeing him even now—I look out there, and it's pretty amazing. It's funny, though, the game at Shea—my wife and I flew in—it was a night game, and the plane was late and the traffic was horrible and we're trying to get through New York. You can imagine that—on a Friday evening, I think, is what it was. We were late getting to the game, maybe, as fate might [have it]; it was a rainout, so we didn't miss anything.

"So we get to the stadium about an hour or two hours late, and people are still kind of waiting around, but they rained it out and we were able to go for the rest of the series. That's how we were able to get to his first game."

Tom said he experienced myriad emotions, but focused on how incredible it was, how proud they all were, and that he "was just happy for him [Adam], because I knew that it had seemed like once he got into college and started playing baseball, that he became superfocused. You know how it goes: the talent level kind of evens off—in other words, you could go through the minor leagues of baseball and not see a great deal [of disparity]. Among all, say, the Triple-A players, the talent level is relatively consistent. Of course, there will be a very few that will stand out.

"Then there's got to be that other variable that kicks in, that other intangible that kicks in that gets guys to the next level. And I think that's what Adam [had], with his focus so one-minded. I think this began in college, when he went to Cal State Northridge. He was going to make a run at it [the majors] and not be distracted. He just had his sights set on the bigs, and it happened." He shoved his basketball aside and locked in on the horsehide leather and lumber.

Shea Stadium provided two moments of frustration, however, before Adam collected his first base hit. "He went hitless in his first game, then Orel Hershiser was throwing in the second game, and he got his first hit off Orel," Tom said. "I believe it was a single to right-center. Then in his next at bat, Orel plunked him."

But Tom didn't feel that Orel, the crafty veteran, was sending a message to the raw rookie. "You're just an upstart; respect your elders" was the way he interpreted it. Instead, said Tom, "I think he was just trying to pitch inside." Nevertheless, Tom said there was a message delivered anyway: "Welcome to the bigs. He goes and gets plunked. Then he went on to get two more hits that game, so I think he was three-for-four."

From then on, Tom continued to follow his son's career faithfully. During an interview in the latter part of the 2000 season, Adam said, "He comes to pretty much every game, especially now that he's out of school in the summertime—he pretty much comes every night [for Anaheim home games]. It's only, like, thirty minutes away, and he's made a couple of road trips—he loves it, what dad wouldn't?"

Adam has also taken his father inside the clubhouse—yet another enjoyable experience for Tom, who has been around baseball nearly all his life in one capacity or another. In a way, said Adam, Tom was like a typical fan when he entered the Angels' clubhouse. "He loves it all," Adam said, adding that it's great for his father, "being able to watch his son play in the big leagues every single day. [It] is like—I can't even imagine, the thrill would have to be awesome. I like him to see how it is around here and feel comfortable [around the clubhouse and big-league scene]."

Tom makes no bones about it. He admits that he loves to meet Adam's manager and teammates. "That was one of the highlights of this year—being able to go down into the locker room and have Adam show me around the weight room and meet some of the guys. That was a thrill.

"I've been able to talk to Mo Vaughn a little bit, and, boy, is he a classy guy. He looks pretty intimidating, but he's so polite and soft-spoken. As a matter of fact, he's the one who has sort of taken Adam under his wing of all the Angels. Just a nice man."

When he can't see his son in person, Tom said, "We have a satellite dish. As a matter of fact, Adam got it for us. We've got cable out here, where we get the Fox Sports channels, so we can get games that aren't telecast normally. We get pretty much all [his games], and I've been to virtually every Angels home game so far this year myself. We couldn't be any closer [to the park].

"It's funny," Tom continued. "Early in the season Adam took me downstairs and introduced me to Mike Scioscia, their manager, and he was very nice to me. We were talking and I said, being sarcastic, 'Gosh, it's just a shame that Adam's so far from home—thirty-five minutes.' And Mike says, 'Well, we can fix that. Our Single-A affiliate is right out there in Lake Elsinore, right there beside you. Will that work out?' "

Needless to say, Adam, who resides in Newport Beach, California, has stuck it out at the big-league level, learning and improving as time passed. To an outsider, it might seem odd that a son could get to a point where he'd know more inside baseball than his father does, as if he'd outgrown his father. The Kennedys don't entirely feel that way. "I never really stopped and thought about that, and I don't think he does, either," Adam said. "It's not really a competition of who knows more."

The two men share insights in their love of the game. "We've both watched baseball our whole life," Adam said. "So he knows about players just like I do." Still, it must be nice to discuss the game you love at such a high level of understanding. Furthermore, they live so close to each other that they still spend a lot of time together. "As a matter of fact," said Tom, "they had an off day last week, and he came home for some home-cooked dinner and then headed back that night. We've got a La-Z-Boy chair, and I think every now and again he just likes to kick back, get a meal, and sit for a little while—just touching base at home."

One instance of them watching a game together that the Kennedys will, no doubt, never forget was back in 1988. "He took me to the 1988 Series at Dodger Stadium when [Kirk] Gibson hit the home run," Adam recalled. "I had to be 12." Considering that the Gibson blast remains one of the most dramatic World Series homers ever, it was only natural that that moment should be etched in Adam's mind.

Tom related how they wound up seeing history being made. "I remember that a friend of mine who had a son that was Adam's age called and said he had some tickets, so we went down together," he said.

Although Adam doesn't have a son, if he ever does he says he would, of course, be happy to share the game with him. "I'm going to offer it to him," he said. "I mean, one thing that I love my parents for especially is that they never made me play anything I didn't want to play. The fun was never taken out of it for me. That happens to a lot of kids—I grew up with kids that happened to. Some were better than me, or the parents thought they were going [to be] a major leaguer," he scoffed, adding, "Who's to tell you're going to be a major leaguer when you're a teenager? I think that's when people get in trouble."

The Kennedys present a living, warm, and affectionate family portrait. Some players, upon getting older, leaving home, and becoming professionals, may drift apart from their fathers. Not so Adam and Tom Kennedy. "We just keep getting closer and closer," Adam said. "He doesn't have to have that guidance over me anymore, which, I think, opens up a lot, being able to get closer. He knows if I'm going to make a mistake it's not because he didn't tell me it was the right or wrong thing, it's that I messed up now. He taught me everything that I'm going to learn, pretty much, as far as right and wrong. I think he's done a great job with that. Everything I have, everything I'm doing, or I've done, is from him and my mom.

"I just strongly feel like them not ever pressuring me or making me not have fun—giving me choices [is so important]. I see so many people not give their kids that choice and push it [sports] on them too much. You can't groom your kid.

"One of our coaches has a son who doesn't like baseball at all," Adam continued. "His son loves skateboarding, and he loves him for that—loves the fact that his son does his own thing. It's great. You can't make somebody into a baseball player."

Trying to put one's feelings for one's children concisely is never easy, but Tom tried. "I'm just very proud of them," he said. "I'm almost—I don't know if 'awe' might be a little too strong of a word, but I'm awed by them. I'm very impressed by them, and very proud of what they've done and what they've been able to achieve, and the quality of people that they are."

He recognizes, too, that the relationship that he and his son have is a bit different from what it was years ago, in that he feels Adam knows the game more than he does now—the classic scenario of the student going beyond the teacher. "I kind of do [feel that way]," he said. "That's a little bit of that awe I was talking about. I know they talk a lot about Mo's dad guiding him still and coaching him; well, I don't even go there. Adam's got guys, professional coaches and things like that, that he can talk to. I just don't feel like I can really help at this point."

To the contrary, if Tom was still coaching, he would unashamedly ask Adam for pointers. "Oh, sure," he said. "As a matter of fact, after Adam signed and was in the minors, and I was still coaching high school baseball, I had him come out and work with my kids."

So when it comes to addressing the subject of his son's talents, Tom humbly remarked, "I'd like to maybe somehow take a little bit of the credit, but

I don't think I can take very much of it. I just think what they've done, they've pretty much done on their own."

While Tom clearly does have the right to take credit for starting them off and guiding them, he still wants the bulk of the credit to go to his two fine sons. And make no mistake—Tom does see Adam and Bryan as fine young men. He made it clear, for instance, that he is prouder of Adam the man than he is of Adam the ballplayer. "I think I have the realistic view that playing ball could end tomorrow, but he's going to have to go on," he said. "There are other qualities that will carry him, of course, more than just athletics."

Chapter Sixteen: The Moehlers

When I contacted Jim Anderson, the public-relations manager for the Detroit Tigers, I asked him to help me get in touch with Gregg Jefferies. I knew about Gregg's relationship with his father, Fred, and I felt that a section on them would strengthen the book.

After a short time, I got a call from Anderson informing me that Brian Moehler had volunteered to do a telephone interview for the book. He wanted to express his feelings for his father. While that desire is hardly unusual, the idea of a busy major leaguer volunteering to give up his free time *is* rather rare. As it turned out, Anderson knew of Moehler's deep devotion to his father, approached him, and Brian readily agreed to help out.

Brian told how his involvement transpired. "He [Anderson] came up to me, actually, and he said, 'Do you want to do it?' I said, 'I'd be glad to.' I think he'd heard stories about my father and how our relationship was."

Brian said that players get approached so much that they learn to say no, but that he is usually amenable to suggestions, especially this one. "In this business you get a lot of people that sometimes want to take advantage of you," he explained. "You have to say no, but something like this, I enjoy doing." He said it was a way of honoring his father. Brian is now a father himself, with two daughters.

Brian was the winning pitcher in the last game ever played at Tiger Stadium, back on September 27, 1999. He was also given the nod for the first start in the debut of Detroit's new park, Comerica Park, on April 11, 2000, a game in which he earned the win. Those feats made him part of baseball trivia, but he has done much more than that. He has victory totals in the double digits for each of his four seasons as a Tiger, with personal bests of 14 wins and a 3.90 ERA in 1998. Through 2000, the sixth-round draft pick from June of 1993 owned forty-seven big-league victories.

Brian Moehler was born on the last day of 1971, exactly one year before the death of Pirates legend Roberto Clemente. He grew up in Rockingham, North Carolina, a state often associated with basketball. While Brian did play that sport, it wasn't long before everyone realized that he was destined for baseball stardom. "I think [it's] because I grew up in such a small town," he said matter-of-factly, with no trace of bragging.

"We've had other athletes that have played pro ball—Franklin Stubbs played ten years for the Dodgers, Houston, Brewers, and Detroit. There have been a few others—Mike Quick [a wide receiver] played in the NFL, and some other guys who were all older than me. It was always a good, rich baseball community, always good talent. I just felt like I could compete with the guys that were in my area and outside my area.

"I always felt like that [playing baseball professionally] was what I was going to do—from when I was probably 10 or 11 years old," he went on. "I remember telling my mom and dad I was going to do that. I think they really believed that I could. It was just something I believed that I could do, and they allowed me to do that."

Brian said he doesn't view his success as a way of living up to the family name or even of paying tribute to the family. "No, my mom knows me— that I don't like the attention. And some friends of hers, who she hangs out with, our family members, they don't understand why I don't like the attention. Sometimes they'll wear MOEHLER jerseys or whatnot. They say, 'Well, you do something special.' I say, 'I know that, but to me it's just another job.'

"Maybe someday, when I'm done playing, I'll look back on it and think, Hey, I had a unique opportunity that very few people get to do. But I'm very grateful for what I do, but I also know I don't get very complacent. This game can come up and be very humbling. I could be here today and gone to-morrow. If that happens, I know it's not because I didn't work hard; I can live with that."

In the meantime, during a start in the 2000 season, Detroit's Brian Moehler's last six innings of his complete game victory over Baltimore featured pinpoint control on his part. He threw only ten pitches out of the strike zone. He accounted for his control quite simply. "My first catcher was my dad, who refused to wear pads," he explained. "To avoid hurting my father, I learned to throw strikes."

During Brian's interview for this book, he elaborated that back then they didn't have a good glove or a catcher's mitt for his dad. They used a glove that was "given to me by my uncle, and it was a glove used in the sixties—that's all we had," he recalled. "He didn't have a face mask or shin pads or anything. The plate was a block of wood sitting in front of him. I tried the best I could to take it easy on him, as far as throwing pitches in the dirt. You know, when you're that age you don't pitch like you do now—you don't have as much control. I was really trying to take it easy on him, but he would sit there and say, 'All right, throw me a curveball here,' or, 'Throw me a fastball here.'

"I can remember countless times hitting him in the legs or the shins. He'd just get up, go get the ball, and come back and throw it to me." Many times, the ball would even shorthop off the makeshift plate, with a result that was usually painful. Worrying about his dad made Brian more conscious of his control, so he attributes his big-league control today to that concern for his father. Also, that training went back for years. "He used to catch me from when I was 8 or 9 years old up through college," Brian said.

"I remember always when I was in college ball—we started right after Christmas, and he would always have the first catch of the season with me." By that time catching him had to be a challenge, as his father was getting on in age and Brian guesses he was throwing in the 88- to 90-mph range. Of course, he added, "I wouldn't throw it as firm as I could, but he would still get up there and catch me." He estimated that he would throw to his dad at about 75 percent of his full speed. "He was always a sport—always there to help."

It's worth noting, too, that Brian's dad was willing to help even though he wasn't a baseball player himself. In fact, Brian said, "He played hockey. He grew up in Chicago, and for him baseball [weather] was just too cold, but he did play a lot of hockey. He told me that the tennis courts would freeze up and they would go there, put their skates on, take the nets down, and play hockey." Maybe that background, Brian joked, toughened him up for their grueling games of catch. Fred Moehler's deep involvement with Brian and baseball makes one wonder if he finally grew to love baseball, or if he played the game simply for love of Brian.

"He treated all of us the same," Brian said. "He loved his kids the same, but he helped us in different ways. Again, he really didn't grow up playing baseball. He never mentioned anything to me about playing baseball. It was just something I think he saw me doing that I enjoyed.

"He used to go to clinics with me. I was at a young age, where your attention span isn't what it is today, and *he* would take notes and come home and work on things with me. He enjoyed helping me, and he did that with my sister with her studies and my brother with his golf. It was just different for each one of us," said Brian, telling a story of parental sacrifice. He said his father's attitude was basically one of, "I don't really know the game, but I'm going to learn as much as I can in order to help my son."

So it wasn't unusual to see Fred Moehler buried in a baseball book or listening to a lecture by college coach. "He enjoyed it. I think he got more of a kick out of it than I did," Brian said.

There is no doubt that baseball was a bonding agent between Brian and his father. "The way people look at it, [they think of bonding] when son and father are always playing catch, and I think that's the way it was for us. There was never a Saturday or Sunday when, if I asked him to play catch, he wouldn't help me; he always did. Sometimes *he* dragged *me* out there. It was just that way."

Their involvement in baseball actually began when Brian was in tee-ball, at the age of 5 or 6. "I can remember playing [back then] and he built me a tee," Brian said. "I played outfield through college. Pitching at a young age is fun, but if it's the only position, it's somewhat boring. I enjoyed playing other positions, because I was such an active kid."

Brian feels that he learned a great deal from his father. "My dad was a lot like me," he said. "I don't really want attention, I don't draw attention. The way I look at my job is like anyone else's. My hours are a little different, my pay might be a little different, but it's no different [in that] I show up at 1:30 at the park and I don't go home until 11:00 at night—the same amount of hours as a working person would put in."

So, he says, there is no doubt that his work ethic came from his father. He bases that on "the fact that my mom and dad worked nine to five until they retired, and put three kids through college."

Brian Moehler is the kind of man who, if he played in the NBA, would never be featured on a cacophonous, flashy pregame lead-in—the ones that, typically, are full of hype, of sound and fury. He prefers to go about his work quietly and efficiently, without fanfare. He said of his childhood, "It was really nothing different from anyone else's, probably. I had a mother and dad who worked from nine to five. He worked for the North Carolina Forest Service. He worked until he was probably 60, 61 years old.

"They were always there for us in the evening and whenever we needed them. Everything was structured: Sunday was cleaning day, we had church in the morning, we'd come home and clean house—everyone had their chores. It was a very structured life; they always knew where we were, and they wanted to know who we were with. And we had an allowance, just like everyone else. I was fortunate to grow up in such a caring environment," he said.

Brian's love for his father is as obvious as it is understandable. He said of his father, "He was just one of those guys who was always there for the kids, always there at dinnertime, and always there for us when we needed help with schoolwork, or athletics, or whatever—he was always there. If I was struggling with something, they would talk to the teachers or get me a tutor. Yeah, I think I was lucky to grow up in such a good, family-oriented lifestyle."

Of all his memories of moments spent with his father, Brian said, "The one time that really sticks out in my mind was when I was 12 years old and we were playing in our hometown [for the right] to go to Charlotte, North Carolina, which was the [site for the] regional for the Little League World Series.

"We had, I think, a one o'clock game that day. It was a Sunday morning, and we had gotten back from church and my dad wanted to know if I wanted to go hit a little extra. So we went over to the park and we got in one of the cages—there were no screens in the cage. So he was basically throwing to me with no net in front of him.

"I hit a ball right off his face, right underneath his left eye. It shattered his glasses; he had about an inch cut underneath his eye, and it was bleeding pretty good. I thought I killed him. He got up off the ground, and he always carried a little white handkerchief in his pocket, and he put it over his eye and said, 'Let's go, let's keep hitting.' I was like, 'Oh, my gosh.' I couldn't believe it, but that's the kind of guy he was."

Although he loved baseball, Brian never really saw many games while he was growing up. When he was asked if there was a minor-league city nearby, he replied, "No, and you know what, I didn't know anything about it, either, if there had been.

"I went to college at U.N.C. Greensboro, and there was a minor-league team there then, the Greensboro Hornets, which were with the Yankees at the time. The only baseball team I knew were the Braves—that was the big-league team, and that was it," he said. So, other than the radio and television broadcasts from Atlanta, Brian wasn't too much into pro baseball. It goes without saying that sitting right next to Brian, taking in the broadcasts, was his father—although, Brian admitted, his father, like so many dads, "enjoyed his thirty-minute programs also, the sitcom types."

Brian said he did collect baseball cards as a kid, adding, "but if it wasn't a Braves player, I didn't care. I didn't even know Detroit had a team when they drafted me, to be honest with you."

Later, he said, "My first [big league] game I saw the Cubs play the Pirates at Wrigley Field. I was 11 years old then, and we went up to visit my grandmother. We went to a game with all my dad's cousins and family members. It was just something that we just wanted to do, and he knew I liked baseball. Obviously, I wanted to go—it was something I'll never forget. I remember where I sat and everything. We had a good time.

"I didn't know the history behind [Wrigley] at the time, I was just going to a baseball game. But when we [the Tigers] went to Wrigley last year, that was the first thing that popped into my mind—how I sat right behind first base in the upper deck. But now the history behind the field is much more entertaining to me than seeing a game," he concluded.

Although Fred had always helped Brian to the best of his ability, he found that when his son was ready to sign a professional contract, that was out of his league. He didn't, for example, help Brian negotiate a contract. As Brian said, "My dad was like, 'Just give it everything you've got. See what happens. Enjoy playing it.' That was basically it.

"They were more concerned about me getting my education than anything. That was their main concern. Basically, the bottom line was they were happy I got drafted, but they wanted to make sure that somewhere down the line I was going to take care of my education."

So Brian used his baseball scholarship to get him to college, stayed for three years, then moved up to the pro level. He did, however, say, "I'm definitely going to go back to school; I promised that to my mom and dad. That's one of my goals." He plans to get a degree in exercise and sports science. And if his background is any indication, there's no doubt that he will indeed keep his pledge, and not become one of the thousands of athletes who swear they'll go back for that diploma and never do.

Throughout his life, Fred Moehler guided his son, but he never became a stereotypical "stage mother," meddling in his life. "He never pushed me to the point where you have to do this, you have to do that," Brian said. "Never, ever, at one time did he ever do that. He might have guided me to say, 'Look, you might want to consider this,' but it was never, 'You need to go out there and throw 200 pitches today,' or anything like that. It was like, 'You're happy? Then keep doing it.' That's all he wanted, was for his kids to be happy.

"I think every parent wants their kids to have a better life than they did; that's all he wanted for us," said Brian.

Fred Moehler passed away early in 1995 and, regrettably, never saw Brian pitch in the big leagues. He did, however, get to see Brain take to the mound in college and in the minors. Fred wouldn't offer advice—by that stage perhaps he *couldn't,* as Brian's understanding of pitching had to be far beyond his own. Still, Brian said his father would "come in and say, 'You just had a good night,' or 'You had a bad night.' And that would be the end of it. He would always say, 'We're proud of you no matter what.' "

Furthermore, Fred Moehler's pride was simply based on his being happy that his son was doing something that he enjoyed and was doing it well, since he didn't care so much what Brian did as long as he wanted to do it. "I could have been a doctor, as long as I was happy—whatever," Brian said.

Brian also said that he introduced his father to other minor-league players, but he never took his father into a minor-league clubhouse because "there wasn't a whole lot to see. I wish today that I could, but I don't dwell on it, because it's not going to happen," he added. "I think about what it would have been like to have him sit in the clubhouse after a game, because he would have enjoyed that."

Fred followed his son's career by subscribing to USA *Today / Baseball Weekly.* They also stayed in touch via the telephone. "I'd call, but he knew," Brian recalled. "They could tell by my voice when I had a good game, or not. He was thrilled if I did [have a good outing], and if I didn't, well, 'You can get 'em next time.' He was just happy that I was happy."

Of course, the family also kept their own archives of Brian's baseball career. "We've got scrapbooks back home of me that go way back to, oh, gosh, 10 to 12 years old. My mom and dad did that," Brian said.

While Brian doesn't view his success as an homage to his mother and father, he did grant that his success was gratifying, in that it gave feedback to his parents and was a way of pleasing them. "I would never boast," he said. "Even if my dad were alive today, I would never boast in front of him, and he wouldn't boast, either." Basically, then, it boiled down to Brian feeling that his making it to the minors, on to the majors, and lasting there pleases him because it would have made his father feel good. "Definitely," Brian said. "He enjoyed watching games, and I think it would have made him very happy—very proud to come to a game and say, 'Hey, that's my son.' "

And, in fact, there were countless times when Fred was sitting there on wooden bleachers saying words to that effect. "He was always there, no matter what," Brian said. "Even for basketball, he was always there. I could see him there, sitting in the corner of the gym—he was just there."

As Brian grew older, the relationship between him and his father became closer. "We became more of friends," he explained. "We were close when I was growing up, but then you hit that stage, when you're 13 until you're about 16 or 17, when you don't think your parents know as much as they really do, but you're too young to realize that. I think as I got older we became closer, as I got out of that stubborn stage where it wasn't cool to hug your dad in public—you always used to shake hands."

Although Fred never saw Brian in the majors, every time Brian gets a start he performs a ritual that's designed to pay homage to his father. Prior to his first pitch, he puts Fred's initials on the mound. "It's just to remind me that without him I wouldn't be where I am today," he explained. "It just basically reminds me of how far I've come, and without him I wouldn't be there."

The tradition began several years ago, shortly after his father's demise. "I was at Double-A in '96, and for some reason I just did it," Brian recalled. "It just kind of stuck with me." And unlike some rituals done by rote, which lose their emotional impact, Brian puts some thought into each and every time that he scrawls his father's initials on a mound. "I do," he said. "It means a lot to me. It's not [merely] out of habit that I do it."

Looking back, Brian said, of all the things his father taught him, he thinks the most important was "the value of hard work. I sat there and watched him work every day. [With] my father and mother's combined income, we didn't grow up rich, but we weren't by any means poor. They belonged to a club, and on Saturdays and Sundays we would go out there and clean it up in the mornings after they'd had parties. They got paid seventy-five bucks for that, but that $75 went to help my brother for spending money at college."

Instead of joining his friends at the club, Brian had to work, and he worried that they would see him doing such unglamorous things as "vacuuming floors and taking out trash." He added, "We used to do that from when I was 10 to 16. I was at that age when doing things like that was embarrassing to me, because my friends would go out there to the pool. At the time, I didn't look at it like it was helping my family out, the way my mom and dad did. Now I look back on that and I think they were doing what they had to do for the family. Stuff like that made me a better person as far as doing hard work and doing the little things."

Brian said that it's impossible to sum up his feelings for his father concisely, but he tried, nevertheless. "I was very happy with my childhood and how I was treated," he said. "I respected him, but at the same time I knew if I did something wrong I was going to get punished. There was a respect there, and a love for him at the same time. I didn't take him for granted. I wish he could have seen a lot more things in my life, but it just didn't happen that way. But I value the time I had with him."

Chapter Seventeen: The Franconas

The Franconas, Tito and Terry, are from a hotbed of athletics in the Pittsburgh area, a region that has produced a slew of fine athletes. Tito is from Aliquippa, a tough steel town, where he spent the first ten years of his life, and his son is from New Brighton, about twenty minutes from there.

Aliquippa loves its sports, especially football. The city's program, which is nearly 100 years old, does it up big. Prior to a home football game, the mascot, an Indian sitting atop a pony, races to midfield and embeds a burning spear into the team's logo. Much of the football facility, along with the Indian props, is courtesy of a devoted booster club. Lavish banquets, new uniforms, trophies, fireworks, and even sky divers are supplied by that organization. Since 1985, private donors have given a quarter of a million dollars to the football program.

Famous ballplayers, such as Tony Dorsett, Mike Ditka, Dan Marino, Joe Namath, Jim Kelly, Joe Montana, Stan Musial, the Griffeys, and a host of others all hail from the Greater Pittsburgh vicinity. In fact, Dorsett's family moved to Aliquippa when he was young, and Ditka also went to high school in that steel town. For that matter, pitcher George "Doc" Medich came from Tito's hometown, too.

Tito has a daughter, Amy, who is three years younger than Terry and lives in Tucson, Arizona. "She's Terry's No. 1 fan," Tito said.

Terry is proud of his dad's longevity, saying it's not easy for anyone to last in the majors as long as his father did. "He was a good hitter," he said. He added that his dad's zenith was "1959, the year I was born; he hit .363. That was a pretty special year for him. He had been battling the first couple of years of his career, trying to be an everyday player and to stay injury-free. Then, all of a sudden, Cleveland trades for him [from Detroit] and, boom. Man, he jumps in there and just goes bananas. That had to be pretty special," Terry said. That .363 batting average was the highest by an Indian in sixty-five years.

Tito was a fine hitter, nearly winning a batting crown that magical season. In fact, his average was a full ten points higher than that of Harvey Kuenn, who did win the crown. Tito was denied the title because his 399 at bats (plus other times at the plate for walks drawn, hit by pitch, and so on) over 122 games fell shy of the requisite number of plate appearances. He didn't miss by much, coming up a mere thirty-four appearances away from the number that was then determined as the minimum for a title winner.

There were times in baseball history that a batting crown winner needed to play in just 100 games, or bat in two-thirds of his team's games to qualify. Under those conditions, he would have won the title. In fact, the Cleveland *Plain Dealer* reported that five batting crown winners had fewer at bats than Francona did in 1959. In 1956, a player needed just 400 at bats to lead his league, and Terry would have squeezed out one more at bat if those rules had still been in effect, but they changed in 1957.

"I believe between not playing at the beginning of the year and being injured—a quad pull, or something, he missed out on enough at bats," Terry explained.

On August 3, 1959, Tito's bat was smoking. He would have had an incredible eight-for-eight doubleheader, but a diving Brooks Robinson snared a line drive to rob him of a hit. Still, when the dust settled that day, Tito was hitting an ungodly .417. His average did tail off, though, because of a thigh injury, which rendered him almost unable to walk. There was a risk of losing the leg if he didn't rest.

Tito also enjoyed a solid season in 1960, leading the league in doubles with 36, and he hit .301 in 1962. In all, he hit .272 over his fifteen-year stay in the majors.

As for Terry's grandfather, Tito recalled, "He played a lot of sports, a lot of baseball, but no organized baseball, just local. He was a good teacher. Just like any other father, he taught me the fundamentals. He encouraged me very much."

However, unlike Terry, Tito seldom got to go to big-league games as a youngster. Although he lived within a lengthy, say, 5:00 shadow of venerable

Forbes Field, he said he seldom went there. "We couldn't afford to do things like that," Tito said.

"When I was growing up, Mel Ott used to be my favorite ballplayer," he continued. "The first glove that I ever owned had Mel Ott's name on it. To top it off, when I went to Detroit, lo and behold, who's the radio announcer over there? Mel Ott. We became good friends.

"I was just sitting the bench over there, not playing. At the end of the season, I told Mel, 'If there's any way you can help me, I'd really appreciate it. I'm not playing [much]. Anything you see that I'm doing wrong, I'd appreciate your help.' He would give me some tips; he tried to help me. The next season, I went to Cleveland and had a super year." He attributes at least part of his .363 success to Ott, who, unfortunately, died before he had the chance to see Tito's breakthrough year.

Even though Tito had reached the major-league level, he said that when he first approached his childhood idol, he felt like a little kid. "Here's one of the best hitters in baseball," he said. "[His help] was sort of on the q.t., because he's an announcer, not one of the coaches over there, but I went to him on the side."

Speaking of gloves, Terry's first glove had his own name on it—well, his last name, that is. "His first glove was one of my old gloves," Tito explained.

At one point in Terry's youth, he lived by a swimming pool, but he didn't want to dive into the pool. "I told him if he learned to swim and dive, I would get him [some equipment]," Tito recalled. "Terry wanted shin guards. I said, 'What the hell you want with shin guards? You're left-handed, you can't [use them].' Boy, I tell you, when I came back from a road trip, he was waiting for me to do it. And early that morning I had to take him down to a sporting-goods shop and get him a pair of shin guards, because he learned to swim and dive. He made me get good ones, too."

Actually, Tito said that his son did mess around with catching, even though he threw lefty. "He'd get back there once in a while. When he was in Little League, he'd do anything. He even pitched. I used to pitch in high school, and I used to call him a junkballer, but he was a good pitcher; he'd win. He threw a knuckleball and a curveball in high school." Tito compared Terry to a major-league pitcher such as an Eddie Lopat.

Terry is now working in the Cleveland Indians organization as the special assistant to Baseball Operations, after a short stint as the manager of the Philadelphia Phillies. However, he enjoyed a solid career at the big-league level as well. Over 708 games and parts of ten seasons, he hit a very respectable .274.

Primarily a first baseman and an outfielder, he also spent 62 games as a designated hitter. He even played third base once and, perhaps relying on his savvy à la Lopat, pitched one game in a mop-up role in the majors in 1989.

He played for the Expos, Cubs, and Reds before ending his career with two clubs that his father had played for, the Indians and the Brewers. In the 1981 Division Series with the Expos he hit .333, with two steals over the five-game series. Both he and his father are listed in *The Baseball Encyclopedia* as 190-pounders who hit and threw lefty.

Terry Francona said it would be impossible, within the time limits of our interview, to recount all his childhood memories involving his father and how baseball had helped them bond. "First of all," he began, "my dad was never, ever my coach—never, which I think people find surprising. But baseball linked us. I mean, that was our *love*. He did it for fifteen years, and I grew up, from the time I can remember, *wanting* to be a baseball player. And it's been my livelihood my whole life, and it will continue to be.

"So it linked us, and it gave us a common ground, but he was, and my mom, too, wonderful parents. Baseball was a love that we both had; we certainly spent a lot of time talking about it."

Tito agreed that baseball had been an important part of their lives. "I remember when I was playing in Milwaukee," he said. "Other kids were running around the ballpark, but I used to see him from the field there, and he'd be sitting right behind home plate. He had his hands on his chin, leaning against the rail, watching the pitchers.

"He knew everything. I never had to tell him, teach him, how to run or throw the ball, where to throw the ball. He had real good baseball instincts." Tito said he believes Terry was, therefore, always more mature than his years, and was far ahead of his peers. "I think that's why [I knew] he would be a good manager.

"When he was playing in high school, he had a cousin who was a catcher, and Terry used to tell him a lot of things," Tito continued. "But I remember Terry said, 'Dad, how come you don't tell me things?' I said, 'Well, Terry, if you want to become a good ballplayer, you've got to learn these things yourself.' And he did. Then he realized what I was talking about."

As Bobby Bonds would do years later, Tito attended his son's games, while making it a point not to be a distraction or to interfere in any way. There was a time, though, when Tito decided that, while he wasn't worried about his son, it wouldn't hurt to pass on some of his big-league knowledge to Terry. However, the message did not involve the strategy of the game but, rather, was about baseball life in general.

"I told him all the good points and bad—everybody's trying to hustle you," Tito said. "But I always thought Terry had a good head on his shoulders." In any case, it doesn't take a player long to realize that not everyone he meets is sincere, that the world isn't full of altruists.

Terry loved watching his father play. "I saw my dad play a ton," he recalled. "For the last couple of years, I was 10 and 11 years old, so I can remember it pretty good. By then he was pinch-hitting a lot, so he didn't play every day. When he played every day, I was pretty young. But I remember, always in B.P., watching him hit. I remember thinking, not because he was my dad, what a good hitter he was."

When it came to having a hero or a favorite player, Terry said, his father "was always my favorite guy, but I always kind of latched on to one guy on every team he was with. It was funny, because in Milwaukee it was Al Downing. I didn't want to be a left-handed pitcher [like him], but Al was a gentleman. To this day, if I see Al, like when he was broadcasting for the Dodgers, he's a gentleman.

"There was a guy in Oakland—it was Rick Monday, and a guy named Tommy Reynolds. I don't think Tommy was even playing much, but I liked him. Every team we'd go to, I'd find somebody else and [become] just like their shadow—guys who would play catch with you in the outfield. I was just happy to be there."

Terry thought back on how he was raised. "I knew, and I guess I thought it was normal, but I had a very loving family and parents that I respected," he said. "I mean, I went through all the normal growing pains, and I talked back to my mom—not my dad. But when I got away from home and went to college, got into the minor leagues, it wasn't so much normal as I was actually very lucky. My parents taught me to respect people."

Terry stressed that while he may have sassed his mom on a few occasions, he never dared to argue with his dad. When Tito was told what his son had said, he laughed. "You know what? All I had to do was look at him and he'd cry," he said. "When he'd do something wrong, I just looked at him, and he thought I was killing him. My daughter was the opposite way. I used to pound her on the fanny, and she'd just look at me and say, 'Are you through?' "

In retrospect, Terry said he wasn't sure when he and his father first realized that he had a special talent for the game. "I don't know. I mean, for a little town, I guess I thought I was pretty good. But everybody does. I knew I *wanted* to be a major-league player.

"When the high school guidance counselor passed out those [forms] about your occupation—what you want to be, I'd always put, 'Professional Baseball Player,' " he continued. "He'd call me in every year and say, 'Terry, you can't write that.' And I said, 'Well, that's what I'm going to do.' Little did I realize the odds that are against you—they're stacked against you. I was real fortunate to be able to realize my dream."

Tito disagreed with the counselor right away. "I could see it," he said. "I didn't know how far he was going to go, but I could see he had talent. I never told Terry much; he just learned it. I guess he thought it was the thing to do, because he was always around the ballparks. He just learned by what he saw."

Terry didn't feel that he was treated any differently from the kids who didn't have a major leaguer for a father. "I grew up in a town of about seven or eight thousand people, so you know everybody. I'd eat dinner, I'd walk down to the bottom of the driveway, put my thumb out, and hitchhike to practice. You can't do that anymore. In the town where I grew up—and I don't think that was because I was the son of Tito Francona—I just think it [was because of] the fact that you knew everybody."

As children, some future players had special memories about going to a major-league park in their area. Terry said, "Oh, man, I went to *every* field. That was one of the luckier things about being the son of a professional baseball player, because there were some drawbacks, like not being able to see him as much as I would have liked.

"I think that one of the memories [he has concerning ballparks] is the last year he played for the Milwaukee Brewers. I was 11, and I was old enough where I could go into the ballpark with him when he went in at, like, 2:00. The big thing was if I behaved myself, I could go. If I didn't behave, I had to stay home. I know that summer I did not miss one game, so that was a good way to keep my behavior in check.

"I think my dad knew from an early time that I was very respectful of the players. It's always been that way, and I'm sure I got that from him. He taught me to enjoy and respect the game of baseball. That's probably the most important thing I've got from him about baseball; not about where to hold your hands when you swing or things like that. I think he knew that I was attentive enough as a young kid that I would watch and learn and I would kind of pick up what I wanted to do."

Tito looked back on that time period and said, "He loved to get in that clubhouse. When I was in St. Louis they used to get in there; we had a lot of kids on that ball club, and, man, they'd get the candy bars, pop, and everything. He came to me and said, 'Dad, boy, this is free.'

"The old clubhouse guy would just be sitting on a locker there, just watching everybody, and keeping track of it [the costs] in his mind. He'd put it on your bill." Tito paid his tab, of course, never once telling his son the truth about the "free" goodies he had consumed so voraciously.

Terry got into another too-good-to-be-true, get-rich-quick scheme in St. Louis that would have made Ralph Kramden proud. "One time he [was with] Curt Simmons's two sons; they were a little older than Terry," Tito said. "Terry was about 7 or 8 years old, and they were about 10 or 11 years old. The kids were in and out of the clubhouse a lot, and when you come out to the dugout there's [the rack] where they keep the bats. Well, people were leaning over there, looking in the dugout. One day Terry came in the locker room, right after we took batting practice, and he had all this money in his hands, about $10.

" 'Where'd you get all this money?' He said, 'Hey, we're selling those bats out there.' Here, they were the guy's gamers. I just told him to keep quiet." Luckily for Terry, nobody ever said a word about it, but he may have learned an early lesson back then: nobody messes with a player's 'gamer.'

Tito added, "The Simmons boys were encouraging him: 'Here, sell these bats.' They were going cheap."

Tito also laughed as he recalled the time he took Terry on a road trip with him. It was in Tito's farewell season, 1970, when, he said, "we went on a two-week trip, and when he came back—man, he was just beat when he came home. But every place he went for two weeks we put a Milwaukee uniform on him. He did everything; he'd go out and shag [fly balls], he did the whole works." That even included being a batboy for the team.

"I don't think he'll ever forget that time," Tito went on. "We'd be in the hotel. We'd get in there at two, three in the morning—the poor guy. Then riding the bus, you know how the guys can be, sitting in the back of the bus. I always had to put my hands over his ears. He really got educated."

Tito's decision not to coach his son, per se, was not a case of his distancing himself from teaching Terry the game. As Terry indicated, "We talked so much, but, again, I'd sit in the backseat when they [his father and different players who drove together] came home from a game at midnight and listen to them talking. I probably learned more like that. I think he knew that I cared a lot about baseball, and I kept my eyes open and my ears open. I just kind of watched.

"I'd always come home late with my dad and whoever he had driven in with. My sister was younger, so she couldn't [stay out late]. So my mom would either not go to the game or they'd come home early."

Since players almost invariably talk shop, perhaps there was no better way for young Terry Francona to get indoctrinated into the game. "I was the only 8-year-old who knew you pitched up and in, down and away," he said, half joking. "I used to listen and listen and listen. I felt like I had died and gone to heaven."

Interestingly, when Tito was told the tale of Terry's eavesdropping, he chuckled. "I never realized that, but he was all ears," he said.

Terry didn't get to play many games of backyard catch with his dad, because "he wasn't really around during the summer," he said. "As I started getting older, that started not being as cool—you know, being the son of a major-league player is pretty cool, but then, all of a sudden, you get to be about 11 years old and, 'You know what? The heck with this, I want him around.'

"I'm sure it was difficult on him. I'm sure that played a part in his retiring, because I think he still could have played. But we got to the point where we missed him, and those are the things I'm going through now as a father. You've got four kids, and you're trying to balance your life and your commitments to work, and it can get very difficult."

As tough as those dilemmas are for him, Terry said, he felt that "it was more difficult for my dad because of the money. They didn't make very much money back then, so you had to make a lot of decisions based on financial [issues]. Nowadays, when I was a major-league manager, not that I was making millions, I was certainly making enough money where we moved my family to Philadelphia. It makes it a little bit easier to try to keep your family together."

When Terry was managing in Philly, he displayed the tenacity (with a splash of humor) that many people associate with his family. By August of 2000, his team was losing, and he was taking a lot of flak in the papers. He responded by saying, "I'm bald. I have a big nose. I've been released five times. I have a thick skin. I'll make it."

He was fired that season, but, like a true survivor, he rebounded quickly and was hired by Cleveland. In December of 2000 he said, "I came here to learn. I want to learn about scouting. I want to work with minor leaguers. This is what I want to do at this time in my career."

At that time, Tito was recovering from a heart attack. "He was at a dance for all these doctors about a month ago when he had the heart attack," Terry said. "The doctors told me he was dead, but one of them had a defibrillator in his car. They put the paddles on him and brought him back."

It's not surprising to learn that Terry said he took his current job for several reasons, one of which was consideration for his family. "Part of the reason was so I could stay in Philadelphia, not move my family. And it's not as time-consuming, certainly, as being a manager.

"At the same time, this is what I enjoy doing. I was home the first week of the season, when spring training was over, and I didn't know what to do with myself. The season started, and I'm supposed to be doing something, so it was a little different. I've always liked being busy with baseball stuff, and I don't think that will ever change."

Terry has a son, Nick, who was 15 in 2001, and three girls, who are 13, 11, and 7 years old. He says his son "loves to play." They started playing when Nick was very young. "I think every dad plays catch with their kids regardless of what their job is, but I certainly haven't—and won't—push baseball on him—or anything, for that matter," he said.

"What I wanted to do, with my girls, too, is whatever they do, do it to the best of their ability," he went on. "Whether it's baseball or playing in the band, I don't care. I just want them to fulfill their ability."

As for predicting Nick's diamond prowess and his future, Terry's voice took on the quality of a shrug. "Ah, you know, I can't tell. He's O.K. I guess maybe it's because I've seen the odds of becoming a professional player—it's such a long shot." Nevertheless, Nick is playing the game now, and enjoying it in typical Francona tradition.

A lesson Terry learned from his father was to keep a low profile when dealing with his son's youth baseball career. "My dad used to get a lawn chair and go sit out in the outfield and leave everybody alone," he said. "I do the same thing. I don't want to put any pressure on him or his coaches. I like the fact that he enjoys it, but I want him to continue to enjoy.

"I think nowadays people are making Little League baseball way too tough on kids. If anything, I'll back off. I love to throw to him, and if he wants to hit, that's fine, or take grounders, but I kind of stay out of the way."

While Tito may have tried to stay away from Terry's youth-league career, he has followed his son's big-league days faithfully. As a matter of fact,

Terry said, "He negotiated my first contract with the Expos. I didn't get an agent; he did it. When I speak to Jim Fanning, who was the guy that negotiated for the Expos, and I ended up playing for him [when he] was the manager, he laughed. He said it was the easiest negotiation he's ever had in his whole life.

"He came to the house, my mom cooked him a dinner, and it was done as cordially and as professionally as you can imagine." He said that was quite different from the friction that often goes on now between agents and front offices. "My dad knew the number I wanted, Jim Fanning knew the number I wanted, and I told my dad I needed a week's rest [before reporting]. Jim came on a Sunday, and I signed the next Sunday."

Tito explained the tactics he applied to his son's pro contract. "I knew Jim from way back," he said. "[The signing] was when Terry was ready to get out of school, the summer when he was a junior. I thought it was important that he get out and get to finish the rest of that [minor league] season out, because every year he would have got experience. If we kept negotiating, we probably would have made more money, but he would have lost a season. I thought it was very important for him to get out, so we set a figure for what we thought he would be happy with and we signed. We really let Jim off the hook. So Terry played his junior year, but he didn't play his senior year." From there it was a trip to the minors and, eventually, to the bigs.

During Terry's playing days, his folks "would always make a trip down to spring training," he said. "We [Terry's team] went to Pittsburgh every year, so I'd see them there. They'd always make a trip wherever. It would be to Cleveland or somewhere close, which was always a treat for me." Tito's idea of "somewhere close" even extended all the way up to Montreal, when Terry played for the Expos. Like any good father, the trip itself meant nothing to Tito—he simply had to see his son perform.

Tito said that he was able to catch Terry play in person during his minor-league days, too. "When he was playing for Triple-A [in the Expos farm system], I think he played for Felipe Alou. We drove down to Indianapolis, Indiana, to see him play a game." Interestingly, Alou, a teammate of Tito's in Atlanta, also went on to produce a son who rose to the big-league level, hard-hitting Moises.

Tito may have exchanged pleasantries with Alou and Terry's other managers, but other than that he wasn't very obtrusive. "I tried to stay away from them," he said. "It was his thing. I let him do what he wanted to do, and I didn't put any pressure on him, and didn't put any pressure on his managers, like Alou."

One treasured memento from those days took place in 1981, Terry's rookie season. "We got a picture in spring training that was me and him and Cal Ripken and his dad," Terry said. "They took the picture, and it was in *Sports Illustrated*. They were predicting, I think, the [top] rookies of the year.

"It's funny how things work out, because I ended up getting hurt that year, and Cal went on to play in how many games in a row? But it was a neat picture, and I have it in my basement. I had Cal put an inscription on it."

Terry carved out a decent career for himself, but he quit after three games in 1990. Still, even after his retirement from playing, Tito continued to follow his son. "When I was managing, he had the dish at home and lived and died with the Phillies," Terry said. "It was kinda neat, because I think it brought him back to baseball. Since I was done playing, he hadn't really paid attention to baseball a whole lot. Then, all of a sudden, I got back at the major-league level, and it gave him something to do at nights."

Tito conceded that that was indeed the case. "When I played my last game in 1970, I never went back to watch a big-league game until Terry played," he said. "That represented a period of time over a decade long." True, he continued to watch games on television, he said, but "going to the ballpark? I didn't get excited."

Despite Terry's success, Tito said that he always viewed his son differently from the way other people viewed him—and that's natural. To others, Terry was a big-league player or a skipper, but, Tito said, he was his "blood." He added, "I know I would get excited when he'd come to bat, when I'd watch him play. It was difficult, but it was enjoyable to watch him play."

For Tito, the enjoyment and the excitement of seeing his son brought a certain nervousness. "You want him to get a hit every time they come to bat," Tito said. "You know that's not possible, but you feel like you're in his position, you're hitting right with him.

"But, you know, there was more pressure, I thought, when he was a manager. Instead of worrying about one guy, you're worried about all twenty-five players. We're looking forward to his career—I'd like to see him get back into managing. I think he relates to this new breed of kids. I think he handles them very well. He just ran into a bad situation over there with all the injuries, and they didn't make any trades for pitchers. He'll be back soon as a manager," Tito prophesied.

Thus, even in adulthood, the Franconas were still bonding through baseball. "Baseball was just good to me," Tito said. "Everything that I have, I owe to baseball. It was very, very good to me."

He added that the game has also been good to his son, and that they relate through the game, too. For example, when Terry was still managing, Tito might ask him a question not unlike the kind of information a fan might want to be privy to. "I asked him about a lot of ballplayers," he said. "I can remember the last year [Terry was managing]. They were playing in Pittsburgh, and he had one of his players in a slump—his third baseman [Scott] Rolen.

"You know when you get in a slump, everybody has different theories what you can do. So I walked in the locker room and into Terry's office, because I was never one to want to be in the locker room where the players were. Terry called Rolen in the office and he said, 'Dad, tell him what you did when you were in a slump.' I just grabbed a bat and walked up like I was walking to the plate, and I jumped in there like I was jumping in with two feet.

"Rolen looked at me like I was crazy and said, 'Well, why do you do that?' I said, 'Because when you do that, you don't think. When you think, you're dangerous.' For some reason, he went out there that night and had about three hits."

Tito liked Terry's managerial attributes, such as the fact that he had good rapport with his players. That even included handling basketball legend Michael Jordan in the minors at Birmingham. Terry made it a point to treat Jordan as he would any other player on the field. Once Jordan told Terry that he had doubts about continuing his attempt to make it to the majors. Terry replied, "You can't quit. My dad's coming down to see you play."

When Tito visited his son in the newer facilities, he marveled at how different the amenities and the environment are from those of his era. "My wife and I went up to Jacobs Field in Cleveland, and one of the guys took me through a tour," he said. "Holy smoke, I couldn't believe what I saw. Beautiful. It has everything in the world they want there." Tito must have felt like a pioneer who had endured primitive conditions, but he was pleased that the next generation could live in luxury.

At times, while watching his son, he couldn't help thinking that there, in the batter's box, stood the same person who, seemingly just a few years ago, had been a little kid playing on much smaller, local fields. The same little kid who sold some bats, who loved being around players, and who would hitchhike to practice.

"I remember I used to play in Cleveland and we played a doubleheader on Sundays," Tito said. "He was only about 4 or 5 years old, and I'd be coming home—it would just be getting dark, and he'd be sitting on the step waiting for me to play with him and I just finished playing a doubleheader.

Terry [later] said, 'Dad, I never realized what was going on. I'd be waiting for you and not knowing how tired you'd be.' "

As Terry grew older, such insights came to him from time to time. For example, as he began to experience just how difficult it is to hit big-league pitching, he gained an even deeper appreciation of his father's hitting skills.

"They realize [such things] when it's later," Tito said. "When I watch the game now, I think the game is so hard. They always say it's easier when you're watching now [retired], but to me it seems so hard. I watch these guys, 'Wow. It's tough.' " So even a star like Tito has come to appreciate the difficulty of the game as he grows older.

Like his father, Terry said he's glad that he's been able to expose his son to the big-league scene—taking him into the clubhouse, for example. "I think he understands the respect part. If I ever got a report that he wasn't behaving, that would be his last time in that clubhouse. But I guess, like me, when you spend your whole life around it you're comfortable.

"When he walks into a major-league clubhouse he's not intimidated, but, at the same time, he respects the players," Terry said. "That's kind of the way we've lived our life. When he walks in next to a $10 million player, besides the fact that he likes being there, it's not like he's in awe."

Terry, therefore, feels that baseball has helped him bond with his son, but, he said, "Regardless of whether it's baseball or not, we would be a close family."

The Franconas' baseball roots go back not only to playing catch but also to the days of collecting baseball cards. "I did it when I was a kid, and my son did it up until about two years ago," Terry said. "He's got quite a collection. I never collected an autograph when I was a kid. Then, when he got into that, I tried to get him some balls. He's got a pretty good collection of baseballs—a bedroom full of baseballs."

Terry said of his relationship with his father, "If anything, my respect for him has grown. We're probably more friends now than we were when I was growing up, but I've always known that my dad was a good guy.

"You hear people talk about their 'old man'; I've never used that comment, that adjective for my dad, in my life. When people say, 'How's your old man,' I'll stop them and say, 'Nah, that's my dad,' because I think you understand the amount of respect that I have for him. He's a good dad."

An old Mark Twain maxim stated, "It is a wise child that knows its own father, and an unusual one that unreservedly approves of him." Terry is one of those unusual ones.

Given the intense respect that Terry has for Tito, one would expect him to want to live up to the family name. He concurred up to a point, saying,

"Well, I tried always to do the best that I could, obviously. But, again, that comes back to my dad. I *never* felt that I had to live up to anything. I've seen some other kids of ballplayers, and saw the pressures that they felt; I never went through that. I was fortunate.

"My folks tried to let us have a real normal childhood. I felt like it was, but it obviously wasn't—we traveled to different teams and were in a professional-baseball atmosphere, but I always thought it was normal."

He reiterated the importance of his father's lesson of giving respect to others. "That was No. 1," he said. "It doesn't matter the color or religion or anything—just have respect for people. Try to be a good person and usually things have a way of working themselves out."

Terry further said that if there is one thing his father is probably most proud of, it would be that he, Terry, has learned the lesson of respect for others. "I hope it's that," he said. "If he said that, that would make me feel good."

What Tito, who does appreciate the fact that his son is a highly respectful person, actually later said about his son and their relationship was this: "First of all, not as a ballplayer but as a son, he's been everything to me. He's been a joy." And *that* should also make Terry feel good.

Tito went on to say, "When I was playing ball and I would see the old-timers come around and they opened the gate for us, boy, I always made it a point to make them feel comfortable and know that we respected them for what they had done when they played ball.

"Players today don't do that as much as we did. They're in a different situation; maybe they don't think they should do it." However, Terry is well known for showing deference to one and all, and Tito says that is something he tried to instill in his son. It worked.

Tito had further praise for his son's consideration, of how Terry tells people things that will make them feel good. "You know what I like about Terry most?" he said. "When we talk, he always says, 'Geesh, Dad, I'm always running into guys you used to play with.' And I'm always proud, because he said, 'Dad, they always respected you.'

"Just like Darrell Evans—he was just a young kid down there [in Atlanta] and he'd get in the batting cage and hit the ball, but he was having a tough time with the curveball," Tito continued. "These guys [veterans] were always laughing at him, and I sort of got him aside and said, 'Darrell, don't let these guys discourage you.' Then, when he saw Terry back a few years, he told him, 'Boy, I'll never forget your dad—what he did for me.' That really felt good.

"I think that [type of helpful behavior] rubbed off on Terry. I see guys who are respectful of Terry. I know some of my guys [I played with], like

Mickey Vernon—somebody would come in the clubhouse before the game and Terry would get on the phone and call me. 'Hey, Dad, here's somebody who wants to talk to you.' That's really nice." Obviously Terry grew up to be a thoughtful adult.

In a way, Terry was always adultlike, according to Tito. "Terry was never a small child," he said. "It seems like when he was born he grew up real fast. When he got out of school, he went to the University of Arizona in Tucson, and he was just growing up all the time—he never had the chance to really enjoy life at that age. I mean, he enjoyed baseball, but, geesh, he just grew up so fast."

In college, Terry played under legendary collegiate coach Jerry Kindall. "We played together in Cleveland," Tito said. "Terry was a pretty good, hot prospect when he was in school. Then, right before the draft, he broke his shoulder. He fell on his shoulder, and they had to put a pin [in].

"My wife had kept a legal pad with about three pages of everybody who was calling [to recruit Terry]. When he broke his shoulder, the phone stopped ringing. The only guy that kept interest was Kindall.

"So when Terry went to the University of Arizona, all these other schools said, 'Tito, we thought you were going to come [to us with your son].' I said, 'Jerry was the only one who kept interest in him; nobody called to see how he was doing, how his shoulder was, and that's why he went to the University of Arizona.' "

Apparently, integrity also ranks high, along with respect, in the Francona scheme of things.

Chapter Eighteen: The Rest of the Clans

Gary and Daryle Ward

Daryle Ward is the son of former big-league outfielder and current major-league coach Gary Ward. The 25-year-old outfielder was a fifteenth-round selection of the Detroit Tigers in the 1994 draft. His first cup of big-league coffee came in 1998, but he didn't appear in 100 or more games until 2000, the year he exploded for 20 homers in just 264 at bats. A career .304 hitter in the minors, he sports a .264 lifetime average in the majors.

Daryle now resides in Riverside, California, but he was born in Lynnwood, California. He and his wife, Shannon, have a daughter, Jordan, and a son, Jaylen.

His father played for twelve seasons—from 1979 to 1990—with the Twins, Rangers, Yankees, and Tigers. The Los Angeles native was a career .276 hitter who smacked 130 home runs. His season highs include 26 stolen bases, 28 homers, 91 runs driven in, 97 runs scored, and a .316 batting average.

Daryle said that he didn't think "baseball has anything to do with a normal family bond—that comes at home, not at the baseball field. Just me being close to my dad at the house made me come closer than with baseball."

However, he then added that baseball had provided them with a common ground. "We talked about it a lot," he said "It was something that we discussed probably 50 percent of the time. He'd give me some inside tips; he wouldn't give *all* the information. He said I had to learn a lot of the game on my own." Therefore he learned from his father and from observing others. "I see some [things] that he had told me already, and I just go with it and do the best I can and handle the situation the best I can."

Daryle feels that his father's approach to teaching was wise. "Nobody knows everything," he said, "and the person who thinks they know everything usually causes a lot of problems—you don't really learn much, you become stubborn."

Gary said Daryle started "at a real early age. I think he was around 4 years old when he first started. We bought him one of those little plastic pitching machines, and he got past that real quick.

"I saw [his good hand-eye coordination] at an early age—oh, around 5," he went on. "And when he got into Little League he always had to play in a league above his, because he was a little more advanced than the other kids because he grew up around the game."

However, Gary said there were few similarities between their games. "I'm a right-handed hitter, he's a left-handed hitter, and it's not the same stance. He's totally different, but you can see in him a little bit of a right-hand approach, because it was tough for me to teach him because he was left-handed.

"He has a good work ethic, like I had, but he's a little bit more laid-back than I was. I was a little meaner than he is; I didn't take a lot of stuff from a lot of people, and I taught him a little differently as far as that goes, so he can have more patience than I had."

Like many sons of players, Daryle said that he "went all the places that I could go when I wasn't in school—winter ball, spring training, then in summertime, the regular season. We did that almost every year."

He said he was old enough to remember his father's career—"almost the whole thing," adding, "I still remember days of going to Toledo when he was in Triple-A with the Minnesota Twins. When he made it to the big leagues I was probably about 6 years old, so I've "been around.""

"He grew up around baseball; he was at the ballparks with us a lot," Gary recalled, "He would go out on the field. We would throw batting practice to him. He worked hard at it, and I taught him a lot of the things that I learned as far as hitting and playing the game goes."

Because of his familiarity with the players, Daryle said, to him they became "just other guys." He added, "I never really got too excited about being around a lot of players. Some of them are my favorites, like Dave Winfield and Rickey Henderson. Now it's guys like Jeff Bagwell and Mo Vaughn. They're my favorite players from today."

Daryle also said that as the years have passed, he and his father have become more like friends than father and son. "I think it works out that way once you get older and you get out of the house and the rules aren't being laid down anymore," he said. "Now it's just father-son relationship [but] you just talk more, like friends—like you would with your friend at school, that's how I talk to my dad now."

Gary concurred. "He's a grown man now," he said. "He's 25 years old, he has his own family, and he has to do for his kids like I did for mine."

Speaking of kids, Gary said he still remembers the time when Daryle was a child and "I had him in the cage at home one day and I asked him if he really wanted to play the game. He said yes. It was cold that day, and I had thrown him a couple of balls and it sort of stung his hands. He wanted to stop, and I wouldn't let him. He got a little teary-eyed, but he hung in there and stuck with it. That was an incident where I had to let him understand you can't worry about the weather. You've got to be able to endure it all, regardless of the climate outside. You have to go out there and get yourself ready, prepared to play."

Daryle was also like many of the major-league sons who say that after they clawed their way to the bigs they began to see more clearly just how difficult it must have been for their fathers to make it. Those sons began to see their fathers in a different light. "It makes me appreciate it a lot more, because he had it a lot harder than I did," Daryle said. "I'm fortunate to be here when I'm here because he was a rookie when he was 28 years old, and I got to be a rookie when I was 24."

When he was asked to sum up his relationship with his father, Daryle fumbled for a moment, then said, "Let's just put it this way. After our games get done, I watch the TV and see how the White Sox did and hope that they win, because I want him to do good, too. If that can't explain it, then I don't know what can."

Gary helped guide his son's career even when it came to Daryle's signing. "When I first signed," said Daryle, "we did most of the negotiating; I didn't have an agent at the time. He did that for me and kind of guided me through rookie ball and stuff like that. After that, he just kind of let me go on my own because I was a man."

Gary commented on the pride he takes in Daryle and how pleased he is with his success. "I'm real happy with that, because we did a lot of work. We still do a lot of work in the winter to make him better. I also have to let him understand that your season is made from what you do in the winter, not from what you do in spring training."

Brian and Marcus Giles

If there is, in fact, a universal need for (or desire for) sons to gain acceptance from their fathers or to make their fathers proud, then Brian and Marcus Giles have certainly succeeded.

Brian was born in El Cajon, California, in 1971 and was the Cleveland Indians' seventeenth-round selection in the June 1989 free-agent draft. He played well for Cleveland from 1995 to 1998, before being traded to the Pittsburgh Pirates in 1999. A lifetime .301 hitter, the strong outfielder ripped the ball in 1999 and 2000, hitting exactly .315 both seasons. During those two years, he also collected 74 home runs and 238 runs driven in.

Meanwhile, his brother is the opposite of Brian, in that he throws and bats righty. Marcus was the Atlanta Braves' fifty-third–round pick in the free-agent draft of June 1996. In 1998 and 1999, he was his minor league's MVP. In 1998 he led the South Atlantic League with his 321 total bases and .636 slugging percentage. In 2000 he led all Southern League second basemen, with 655 total chances accepted and 70 double plays turned.

When Marcus broke spring training camp in 2001, he was assigned to Richmond, the Braves' Triple-A team. Soon the second baseman was called up to the majors. Even though he was such a low draft pick, he quickly established some glittering credentials, winning two league MVPs in the minors. For example, he hit .348 in 1997, his first full season in the minors, with 37 homers and 38 doubles for Macon. Furthermore, in 1999 he led the Carolina League with his .985 fielding percentage for a second baseman.

The day Marcus was called up to Atlanta, he critiqued his play, saying modestly, "I'm always going to have to work hard on my defense. I'm not gifted." Like Brian, Marcus is a hard worker, and the general consensus is that the brothers got their dedication from their father.

Brian concurs. "He's somebody that raised his sons the right way, and a lot of times it doesn't have to do with baseball, it has to do with just the way you're brought up," he said. "He's always instilled hard work and discipline. And going through the minor leagues to get to the big leagues, you need that to get to this level."

Brian said his father was a man who played baseball up through his high-school days. He was a fine athlete who, Brian noted "went on to Illinois and wrestled, but he wasn't a baseball player. It probably was something he'd liked to do, but just wasn't good enough, but I'm just fortunate to have parents who threw me into sports."

Brian said his father introduced him to "youth sports and let me play." He added, "As a kid, when you start liking it, you do it more and more, and they [his parents] were an influence. They took me to every sporting event and let me choose which ones I wanted to play.

"I always enjoyed going to the Padres games back in San Diego [with his father] growing up. I really never went there to get autographs or anything. I'd go there, just sit there, and enjoy watching a baseball game. It was a good time.

"That was our time alone, just going out. You get to go to games and sit there with your dad and watch them and [have him] try to explain why people are doing certain things in situations. He's been a big positive towards my career."

The elder Giles's payback, in part, is the pride he now takes in having two big-league sons. "He's really proud right now," said Brian not long after Marcus was recalled to the big leagues with the Braves. "He was just out here a couple of weeks ago, and you can see it in his eyes. He's somebody that made sure we were disciplined, but he guided us in the right direction, and you can see it's paid off now."

Brian never had much of a chance to see his brother play during his developmental years, although his father did, of course. "Marcus and I are seven years apart," he said. "When I signed it was tough, because I went out and played minor-league baseball and didn't really get to see him grow up and play at different levels. He was 12 years old [when Brian began his pro career], but hopefully that will all change soon."

His father, however, not only got to see both of his sons evolve as players but also "coached me occasionally and then coached my brother's teams some, so he was busy," Brian said.

The Alous

Felipe Alou, a highly respected manager, was an outstanding major-league outfielder, beginning in 1958 with the San Francisco Giants before moving on to play with the Milwaukee and Atlanta Braves. Later in his career, he kicked around with the Oakland Athletics, the New York Yankees, and the Montreal Expos (where he later managed) before finally ending up with the Milwaukee Brewers in 1974.

A solid .286 hitter, he had some sting to his bat, compiling 206 home runs, 359 doubles, and 852 RBI. His personal bests included 218 hits, 122 runs scored (both league-leading totals), 31 homers, and a .327 batting average in 1966, when he also led the National League with his spectacular 355 total bases. That season he was selected as the first baseman on the *Sporting News* N.L. All-Star squad. His top season for driving in runs came in 1962, when he compiled 98 ribbies.

Born in Haina, Dominican Republic, in 1935, Felipe is the brother of major-league outfielders Matty and Jesus, and is, of course, the father of Moises, yet another fine outfielder.

Matty, whose real first name is Mateo, was born in 1938. He debuted with the Giants in 1960, and would go on to play for fifteen seasons with six different teams. He once led the league in stolen bases, with 45 in 1963; in hits (231) and doubles (41) in 1969; and won the 1966 batting crown with the Pittsburgh Pirates when he slapped the ball, drag-bunted the ball, and Baltimore-chopped the ball to the tune of .342. He eventually wound up with an impressive lifetime batting average of .307.

Jesus also played major-league ball for fifteen seasons. In 1963 he began his career with the Giants, giving them all three Alou brothers on the same squad. As alluded to earlier, it was in San Francisco that the brothers manned all three outfield positions during a single game, an oddity that has yet to be duplicated. Later, Jesus moved on to enjoy his finest season with the Houston Astros. In all, he played with four teams, hitting .280 for his career.

Finally, there's the Alou who is on pace to become the best of them all, Moises. Born in Atlanta the day before Independence Day 1966, Moises began his big-league stint in 1990. He was a first-round pick, and the second player taken overall, tabbed by the Pittsburgh Pirates in January of 1986, but was soon dealt to the Montreal Expos.

Since then, he's been to the playoffs with the Florida Marlins in 1997, advancing to win the World Series, where he hit a blistering .321 with 3 homers and 9 runs chased home, and with Houston in 1998.

Twice, in 1994 and 1998, the same seasons he was on the N.L. Silver Slugger team, *Sporting News* selected him to its All-Star team. His single-season high-water marks include a lusty .355 batting average in 2000, and 34 doubles, 38 home runs, 104 runs scored, and 124 RBI, all in 1998.

In July of 2001, Moises Alou broke the family record for the longest hitting streak. Felipe had the former longest Alou skein at 22, which he set as a member of the Atlanta Braves in 1968, too far back for Moises to recall.

Upon eclipsing his father's mark, Moises said, "They still consider my dad one of the greatest Dominican players ever. For me to surpass some of his career statistics really lets me know I've had a great career so far. I'm sure he wants me to surpass all his career statistics."

Jose Cruz, a coach on the same Houston team with Moises in 2001, commented, "The Alous are special because they had a father playing in the big leagues for a long time and now Moises is doing just as good as his father, probably better, making a lot more money than his father made. They're good ballplayers—a good combination."

And what a fine combination they made when they were together for several years with the Montreal Expos. "It was a great experience because my parents were divorced when I was 2 years old and I didn't get to spend very much time with my dad," Moises said. "I was kind of like a fan of my dad's, because my dad was a baseball player and instead of being his son, I was another fan because we didn't live together.

"So baseball gave us the opportunity to be together six years, every day and night. It was a very beautiful experience. I kind of took it for granted afterwards because I got used to it a little bit, and now after I left Montreal as a free agent I really miss him a lot."

Moises leaves no doubt that baseball helped him bond with his father. "Yeah, I've been very thankful to the game. I mean, first of all, to God, and then to the game for bringing us together."

Interestingly, Moises played alongside another relative, relief pitcher Mel Rojas, for "five, six years. He's my father's half brother's son," he said. "I am very proud, and I'm proud of myself that I kept that tradition going. Hopefully, my kids can do the same thing."

Moises spent a lot of time with his uncle Jesus. "He's my godfather," he said. "And I still spend a lot of time with him. Matty, not much, but now we are spending a little more time [together] because we go to the track together in the Dominican."

In comparing the Alous as hitters, it seems safe to say that Moises, a powerful hitter, is more like his father than like his uncles. "Matty was a Punch and Judy [hitter]," acknowledged Moises, who called Jesus a "bad-pitch swinger." He added, "He would kill the bad pitch—high, low, anything." In that respect, Jesus was typical of the old saying that a player can't make it to the majors by drawing walks. As some Latin players, dating back to free swingers such as Rico Carty, put it, "You can't 'walk' your way off the island."

Moises, who played with the Santurce Cangrejeros [Crabbers], said that coming from such a great background did have a downside once, concerning others' expectations. "To tell you the truth, earlier in my career the only pressure that I had about being an Alou was when I played winter ball in the Dominican," he said. "I was a player out of 'A' ball, playing in one of, if not the toughest winter leagues ever, and I was struggling a little bit.

"The fans were a little hard on me because I was Felipe Alou's son; they expected me to get a hit every at bat. That's been the only pressure that I had, and after that everything has been easy, because I play well. But, you know, I kind of feel bad for my kid, because to be Felipe Alou's grandchild and Moises Alou's son, they still have it coming."

Although Moises is proud of his family's baseball heritage, he says that he never really discussed such matters with other families, such as the Alomars. He felt there was no need for him to do so. "No, because I've been through it, and I know what it's like, unless I would have had a bad experience with my dad—which I didn't have," he said. "So I never shared any of those feelings with anybody else."

Now, with three sons of his own, Moises says baseball is bringing them close together. "Yeah, it does, because they come to the clubhouse after the game every night and I have to pitch to them for about a half hour. That's pretty much the only time that I have to play with my kids, quality time, because it's so hot in Houston, you don't want to go out in the morning because you'll be tired for the game. So after the games—when we win, that's the only time we have some time together. I take them in the cage. I'm working a little harder with the older one. He's 9, and he really hasn't played much, and I think he's a little bit behind and I want him to be a good player."

Mike and Andy Hargrove

Mike Hargrove was a star-caliber player from 1974 to 1985, spending only 200 games in the minor leagues. A one-time member of the American League All-Star squad, he won the Rookie of the Year Award in 1974, then went on to carry a .290 average throughout his career, while drawing 965 walks as opposed to just 550 strikeouts. Called "the Human Rain Delay" for the antics he engaged in preparatory to hitting, he hit as high as .325 once, with six .300 seasons to his credit. He even led the league in on-base percentage in 1981.

His son, Andy, was a star high school pitcher at St. Ignatius High School, a school in the Cleveland area that has a reputation not unlike that of Cincinnati's Moeller High. In 2001, Mike gave a progress report on his son. "He's playing baseball at a junior college out in Arizona, Yavapai Junior College," he said.

Mike readily understands how much baseball helped him bond with his son. "Well, it did," he said. "Andy's a good kid. He has a good heart, and that's the thing I'm probably the most proud of, the fact that he's a good kid. And I think that baseball had a lot to do with that. It gave us, from the get-go, a common interest, something that kind of connected us. I think that a father and a son especially need some sort of basic connection other than the fact that they're the same blood, and baseball certainly did that.

"Andy was born in 1981, and I can remember, at the end of my career in '84 and '85, I was having a tough time. I had been an everyday player my entire career. Then all of a sudden the Indians decided to go younger, and so I became a part-time player, which was very difficult for me to accept. And having Andy to be with, even though he was only 3 or 4 years old at the time, helped. It helped take away some of that pain.

"I've got a picture at home of me sitting in front of my locker after a game, and Andy's sitting in my lap eating a Twinkie," he said with a chuckle. "I can remember that time and just how having him around helped.

"After that year, I went down to the minor leagues as a hitting instructor in '86, and Andy was at the ballpark with me *every* day. I worked for a guy by the name of Tom Chandler, who was the manager of the club at Batavia that year, and he was very gracious in letting me bring Andy to the ballpark with me. He never got in the way.

"That's one good thing about Andy—most baseball kids grow up around the game and know how to stay out of the way, and Andy sure learned that at an early age, so bringing him to the ballpark was not a burden for anybody.

"It ended up, when players had spare time, they were out playing catch with Andy and, at that time, Andy probably threw better than half of them," Mike said, laughing.

"It was something that really connected us all the way through. Baseball has taken away the time that we've been able to spend together during the summers since, probably, he turned 10, 11 years old, when he started his Little League stuff. I didn't get to see a lot of games; I got to every game I could. When he started his high-school season, I probably saw, over his career, three games one year, and I got to see one game his senior year.

"That was the state finals down in Columbus, when they played Toledo. I came home for his graduation, and it just happened that, I think, he graduated on Sunday, and they played in Columbus that Saturday, so I got to go to that game," Mike said.

Gregg Jefferies

Gregg Jefferies and his father worked out in much the same way Ed and Scott Spiezio did. Their training paid off handsomely, as Gregg went on to enjoy a fourteen-year career in the majors, playing for the Mets, Royals, Cardinals, Phillies, Angels, and Tigers. He hit over .300 four times in a six-season span from 1993 to 1998, with a high of .342 in 1993, when he finished third in the race for the batting title.

His dad helped him learn how to play different positions. In all, the affable athlete (who now resides, fittingly, in Pleasanton, California) played every infield position, outfield, and designated hitter. His versatility continued through his final season (2000), when he played D.H., first, second, and third. A lifetime .289 hitter, the two-time All-Star hit .333 in his only postseason appearance, the 1988 National League Championship Series, as a member of the New York Mets.

The California native, an All-State high-school player in both baseball and football, burst onto the baseball scene in the late 1980s and was playing full-time by 1989. In 1985, 1986, and 1987, he was his minor league's Player of the Year or Most Valuable Player. He was also named the Minor League Player of the Decade in the 1980s by *Baseball America*.

He gained a great deal of attention when countless publications chronicled his training, his tools, and his talent. However, not all the tales they told were accurate. Stories about a young Jefferies swinging a bat as many as 100 times left-handed, then 100 times right-handed, while standing in a swimming pool, with the water offering resistance to his swings are, he says, "really exaggerated. I probably did that once or twice and *Sports Illustrated* wanted to make a big deal about it. I just ran with it, but I only did it a couple of times."

As far as training with his father was concerned, he said, "There were some things that we did, but they got the lighted tennis ball thing all wrong. They said I read numbers off a tennis ball, which is impossible. I did a variation of things like that. My dad would 'x' tennis balls and he'd throw breaking balls, so I'd see the 'x' move."

These stories also had Gregg taking ground balls off concrete surfaces to simulate fielding on slick, fast surfaces such as AstroTurf. He said that practice was actually done, but added that the main reason they did that was "when we'd get rain, we couldn't do that on the field. So we'd just go on cement and take [grounders].

"My dad would tape up balls with black electrician tape and it would kind of skip like you were on turf. So that helped a little, without question," he concluded.

During the off-seasons throughout Gregg's career, his father was still a major part of his workouts. "My dad always threw to me," he said. "Usually [for most players working out, it's] with their ex-high-school coach or their college coach pitching to them."

In his final season in the majors, Gregg said, his approach changed somewhat. For example, in the off-season he had learned to relax a little. "I get away from the game; I play golf now," he explained. "I still do the workouts—lift and hit. There's nothing really I do specifically. I mean, last year I worked on my hitting again, because I had a tough year hitting last year. I got out of sync trying to learn how to D.H. So this year I really focused on hitting, and my swing came back. And I always take ground balls, but I got a wife and two kids now, so those are my main priorities."

Don't get him wrong. As a dedicated, diligent professional, he always worked hard and came to camp ready to go. "There used to be a time when spring training was the time you got in shape, now it's the winter," Gregg said. "Guys come in [to camp] in shape. I think that's a credit to the facilities and to the players.

"People keep saying the ball's juiced, but I don't think that's the case. I think the bodies are juiced; guys are bigger and stronger. It's nothing, seeing a shortstop who's 6'3" that hits 40 home runs, like A-Rod [Alex Rodriguez] or Nomar Garciaparra, even [Derek] Jeter. That's today's players. The catchers are becoming more like shortstops; they're not the big, bulky guys—they're really the good athletes: the Mike Lieberthals, the 'Pudge' [Ivan Rodriguez], the Brad Ausmus, Charles Johnson, Jason Kendall, guys like that.

"You look at those guys and they're not real big power guys, body-wise, like they used to be in the 1980s—like Gary Carter and Lance Parrish. Now you got catchers that can steal bases. I think the guys are just getting better, I really do, and it's a more powerful game. Look at the guys, they're all in the weight room; they could be bodybuilders instead of baseball players. The guys are *big*. Players are getting bigger and stronger, and that's a fact."

Gregg is indicative of the new breed of player who comes prepared. That aspect of the game is one he learned from his father and carried out later on his own with a sense of determination.

During his latter years in the majors, his pregame preparation finally was a bit more relaxed, but that came about because his experience helped him compensate. His main method of getting ready to face a pitcher was simply to watch videos. "It's pretty basic," he said. "I just think about the pitcher we're facing and how he got me out last time or how he beat us. It's a lot easier today, because there's a lot more video. You can just go back there and look at the video. That's pretty much it. I mean, being in the league for so long you're a lot more relaxed. When I face a guy, I just think about how he got me out and what he wants to throw."

While some teams use laptops to analyze opposing pitchers in highly sophisticated ways, Gregg joked, "I think it's a new thing. I don't mess with the laptop. The only thing I do with a laptop is play games on it. I don't need to make it fancy."

He reflected back on his youth, when he spent much of his time with baseball and baseball-related hobbies. "I collected baseball cards," he said. "Just to collect them. I never got autographs. I just kept cards to have them."

Once, though, when his father took him and his brother to Dodger Stadium, Gregg obtained one autograph. "I did it for my brother when I was young," he said. "He wanted George Foster's autograph, but he was a little shy." Being a considerate brother, he approached Foster, got his signature, and promptly handed it over to his brother.

Like any young baseball fan, Gregg said that he couldn't wait to peel back the wrapping on a pack of baseball cards. "Oh, I loved it, man, are you kidding? I just loved getting cards. I had scrapbooks of cards and stuff like that."

His hero was Dodgers third baseman Ron Cey. "He was my guy," he said. "When I was real young I used to sign my name Gregg 'Cey' Jefferies. It was a great thrill for me to meet him in '88. We were in the playoffs, and I guess his son's a big fan of mine, so it was kinda nice. I gave him a bat and signed it for him."

While Gregg loved baseball as a child, by and large, he did not go to many games. "I never really had time to go to games. I was always playing," he said. "There wasn't a day when the sun was up that I wasn't out playing baseball or football or basketball. I just loved being outside—that's just how I was." That, coupled with his father's influence, led to a fine big-league career.

Pete Rose and Pete Rose Jr.

Many years ago, Pete Rose gave his young son, Pete Rose Jr., some words of advice. "I told him who to watch," Pete Sr. said. "I said if you want to be a catcher, watch Johnny Bench. If you want to be a right-handed power hitter, watch Mike Schmidt. If you want to be a hitter, watch me."

Pete Jr.—who's still called Petey by many—started the 2000 and the 2001 season in the same organization, the Philadelphia Phillies, that his father spent considerable time with. It was also the same organization in which he once served as a part-time batboy.

However, when he made his big-league debut a few years earlier, in 1997, in yet another familiar uniform (that of the Cincinnati Reds—a team Rose Jr. returned to in 2001), he paid tribute to his father, the all-time hit king of baseball.

In his first at bat, Pete Jr. took one of his father's black Mizuno bats, given to him as a gift in 1986, to home plate and crouched low, imitating his dad's trademark batting stance for the first pitch. He later said that he had saved that bat, carrying it with him for years, while waiting to use it on his special occasion. He then resumed his normal stance only to strike out.

Two innings later, however, he singled (using his own bat). Upon reaching first, he thrust his fist in a "salute to his dad." And this time his father paid tribute to him, too. Rose Sr., the possessor of a major-league record 4,256 hits, held up his right index finger to celebrate hit No. 1 for his son.

Pete Sr. had flown in from Florida and got caught in traffic, but he managed to be on hand, sitting in his front-row seat nestled next to the dugout. After the game, Rose Jr. came up to his dad, they embraced again, and he whispered in his father's ear, "Thanks for coming." It's impossible to imagine him not coming, but it was a nice, respectful thing to say.

Pete Sr. had to be touched and nostalgically elated when the crowd gave the younger Rose the chant they had been giving to his father for years, shouting, "Pete! Pete! Pete!" in unison, some 31,920 voices strong. On that day, Pete Jr., playing a position that his father had played, third base (of course his dad played *many* defensive positions), went one-for-three with a walk.

Earlier in the game, when Pete Jr. took his defensive position, he also found another way to honor his father: he scrawled "H.K. [for hit king] 4,256" in the dirt near third base. Of course, by wearing No. 14 he had also emulated his father.

Prior to the game the two men, whom the press that night would label "the bookends to baseball's all-time hit list," had met in the stadium's parking garage and embraced. The Associated Press wrote, "Pete Rose Jr. got a hug and a hit in a major-league debut yesterday. . . ." With his lone hit, the son placed the Rose family among the leaders for all-time hits by a father and son.

As of the end of 2000, the Roses had 4,258 hits. By way of comparison, the Bell family had 4,829, but their best one-two punch of Gus and Buddy produced 4,337, just slightly ahead of Rose and Son. The Bonds family and the Griffey duo each had just over 4,000 combined hits, while the best Boone twosome was Ray and Bob, at 3,098. If Aaron and Bret are tossed in, the Boone hit total jacks up to 4,372.

At any rate, when Pete Rose's son popped out of the dugout and made his way to the on-deck circle for his first at bat, his father spoke to him briefly. "Just get your pitch," he said. "Look for the hard stuff."

His son replied, "This pitch is for you." And, on that very first offering from Kevin Appier, Pete Jr. took the pitch for a strike, watching the ball all the way into the catcher's mitt, just as his dad had done for so many, many pitches.

Interestingly, before it was known that Pete Jr. would appear in the Reds' uniform that magical night, they had sold a meager 16,000 tickets. By evening's end, though, it had been a fabulous night for many thousand more. "I was shaking," Pete Jr. said. "My mind was racing."

After the contest Pete Jr. commented, "It was everything and more. Those nine years [in the minors] of bus rides, bad food, bad hotels, bad fans— it was all worth it." Experts said he endured the many debits of life in the minors for two reasons: love of baseball and love of his father. They said he had a "need to make his dad proud." At the age of 27, he had finally done so.

As a noteworthy baseball coincidence, Pete Jr. had a clubhouse cubicle next to that of Eduardo Perez, son of Reds great Tony. Those two players had grown up together in the clubhouse of the Big Red Machine years earlier. Way back then, both boys had discussed their desire to follow in their fathers' cleatprints.

"He's [Eduardo] the best friend I had when I was growing up," Pete Jr. said. "When you're a kid, you sort of expect it. It was like, 'This will be my locker, this will be your locker.' For it to come true is definitely special."

Ever the student of the game, Pete Sr. later said that during his son's first trip to the plate he did get a good pitch to hit, but fouled it off. "He missed his pitch the first time up," the elder Rose said. "I know he had to be nervous. And I wouldn't have used that bat if I was him. I would have used a bat I was comfortable with."

He also joked, "After his first at bat, I said, 'He's only got 1,142 [strikeouts to go] to catch me.' After his second at bat, I said, 'He's only got 4,255 hits to catch me.' He did all right." Ironically, the younger Rose would collect only one more big-league hit through 2000. Thus he owns a career batting average of .143 (two-for-fourteen) in the majors, in contrast to his father's lustrous .303 mark. One season, though, he did hit as high as .308 over 112 contests in Class-AA ball, for Chattanooga in 1997.

He felt that he had a chance that year to make it with the Reds, but after his first game he was instructed to sit the bench. He felt that being the son of the Reds superstar merited a better chance at sticking with the big club. "That's just not right," he complained. By the next season, he had been released from the Reds' farm system. Since then he's kicked around for more than a decade, including a stint with the Pirates, but he said in 2000 that he is not ready to call it quits.

"If I didn't think I could get back to the big leagues, I wouldn't be putting myself through this," he said. "And I wouldn't be putting my wife through this, either."

When his father broke Ty Cobb's hit record on September 11, 1985, Pete Jr. was 15 years old. Immediately after Pete Sr. reached first on his historic single, his son was the first on the field to greet him. Pete Jr. hugged his dad and observed up close how he grappled with his emotions. In August of 2000, Pete Jr., then in his twelfth season in baseball, thought back to that event, saying, "Man, that seems like a long time ago, but it was great to be there when he did it."

Despite his father's teasing about his son needing a bundle of hits to catch him, Pete Jr. said, "It hasn't been hard [following after his legendary dad]. If people expected me to be anything like my dad, they're crazy. I was never going to get as many hits as he did. That's insane. Who's ever going to get that many hits again?"

The younger Rose, normally a third baseman, has played every position on the diamond that his father did—first, second, third and left field—with the exception of right field. He says his father doesn't get to see him play often, but they keep in touch via telephone.

He also said that he hopes and believes his father will someday be permitted into the Hall of Fame. "I just hope they put him in before he's long gone," he said. "It would be nice if he could enjoy it."

Randy Johnson

Randy Johnson's deeds on the field are almost as legendary as those of Hall of Fame fireballer Nolan Ryan. He has, for example, struck out over 3,000 batters and counting (with 1,416 of those strikeouts over the 1996–2000 span, the best in baseball). Going back ten years, 1991–2000, his 3.03 ERA ranks third best. His 2,538 strikeouts for the decade also stood as the best in baseball, 437 more than the nearest man, Roger Clemens. He also owns three of the all-time top-ten high-water marks for strikeouts in a season, with a personal best of 364 in 1999 (just 19 shy of Ryan's record set in 1973). And, for that matter, he recorded 1,000 strikeouts over a three-year span, something that only he and Ryan have ever accomplished.

When the 6'10" southpaw got his 364 Ks, he finished 143 strikeouts higher than the next best National League pitcher, the widest disparity ever. In all, Ryan struck out over 300 men in six seasons, best ever; Randy owned four such seasons through 2000, for the second-best all-time total.

In a game played on May 8, 2001, "the Big Unit" struck out 20 Cincinnati Reds to tie the single game high over nine innings. When he struck out his twentieth victim, he shouted triumphantly and raised his left hand to the sky. Any time a pitcher fans twenty, it's monumental, but in his case fans had almost expected he'd whiff that many someday. Randy left the game after nine innings of a game that went 11, but baseball officials eventually ruled that he would be listed as a record holder with his 20 strikeouts over a nine-inning stint.

The three-time Cy Young Award winner, himself the father of a son, Tanner, and three daughters, had shown signs of greatness from childhood on.

In his final start as a senior in 1982, he threw a perfect game for Livermore High School. Then it was on to a marvelous career at the University of Southern California, where he had a teammate by the name of Mark McGwire, a pretty fair player himself.

According to the *Arizona Republic,* scouts had clustered around Randy as early as his high-school days, but they knew that the only people they had to satisfy in order to please (and sign) Randy were his parents. They insisted that he go on to college. Then, when he was ready to sign a pro contract, his father, Rollen, allowed him to negotiate it on his own. He did a fine job, according to a Montreal Expos scout.

Randy's former Arizona manager, Buck Showalter, told the *Phoenix New Times,* "Hitters are looking for something that comes out of a pitcher's hand that looks inviting to swing at. There's not a lot that comes out of his [Johnson's] hand that makes you think, 'I could do something with that ball.' " After one game, he spoke of how he was amazed that Johnson was still around the 100 mph vicinity "with his 120th pitch." He's even been known to reach 103 mph on occasion.

Always active in charitable endeavors, Randy has carved out a tremendous résumé on and off the field. Still, it all goes back to his father in many ways. From men such as Nolan Ryan to Randy Johnson, the love for fathers blazes like a 100-mph fastball. He grew up in Livermore, California, one of eight children. All of the Johnson children were tall, but Randy was the tallest. During the early years of his youth-baseball career, two pairs of pants had to be sewn together to ensure that his pants legs werelong enough.

His father was a policeman, and although he was strict, they formed a strong bond, using baseball as their common denominator. They would talk baseball endlessly. After Randy's stints on the mound, they would critique his performances. Even when Randy became an established pro, his father would scold him about giving up walks.

Randy first played the game at the age of 7, when he sketched a strike zone on the family's garage door. Throwing a tennis ball at his target, he pretended to be a big-league star like southpaw Vida Blue, who was with Johnson's favorite team, the nearby Oakland A's. The *Phoenix New Times* reported that when he was done with his practice, his father would make him hammer back the nails that had popped loose.

Although he was a fine candidate to play college basketball—he was 6'8" in high school—he focused on baseball, the sport that brought his father and him so close. While Randy is a highly emotional man, his intense feelings for his father probably first fully emerged into the public view when his father passed away in December of 1992. He and Lisa, then his fiancée, had made a trip down the coast from Seattle to his home to be with his folks for Christmas.

His father had undergone bypass surgery around Thanksgiving, and was thought to be doing quite well with his recuperation. However, on the first day of their visit they received a phone call telling them that Randy's dad had been taken to a hospital. There were blood clots in his legs.

Randy arrived at the hospital and, as he later said, "My mom walked out of the room and I could tell by her face that my dad hadn't made it." He added, "I said my goodbyes to him—which were kind of difficult when you see your dad dead right there. But I made a promise to him and a promise to myself that I'd work harder and do whatever it took to make him proud of me."

He told the *Arizona Daily Star* that the year after his father's death he "used it as a source of strength to dig down deeper in certain situations." All season he would point toward the sky, heavenward, toward his father, after each victory.

Interestingly, a teammate of his adopted a similar gesture on Father's Day of 2001. Tony Womack, who had been mired in a slump that began around the time of his father's death early in the season on April 22, broke out on the one day each year that is set aside to celebrate and honor fathers. He collected three hits—two doubles and a grand slam, his first home run of the year. Upon reaching home plate on the slam, he pointed two fingers toward the sky, then hung his head and wiped his eyes.

Randy noted of his father, "He impacted my career from Little League to the day he passed away. He was the person I would call after every start. He taught me you have an opportunity in life one time. You have an opportunity to throw that pitch one time. To pitch in that game one time.

"Those 'one times' have come into play a lot for me in my career," he said. "I draw strength from him. He didn't see me get married or watch my kids grow. I've often thought about that. [But] my one no-hitter, he was alive for that.

"He would be proud. He was proud. But he would emphasize not to be complacent, because there's always room for improvement." Randy Johnson also said that he feels he is never self-satisfied, that he is constantly trying to improve and "push the limits."

He added, "I learned how to push myself when he was alive. He was the disciplinarian in our house, and he instilled discipline in me." Even after his no-hitter, when he called his father from the clubhouse and told him what he had just done, Rollen asked how many walks Randy had surrendered.

Before his father died, Randy's lifetime record was a mediocre 49–48, and his ERA stood at 3.95. He even led the league in walks issued in 1992 (144). Over his next 158 decisions, covering just over seven seasons, he reeled off 118 wins, good for a scorching hot .747 won-loss percentage to go with a 2.78 ERA. Even those pesky walks came down; the year after his father's death he walked 99, then 72, and only 65 in 1995. He was undergoing the classic transformation from being a thrower to becoming a pitcher. He also went from being just one pitcher on the staff to being a true ace.

One reason he did not resist the trade that resulted in his leaving Seattle involved a perceived slight. It was written that the Mariners' president asked him how his father was—this coming after his father had passed away months earlier. He took that as a personal insult.

Randy is laid-back and loyal, though, when seen through the eyes of friends and family. The public sees a much more intense man on the mound. So much so that his mother has told him that he should smile more when he's out in public. While he may not do that, when he first steps out of the dugout for an outing, he said, he looks over to his wife and kids and "I tip my hat to them if they're there." After that, it's all business.

Randy still studies martial arts, something his father first taught him when he was a lot shorter than his present 6'10" frame. He also still gets choked up when he discusses his father or, at times, when he speaks of his four children, all of whom are younger than 7 years of age.

Tim Raines and Tim Raines Jr.

In 2001, Tim Raines Jr. (nicknamed "Little Rock" as a tribute to his dad's "Rock" moniker) told *USA Today/Baseball Weekly* that his earliest memory of baseball was when he was around 7. It took place when the "Expos had a father-son game, and I remember getting all dressed up in a uniform with my dad's number and my name, 'Rock Jr.' on the back," he recalled. "It was great. It was the best thing a little kid could ever have happen."

He also said that he would hang around with other players' sons in the Expos park. "We would make up games and steal candy from the clubhouse and stuff." His father said he felt it helped his son to grow up in that environment. "He's used to the big stadiums with thousands of people," Tim Raines Sr. said. "And I think that helps, because he knows what it's like to be here and he appreciates it even more now that he's been in the minors three years."

About twenty years after the days of his son's youth, Tim Raines Sr. retired in July of 1999, only to make a comeback bid with the Montreal Expos in the spring of 2001. The comeback was incredible on many levels. First of all, Tim Sr. had just experienced the disappointment of failing to make the 2000 U.S. Olympic team. Second, not many 41-year-old outfielders can break a big-league team's roster. Further, he had to quit baseball in 1999 because he was suffering from systemic lupus erythematosus, a disease that causes a person's immune system to attack normal body tissue. It is, in fact, a disease that is incurable but treatable.

Part of dealing with the illness was undergoing radiation treatments, along with massive doses of medication. He lost about forty pounds and told *Sports Illustrated,* "My jeans would hang off my body, like the kids today wear them, but it wasn't on purpose."

In 2000, when he was ill, Tim Sr. had his first chance to see his son play professionally. Seeing Tim Jr. live afforded him the chance to give his son pertinent advice. He said, "I spent a whole week in Frederick. It was great. People knew me and took good care of me, and I had fun going to the games."

After an aborted comeback attempt in 2000 with the New York Yankees, when he began to feel better, he went to the Atlantic League, playing for the Somerset Patriots for part of the summer.

Then, on August 12, 2000, Tim Sr. visited Montreal's Olympic Stadium, to be inducted into the Expos Hall of Fame. There he told the team's owner that he wanted to give it another try the following season. Tim Sr. later said, "I'm not sure he thought I was serious, but here I am." And there he was, indeed, back with the team that had drafted him in 1977, in their camp as a non-roster invitee—never a good sign for a prospect, even one with a past as glorious as his. Despite his status in camp as a second-class citizen, he soon became welcome as he hit .414, making manager Felipe Alou keep him on the team.

Tim Sr., a fifth-round draft choice in 1977, said that he decided to return to baseball because he had not left the game on his own terms. He said that two other factors influenced his decision: he felt that he could still play the game, and he wanted to play at the same time that his son was playing.

By May of 2001, Tim Sr. possessed a career batting average of .295 over nineteen seasons. In addition, he had 807 stolen bases, fifth best all time.

Unfortunately, on May 4 the Expos put him on the disabled list as a result of an all-out, headfirst dive into first base while trying to avoid a tag. At the time he was hitting .265 (11-for-34). On May 19, the day he was to come off the disabled list, the bad news hit the papers—an MRI showed that his shoulder injury was worse than had originally been thought. Instead of a mere strain, he had a tear in his biceps muscle and labrum.

When that diagnosis was disclosed, some writers flat out stated that Tim Sr. would never add another steal to his total. Injuries, they said, had finally done him in. They were wrong. On August 21, 2001, he returned to the Expos after spending time with their minor-league team in Ottawa.

When he was there for his final game, on the 21st, he faced his son for the first time in a regular season contest, albeit a minor-league game. Tim Sr. went one-for-three with a double and a run scored for the Ottawa Lynx in a 4–3 loss to his son's Rochester Red Wings, during the opening game of a twin bill. His son also took a one-for-three, smacking a single. In the nightcap, dad suffered an oh-for-four, while Tim Jr. went one-for-four with a two-base hit, as Ottawa won 5–4 in ten innings.

"I think it was a push," said Tim Sr. "We're 1–1. Our main goal is to do it in the big leagues." The games they appeared in are believed to be the first in modern baseball history involving a father and son opposing each other during the regular season.

Earlier that spring, in an almost Griffey-like scenario, Tim had initially played on the same field with his son, Tim Jr. Back then, though, it was during an exhibition game versus the Baltimore Orioles. On March 6 the Orioles squeaked by the Expos, 7–6, in the contest that featured a father-son one-two punch.

Both men batted lead-off, and both provided their teams with a run driven in. The elder Raines, at the age of 41, actually outhit his 21-year-old son by a two hit to one margin.

"It's not every day that you get to play against your son," Tim Sr. said. "This is something special. My wife is here, my father is here. It's a great moment for our family."

Tim Jr. told *USA Today/Baseball Weekly* that his team's general manager, Syd Thrift, came up to him and informed him that it had been arranged for him to play that day against his father. He said, "I couldn't believe it was really going to happen. It was something we had wanted ever since I started playing pro ball, so it was like a dream come true."

Tim Sr. also gave credit to agent Randy Grossman, who, he said, "went to Baltimore's front office and asked if they would work it out, and both sides were real keen on it.

"I came out of the dugout after dressing and looked across the way, and there he was in the outfield," Tim Sr. continued. "I felt so proud. This is what I've been trying to get done the last three or four years, seeing him in a major-league uniform. It couldn't have been better. We both drove in the first runs for our teams. It was just . . . hard to describe."

Tim Jr., a 1998 sixth-round draft pick from the same high school his father had attended, has, according to scouts, his father's speed (he had 81 steals in the minors in 2000 at Frederick, Class-A ball). He commented, "The ultimate would be actually doing it in a regular season game, but for now this is plenty enough for me."

His father secured his team's lineup card as a memento and had his son do the same with the Orioles' lineup card. His son also got the scorecard from that day, pictures, the ball he got his first hit with, his hat, and his jersey. "It was just a great day," he noted. Obviously, the souvenirs will be treasured forever.

Actually, Tim Sr. has been big on collecting baseball items for some time. When he was with the Chicago White Sox in the early 1990s, he spoke about his baseball card collection. As a child "growing up in a small town in Florida, I never had the opportunity to be around major-league players," he said. Then when he had children of his own, he got caught up in the card craze. "My kids are into it for the art of collecting. They get a chance to be around players. All the players know them, so it's easy for them."

He even instituted a policy concerning autograph requests that he received in the mail. For every card that a fan wanted him to sign, he asked that the fan include an extra Tim Raines card for his children to keep as part of their collection. There were so many different cards, put out by countless companies, that he felt he could help his children by making this unique request. Little did Tim realize that one of those children, who would sit with his collection clustered in front of him, would later wind up in pro ball with a card of his own.

Less than a month after playing against his son, on April 2, Tim Sr., already a member of the Montreal Hall of Fame, made big-league history when he broke camp with his team and appeared in the Expos opener. He thus became one of just a handful of men to play baseball at the major-league level in four decades, having begun in Montreal back in 1979. Not only was his comeback remarkable but, one expert said, "He's still faster than most of his teammates."

That is not the only similarity between father and son. Tim Sr. observed, "He's a little taller [5'10" to 5'8"], but I think he'll be built the same. I was probably about his size when I first started, before I got older and stronger and thicker. He plays the same way. He's more of a natural center fielder than I was, and I was probably a better left-handed hitter at the point in my career where he is now."

Meanwhile, his son did not break spring-training camp with the Orioles for the 2001 season. Instead, he returned to Frederick, where he was working on a skill that his father already possesses, switch-hitting. If he succeeds, club officials reasoned, his climb to the majors seems, ultimately, to be a sure thing. By May 4, 2001, he had already progressed to Bowie of the Eastern League, a quick promotion for the youngster.

On April 6 the Expos hosted their home opener, and the crowd of 45,183 went crazy for the man who was a National League All-Star in seven of his first ten full seasons in Montreal. Making his first appearance in an Expos uniform at Olympic Stadium since 1990, he reached base to the delight of his fans. As happens so often and so unavoidably, Tim Sr. may be creating a tough-act-to-follow situation for his son.

Still, the younger Raines already owns some nice statistics. In 2000 his 81 steals at Frederick ranked second throughout all the minors, and he had a total of 167 steals for his three years' work in the minors.

Therefore Orioles officials are thinking that Tim Jr.'s career is in its infancy. Orioles coach Tom Trebelhorn got an up-close look at Tim Jr. in 2001. "I think Timmy Raines Jr. has got a chance to be quite a center fielder at the big-league level," he observed. "The switch-hitter has some of the same problems that his dad had from the left side early, but he seems to have caught on and that has improved.

"He's got great range in the outfield. 'Average' to 'plus' arm at times from center field, and a 'plus' runner, and developing some power. I think he may not hit as many career home runs as his dad hit, but I think he's got good ability. Once again, he's another kid who grew up in the game, which is a tremendous advantage."

Trebelhorn said that Tim Jr. "didn't really start switch-hitting until, I think, his junior year in high school, when he really got serious about it. So that's four years [now]; he's still developing the swing from the left side—it's much better than it was.

"I think he's getting more confident. Early in his professional career he got a little bit frustrated because it wasn't coming as quickly as he wanted it to. He was talking about hitting right-handed only, but I think his dad talked to him," said Trebelhorn, who explained that it had taken time for Tim Sr. to be effective batting both ways.

"Ultimately," he added, "the left side became stronger. You see more right-handed pitching; you hit left-handed more often. I think if you stick with it and have the athleticism, you've got a chance to have your off-side be your best side. That happens to quite a few hitters."

Another Baltimore coach who has had the chance to observe Tim Jr. is Elrod Hendricks. In July of 2001, he said, "Well, you can never really compare fathers and sons, but he's as close as they come. He runs just like his dad did as a youngster. He's a better outfielder than his dad is, but his dad was a better hitter. Possibly he can catch up to his dad; he's a youngster still, and he's just now learning to hit. As a matter of fact, he's off to a pretty good start in Double-A. It seems like he's the kind of player that, the higher the classification he's in, the better off he will be. In the lower minors he really did not hit that well. Now we moved him up to Double-A, and he's having a pretty good year."

Shortly after Hendricks predicted that a ticket to the majors was imminent for Raines, Jr., Tim, Sr., at the age of 42, stole his first base since 1999. At that point, only he, Ted Williams, and Rickey Henderson had swiped at least one base in four decades. Just over a week later, something amazing happened. Raines Sr. was dealt from the Expos to the Orioles, so that he could close out the season playing on the same team as his son. He was swapped for a player to be named later, making the Raines family only the second father-son duet to play together on the same team in the annals of the game, as Tim Jr. had been called up earlier in October by Baltimore from their Triple-A Rochester affiliate to help bolster their depleted outfield.

On October third Tim, Jr. entered the Orioles lineup, batted leadoff, and collected his first big league hit. The night his father arrived in Baltimore, Tim Sr. was used as a pinch hitter, while his son was already in the lineup. Then, on October fourth, both men finally took to the field together as teammates, with Tim Jr. trotting out to center field and Tim Sr. jogging to his spot in left field. "Little Rock" again hit leadoff while his dad batted in the number six slot in the order. The very next night, an inspired Tim Sr. hit a game-tying home run against Boston, capping his inspiring, heroic comeback.

Bob and Joel Skinner

Bob Skinner was a lifetime .277 hitter over twelve major-league seasons, in a career spent primarily as an outfielder for the Pittsburgh Pirates. His season highs for homers and runs batted in were 20 and 86, and he walked almost as often as he struck out.

His son, Joel, spent the 2001 season as the third-base coach of the Cleveland Indians, having worked his way up from being their Triple-A minor-league manager the year before in Buffalo. There, he led the Bisons to the best record in the International League, and won the league's North Division title with an 86–59 won-loss slate. For such feats, he won the Minor League Manager of the Year Award from both *Baseball America* and *Sporting News*. He was also a coach for Team USA in the 2000 All-Star Futures Game in Atlanta.

Some experts feel that he is being groomed to become, eventually, the Indians' manager, as he is highly thought of in the organization. In fact, during his six years of managing in the Indians Player Development system, from 1995 to 2000, he compiled a gleaming .574 won-loss percentage.

As a nine-year big-league veteran, he caught in 560 contests while hitting .228 for the White Sox, the Yankees, and the Indians.

Joel, the father of three daughters and one son, clearly believes that baseball drew him closer to his father. "Any time you have something in common, whether it's fishing or hunting or whatever—I was no different than any other kid. I enjoyed baseball, and my dad happened to play. I got to spend some time with him during the summertime and it was great. It's something that the memories are definitely there, and I'm very thankful for them."

Joel looked back at his father's success in earning two World Series rings. "Every time that you win a championship [it's special]," he said. "I wasn't born yet when they won it in '60. I was born that next February, but I remember when he was a coach in '79, when they won in Pittsburgh. That was exciting; I was 18 years old, and I understood when you're competing and you get to the ultimate goal, it was a lot of fun. It was nerve-racking as a fan and as a relation. He still wears his rings. That's a given."

However, the Skinner family was never one to mull over their success, count their rings, or peruse their statistics. "We never got caught up in that," Joel said. "He was just a dad and those are things that are done on the field, but when I think of my dad I don't think of him as a baseball player; I think of him as a father."

Perhaps so, but being his father's son indirectly caused Joel to drop a college course. He explained, "In 1979 I was back home in San Diego [not in Pittsburgh for the pennant drive] going to junior college—I had just been drafted by the Pirates in June of '79, and worked out with them in San Diego Stadium and in Dodger Stadium. But in the fall of '79 I hadn't signed; I signed in December of that year. I remember having to drop an accounting class because I didn't do the studying I should have done during the World Series."

From an early age, the Skinners were a baseball family. "We played a lot of catch and stuff," Joel said, "but I was busy playing on Little Leagues and things like that. We'd go out to the ballpark when I got a little older, in my teen years, and take some batting practice and things of that nature. That was a lot of fun and helped me out quite a bit."

His father helped him learn the game, of course. As Joel put it, "Whether you're a professional or not, you're working with your dad on something you enjoy doing." However, the two Skinners played very different positions. While Bob may not have had the catching expertise to give Joel many tips, Joel felt that his father shared his knowledge with "the approach to the whole game, what you're trying to accomplish, and things like that—individual things. You're always talking about certain situations, but I think the basic approach to what you're trying to accomplish and how you're trying to get there [is what he taught]."

Joel said, "I don't know if it was the equipment or what, but I always enjoyed catching. I remember I got my first set of gear when I was 8 years old, but I didn't always catch in youth leagues. I played shortstop and pitched but, once I got to my junior year in high school, I started catching full-time and really enjoyed it. It's very comfortable for me, and I went from there."

As for his dad's guidance, Joel said his father didn't talk much baseball strategy, but "more of a philosophy and how to go about doing certain things and treating certain situations. I think the biggest key for me was playing golf with him as a teenager and as a young man when he taught me how to compete, how to battle, how to get through things.

"I think he's always been a real good listener. I think that's a pretty good attribute. I always remember my mom saying how long it took him to come out of the clubhouse after a game, just for the mere fact that they would sit around and talk about baseball."

Joel said that he tries to be like his father in those respects, but it isn't always easy. "Right now I'm trying to raise a family myself, so time is definitely of the essence, but you try and be a good listener," he said. "It's one thing he always told me, 'You can't hear anything if you're talking.' "

Bob got to see his son in pro ball during the baseball strike in 1981. "That gave him the opportunity to come down to South Carolina," Joel said. "I was playing in Greenwood with the Pirates at the time, and he spent about a week down there and saw me play a few games. Then he saw me in spring training when I was with the White Sox, when we went up to Bradenton, and later on when I was with the Yankees in West Palm.

"But the first time he saw me in the big leagues was, I think, probably in '84. I think there was an overlap in the Cubs and the White Sox. It was one of those rare days in Chicago where they played a day game and we had a night game in Comiskey. I was able to go over to the ballpark in the morning and visit with him, and then he was able to come over and watch us play the Mariners that night. I got to play that night, which was kind of a neat deal."

It's amazing how certain aspects of baseball have changed over just one generation. Certainly, the area of training comes to mind. Said Joel, "He played a lot of handball and worked in the wintertime and played winter ball in Cuba and the Dominican, but the weight-lifting part of it came in the mid-1980s, when we got our first strength coach in Chicago, and it's kind of perpetuated. And then with the studies and the education all these people have now, it's really gone full circle, where it's part of the athletics in general. It's not that it wasn't before, but it's geared a little bit more towards, obviously, the professional players. Guys are bigger and stronger. You can just look at videotape and see the different body types that there are nowadays."

Mark and Matthew McGwire

Mark McGwire, the son of a dentist, grew up in Southern California, a hotbed for professional baseball players. His family is full of big, strong athletes who range from 6'3" (which is also his father's height) to 6'8". Mark's brother Dan is the biggest of them all, at 6'8" and about 245 pounds. Dan was a football star who led his high school team to a 36-3-1 record over his four-year career. He fired 65 touchdown passes and became the first draft pick of the Seattle Seahawks in 1991.

Mark was always a big kid, but when he was around 8 years old he still had a lot of baby fat. With his thick glasses and pudgy appearance, he hardly seemed like a future home-run king.

His father first forbade Mark to play in Little League, owing to all the bad publicity he had heard about querulous, interfering, obnoxious parents.

When Mark burst into tears, John finally agreed to let him play in a less structured league. John, who coached his son, appointed him to be the star pitcher.

Mark was so effective as a pitcher all the way into his college years that a parallel between him and Babe Ruth is apparent. McGwire was a fine hurler; in his freshman season he had an ERA of 3.04 while hitting three homers. In fact, when Mark, then a sophomore, told his college coach, legendary U.S.C. skipper Rod Dedeaux, that he wanted to devote full-time to playing first base, Dedeaux balked. It wasn't until, in the same fashion as Ruth, McGwire started to propel numerous home runs that Dedeaux switched him to the status of an everyday player.

He still got some pitching in, going 3–1 with a 2.78 ERA, but his batting statistics overshadowed those numbers. He belted 32 home runs in his junior year, which was a new Pac-10 Conference record. Plus, his 54 career round-trippers set a new U.S.C. standard. The evolutions of Ruth and McGwire from pitcher/slugger to full-time slugger were both monumentally significant in the history of baseball.

Incidentally, in 1974, when John McGwire relented and permitted his son, who was then nearly six feet tall, to play Little League, Mark launched a pitch over the 175-foot fence in his first official trip to the plate—a Ruthian blast for that league. It was followed by 12 more homers, a league record, which simply staggered observers. In high school, they say he was crushing the ball to distances that exceeded 400 feet.

After college, Mark joined the U.S. Olympic team. Then, skipping his senior year at U.S.C., he became the Oakland A's first-round draft pick. Fame awaited.

In fact, in his very first season, he broke the ancient record for the most home runs hit by a rookie, smashing 49. Amazingly, he broke the former record of 38 by August 14 of 1987. Just when it appeared that he would become the eighteenth slugger to reach the 50 home run level, he and his wife, Kathy, then pregnant with a son, Matthew, decided that if the A's were out of contention when their baby was due, he would get permission to leave the team. He played in a handful of games after that but came up empty.

With one game left on the schedule, Kathy went into labor and Mark abandoned his shot at 50 home runs. He said then (and has repeated it many times since), long before he knew 50 homers would someday be a relatively easy target for him, that the thrill of being present for the birth of his son eclipsed the thrill that 50 home runs would have given him. For the record, in 1996 Mark got his 50, while playing in less than 130 games. He wound up with 52 shots, making him the only player ever to top 50 homers in less than 140 contests.

Sadly, late into the 1988 season, he and Kathy split up for good. On the night that McGwire hit his historic sixty-second home run, another power hitter, who was also a divorced but devoted father, Matt Williams, watched and related to McGwire. He could relate on a professional level, in that Williams once had a legitimate chance to break Roger Maris's record of 61 single-season homers. A labor strike robbed him of his own chance for immortality.

However, Williams also could empathize with McGwire on a personal level. In Mike Lupica's *Summer of '98*, Williams stated, "You ask me what was special about Mark's night, and I will tell you it was seeing a father at home plate with his kid."

During Mark's run at Roger Maris's home-run record, his son, Matthew, would join the team and serve as the batboy whenever possible. For instance, he was on hand as early as May and witnessed such shots as number 43 (on a day when Dad went four-for-four), number 50 (he was presented with that ball later as a wonderful souvenir), as well as for numbers 55, 56, 57, and later a few even more significant ones.

The first night the 10-year-old handled the batboy chores, it seemed as if he was also his dad's personal mascot—Big Mac came off an eight-game homerless streak and exploded for three home runs, his fifth, sixth, and seventh of the year. McGwire said he always made it a point to tell Matt that what he does on the field is something that he is doing for him.

Interestingly, just before Mark left his son for spring training, he asked Matt how many home runs he wanted his father to hit. The youngster asked for sixty-five, and did so in all seriousness. The night Mac connected for his sixty-fifth he said that as he rounded the bases all he could think about was how he had indeed reached his son's goal.

Mark, who donates $1 million a year to agencies that work with victims of child abuse, may be a physically large man, but he remains very sensitive. He said, "When I get letters from kids who have been abused thanking me for helping, believe me, that means so much more than someone saying, 'Hey, great game.' That means nothing, absolutely nothing, compared to helping these kids."

The most special child in McGwire's life is, of course, his son Matthew. In July 2000 Kurt Schlogl, one of the St. Louis clubhouse attendants, told *Baseball Weekly* how tough fame can be in McGwire's life. "I have to pick up Matt at the airport because he can't go there," he said. "That kills him. He wants to be there at the gate when he gets off just to see his son's face, but he can't do that. I was never around the Beatles, but that's what it's like when Mark is spotted."

On September 7, 1998, in St. Louis, McGwire tied one of baseball's most revered records, Maris's mark for the most home runs in a single season. What a day for McGwire. His father, John, who, ironically, was celebrating his sixty-first birthday, was in the stands, and his son, then 10 years of age, was in the on-deck circle, just off a plane that had just arrived from California. For that matter, Maris's four sons were in their field boxes just behind first base, McGwire's defensive position. There, in the stadium where Maris had finished his career, they all watched the magic unfold.

Earlier in the day, John later revealed, "I told him [Mark] that I got to 61 [years of age], so he should be able to do it, too." Of course, he meant his son should be able to hit number sixty-one, and he did—in just his 144th game, versus the 163 games needed by Maris (Ruth got his 60 home runs in 154 contests).

And there, at home plate after the landmark home run, was Matt, one of more than 50,000 people anxiously waiting to greet the slugger. McGwire hugged only one of those people, Matt, then hoisted him high into the air. In doing so, he instantly created a famous photo, a true Kodak moment. And, quicker than a Polaroid shot, the father-and-son image was etched into the lore of baseball and of Americana. He then took his son, still airborne, for a short stroll of about ten feet.

Matt had just arrived in the first inning from his home in Southern California. Later, Mark said, "I didn't see him there in the top of the first inning. I went to the hole to get my bat and there he is. I told him I loved him. I gave him a kiss. Next thing I knew I see him at home plate, and what a wonderful feeling a father could have."

Moments later, out of respect to Maris, Mac pointed his right index finger to the sky, tapped his heart, and blew a kiss. Kevin Maris, son of the former record holder, said of Big Mac, "He tapped his heart, like Dad was in his heart." Of course, he also waved a "Happy Birthday" gesture for his own father.

Still later, Mark said, "I don't think I'll ever let go of this moment. I don't know if I'll ever be here again. So how *can* you let go?"

After a while, Mark noted, "I believe in fate . . . today, it just happens it's my father's sixty-first birthday, and I hit my sixty-first home run. And my son arrives. You just can't ask for anything better than that."

The very next day he *was* "there" again, when he drilled his sixty-second homer to rewrite baseball history. He did so with his son in the on-deck circle and his parents in the stands behind home plate. Upon pouncing on the plate after his home-run trot, he grabbed his son, gave him an enormous bear hug, and shared his accomplishment and his love with him. He also shared his emotions with the family of Roger Maris. As part of his celebration, McGwire went into the stands to hug Maris's six children.

Almost at the very end of his long, special day, a writer asked McGwire if he thought someone would ever eclipse his then less-than-a-day-old record. The giant of a man replied, "I hope my son grows up, becomes a baseball player, and someday breaks the record."

Jose Cruz and Jose Cruz Jr.

Jose Cruz Sr. has a parcel of relatives who played major-league baseball. Two of his brothers, Hector and Tommy, made it to the bigs; and his son Jose Jr. has been in the majors since 1997.

Hector lasted nine years, hitting .225 with a personal best of 71 runs driven in during his 1976 season with the St. Louis Cardinals, one of four clubs he played for. Tommy appeared in only seven games over two seasons, going oh-for-two in his undistinguished career. With the exception of 203 games when Hector was used at third base out of his career total of 624 games played, the entire Cruz family is made up of outfielders.

Jose Sr. spent nineteen seasons in the majors with St. Louis, the Houston Astros, and briefly for the New York Yankees. A career .284 hitter, he compiled 165 home runs and 391 two-base hits. His finest season was probably 1983, when he led the National League in hits and assaulted the ball at a career-high .318 clip, one of six .300 seasons for the amiable hitter. He also hit 14 home runs to go with his 92 RBI, both of which represent second-best totals for him.

Jose Jr. was born in 1974, in Arroyo, Puerto Rico, the birthplace of his uncles and his father. He has been with the Toronto Blue Jays since July 31, 1997, where he's done quite well. In 2000, he smashed 32 doubles, drilled 31 homers and chased home 76 teammates, while scoring 91 times himself—all career highs for the youngster. The switch-hitter, who enjoyed an eighteen-game hitting streak in 1998, also led all American League outfielders wih 417 chances accepted in 2000.

"I'm very proud of my son," said Jose Sr. during a 2001 interview when he was coaching for the Houston Astros. "It was pretty hard for him, because I was a player in the big leagues for eighteen years and everywhere he goes people expect him to be a superstar already, even when he was a young man. But I'm glad now he's in the big leagues." He said his family is proud, as are the folks in Puerto Rico.

"The people of Puerto Rico love him because he played in the Winter League there and put up some good numbers," Jose Sr. said.

When Jose Jr. was a kid, he would hang around the locker room and dugout, where he got to see such players as the Alomars. "He used to come and watch us play in the Astrodome, and see a lot of National League players," said Jose Sr. "He was a big fan of Roberto Alomar and [Jeff] Bagwell." Jose Sr. even brought Robbie to the Cruz house at times to visit.

"Every year when I'd go to spring training we'd take my son. He became a good ballplayer, because he grew up around big leaguers. It makes it easier, because you get used to the ballpark and the players," he continued.

Jose Sr. said he didn't dwell on giving his son tips but that he "just threw a lot of batting practice and hit him fly balls and ground balls—that's what he liked to do, especially hit.

"I had a great time watching him play in Little League and high school and college," he went on. "I retired at the right time, when he was in high school, because I got a chance to spend time with him and watch him play. That's why he got better; I spent a lot of time with him and worked out with him. He was a No. 1 pick for the Seattle Mariners, so I was very proud of that and all the hard work."

He was able to watch his son play when Jose Jr. became a member of the Toronto Blue Jays. He'd watch from the stands, and it brought back memories of when he had coached his son in the Winter League. "It was my first year," he said. "I was managing him in Santurce, and he was coming from his first year in professional baseball. I gave it a chance over there, and he did pretty good."

He felt that all their hours spent together clearly helped them grow closer. "Yes, we call each other two or three times a week and keep in touch," he said. "When he does something that I see and I think he's wrong, I call and tell him right away. We have good communciation, and that's the main thing."

Jose Sr. spoke of another son who is in college. "I throw a lot of batting practice to him. I've got a couple of grandsons, so pretty soon I'll have to throw to them, so I have to stay in good shape," he said.

The Stottlemyres

Yankees pitching coach Mel Stottlemyre simply had to feel that his son Todd was destined for stardom. By Todd's senior year at Davis High School in Yakima, Washington, he had posted an untarnished record of 10–0, with an equally impressive ERA of 0.72. In his freshman year at college (University of Neveda–Las Vegas) he hardly skipped a beat, going 10–4. Two years later, he was drafted by the Toronto Blue Jays.

Now he has gone on to win 138 big-league games, making him and his dad the only father and son pitching twosome to both reach the century mark in victories. Plus, he and his dad own a combined total of 302 wins through 2000, the most ever by a father and son. For that matter, only the Stottlemyres and two other families, the Bagbys and the Trouts, had two pitchers appear in postseason play.

Todd, who once struck out fifteen big-league batters, has been active in charity work, such as contributing both his time and his money to the search for a cure for leukemia and other forms of cancer. *Sporting News* was so impressed with him that it named him to a list of the top 99 "Good Guys in Sports." In 2000, he won the Branch Rickey Award for his contributions to his community, for his high ethical standards, and for being a strong role model. He had donated $1 million to the fight against leukemia, and even began a fund to help a 10-year-old girl who was in need of a bone-marrow transplant.

Clyde Wright said that when he looks at Todd "you can tell that's a chip off the old block. I played against Mel for quite a few years, and when you see them side by side they look alike." Mel stood 6'1", at around 180 pounds, while Todd, as is typical of the next generation, is proportionally bigger at 6'3", 200. Comparisons can go beyond that, as both are right-handed pitchers who also share similarities in their approach to the game, not the least of which is their dedication and determination.

Wright said Mel appeared to him to be "more composed inside [than Todd]." As for Todd, "he seems a little bit tougher on the outside. He would let his feelings kind of show."

In March of 2001, *USA Today*'s cover story for its sports section featured the Stottlemyres. At that time Mel, 59 years of age, who had been ill for some time, was finally declared cancer-free by his doctors. His immune system had recovered and he had regained some of his lost energy. Todd, then 35, was quoted as saying, "Now, if he gets a cold, he's going to be like everyone else. He's allowed to get one. If he does, his body will fight it, just like mine would." For the first time in two years, father and son could converse on the phone without discussing cancer.

That was a huge relief for a family that had suffered from the death of Jason, Todd's brother, who had died of leukemia in 1981 at the age of 11. Further, Mel's brother Keith had died of a brain tumor in October of 2000, on the night the Yankees were clinching their third straight World Series title.

"Phone conversations are normal," Mel said. "They start out with everyday stuff instead of 'How are you feeling?' I appreciate my job, and life in general, so much more. I want people to know that there is life after cancer." He contracted a form of blood cancer that forced him to leave the Yankees in late 2000 to begin chemotherapy. The treatment that he underwent left him bloated and caused him to lose his hair, but by 2001 he looked fine.

Todd told writer Mel Antonen, "My dad is the most remarkable human being I've ever been around. To watch him battle for his life made it easier for me to endure the pain to play baseball. The things Pops has gone through allowed me to look at things differently. The things I battled—there was no comparison to what he was going through." He was referring, in part, to a rotator-cuff injury, which first hit him in May of 1999.

He also had to be thinking of how difficult it had been for him to pitch in 2000 with his dad fighting for his life. "I'd wonder, Am I in the right spot? Where am I supposed to be? I was always negotiating with myself. There were so many times I wanted to get on a plane and be with him."

In fact, in September of 2000, shortly before a scheduled start, Todd decided to take the long trip to New York to visit with his father. Reporters wondered if he had any qualms about his decision—if the trek would affect his pitching. Todd responded, "I wouldn't do anything differently." The public was impressed with the fact that he put his father's health ahead of everything else, including his own career.

A month earlier he told the press, "He's fighting for his life, and I'm fighting for my next start. They don't seem to balance out."

When Mel first decided to tell the public about his condition, he gave Todd a call. Todd, who was going to pitch the next day, recounted their conversation. He said, "I could hear a crack in Dad's voice, but the last thing he said was, 'Win one for Dad tomorrow.' I sat in my car and cried and cried and cried. I wanted to go inside and take that cancer right out of him." What he did do was win the next night—for Pops.

Late that year, when Todd got a start against the Phillies, his father made the trip to see him throw. Mel sat next to his son's dugout and got to witness Todd's first big-league home run.

"I'd never done that before," Todd said. "I had never even come close. And he [his father] said that was one of his best days in baseball. With all his accomplishments—a World Series, five-time All-Star, three 20-win seasons—that means something."

After Mel had a stem-cell transplant performed, Todd flew to New York, where he stayed with his father, flying out only to join his team when it was his turn to start. One had to believe that he got the dedication to join his teammates from his father.

Although Todd politely refused to be interviewed for this book, it was understandable. He explained that he was simply drained when it came to discussing his father's condition. Meanwhile, his father officially resurfaced with the Yankees right after they broke camp in Florida. He not only returned as their pitching coach after his bout with multiple myeloma (that was diagnosed in April of 2000) but he also took to the mound once more, throwing out the ceremonial first pitch at the Yanks' home opener on April 2, 2001.

Fittingly, his catcher for the event was former All-Star receiver and current Yankees manager Joe Torre, who said, "I had tears in my eyes. It was not easy to catch, especially because I knew he was emotional on the mound."

Mel has been around the game a long time and has been through a great deal. He pitched as a Yankee from 1964 to 1974 and had served as a pitching coach for the New York Mets from 1984 to 1993 before settling in with the Yankees as a respected and well-liked coach.

Not long after the worries about his father's health diminished around the time his dad reported to spring training, which also happened to be a few days after a story concerning him and his father appeared in *USA Today*, Todd got bad news about his own health. In March of 2001, he had to stop working out in Arizona's spring-training camp. His shoulder was sore again, and when the source of the pain was discovered, there was little wonder that it hurt. He had been trying to pitch with a torn rotator cuff and an irritated labrum.

As gutsy as Todd is, this injury put a crimp in his play. In fact, on June 8 it was announced that Arizona was shutting him down for the season. Another "minor surgery" was required, and this time it was declared that the 36-year-old right-hander would need up to nine months to fully recover. One report said this latest setback could mark the end of his career. By that point, Todd realized that even if that eventuality came to pass, there is still life after baseball—for him and, thank goodness, for his father.

Mookie and Preston Wilson

Preston Wilson, the star outfielder of the Florida Marlins, signed a five-year, $32 million contract in the spring of 2001. His father, Mookie, was also an outfielder, having enjoyed a long and productive career with the New York Mets and the Toronto Blue Jays, and is now the Mets' first-base coach.

Shortly after Preston signed his contract, his mother Rosa reflected, no doubt in jest, "We really wanted a doctor or lawyer, but we're extremely happy now." All kidding aside, what parent wouldn't be pleased that his or her son was financially set for life?

Tragedy struck the Wilson family, though, in 2001 when Preston's infant son, Preston Wilson V, passed away. The child died on July 23, just ten days after being born three months premature. The baby weighed 1.6 pounds and was immediately placed in an incubator, which was hooked up to various monitors and was "entangled in breathing and feeding tubes," according to the Associated Press. "Wilson was by his side constantly, staying overnight at the hospital and never leaving the intensive-care unit for more than six hours at a time," the press release added. At that time, there seemed to be hope for the baby's survival.

Wilson "talked to his son, sharing stories and telling him all the things he wanted to teach him when he got older." He was quoted as saying, "The first couple of days you have the joy of just having a child and you don't really take in the full magnitude of the problems that he had. Each time

I would go and see all the machines and the doctors and nurses, I think it got tougher and tougher."

After the baby's death, Preston left the Marlins to grieve. "There were some moments when I didn't want to leave my house, much less think about playing," he said later. "I didn't want to get dressed, I didn't want to shower, I didn't want to do anything."

He finally came back to the team and, during the weekend of August 10, crushed two home runs. On each occasion, he crossed home plate and looked toward the sky. He then raised his right hand high above his head and extended all five fingers as a tribute to Wilson V.

Although Preston was still in mourning at the time of our interview, he said, "It's one of those things that you go through, where you say, 'If I can make it through that, I can make it through anything.' I had to bury my son. I don't think there's anything tougher than that."

Ellis and Christopher Burks

Ellis Burks is so quiet and unassuming that he is often overlooked. A fine hitter, he has chalked up a career batting average of .293 while pounding out 285 homers and driving in 1,012 runs. Playing for the Red Sox, White Sox, Rockies, Giants, and Indians, he has hit as high as .344 on two occasions, and has reached the 40 home-run plateau with a career RBI best of 128. In 2000, he played in just 122 games yet drove in 96 and homered 24 times. An All-Star twice, he also owns a Gold Glove as an outfielder.

As recently as 1996, he joined the coveted "30–30 Club," stealing 32 bases while powering 40 home runs. That was also the glittering season in which he led the league in runs scored, with 142. It was also his only 200-hit season (he ended with 211 safeties).

Ellis, born in 1964 in Vicksburg, Mississippi, has recently continued to be productive despite having to play with achy, rusting knees. The 1983 first-round pick of the Red Sox (as the twentieth overall selection), he is a two-time All-Star who was named to the postseason All-Star team twice by *Sporting News*. Not only that but he owns two Silver Slugger Awards as well.

Though he now resides with his family in Englewood, Colorado, Ellis graduated from high school in Texas (Everman High), where he earned All-Region honors as both a shortstop and a pitcher during his senior season. In junior college, he gained All-State honors as an outfielder.

The Cleveland Indians were delighted that he signed with them for the 2001 season. Coming off a disheartening season in 2000, when the Indians failed to make the postseason—something rare of late for them—Cleveland's management wanted a proven veteran with a big stick. On November 20, 2000, they signed Ellis through 2003, with a club option for 2004. The thirteen-year vet stands 6'2" and weighs in at 205 pounds. He is clearly a powerful man, just as he is also a tender father.

Ellis refuses to allow baseball to take him away from his family. He has four children, three of whom are daughters. His son, Christopher Ellis, was born in 1994. Later, at the age of 6, Christopher became one of a group of children known as "the Clubhouse Kids," who helped players out when Ellis spent his final season, 2000, with the San Francisco Giants. In fact, almost all of the helpers that year at the beautiful, spanking-new Pacific Bell Park were relatives of players or front-office workers. Their chores included retrieving balls, bats, and gloves for the players; giving extra balls to the umpires during games; placing the resin bag on the mound prior to each contest; and delivering goodies such as sunflower seeds and drinks to bench personnel while games were played.

Ellis explained how it all began: "Well, actually, when I came to San Francisco in a trade in '98 it had already been a thing to do out there—those guys had been bringing their sons to the ballpark: Barry Bonds, Dusty Baker after he had his son, and Mark Gardner. As long as it was under control, it was fine with the management and, of course, the front office."

Ellis was determined have his son around, and when he left the Giants, he couldn't help wondering what his future team's attitude toward the family would be.

"Once I signed here [in Cleveland], it was just one of those things [having his son as a batboy] I wanted to continue to do and I didn't say anything or mention anything to the Indians about that's what I liked, but they just had Christopher's jersey in the locker beside mine when I came in to visit the Indians," he said. "I thought that was very nice." He alluded to a trip he made to town when he was considering making the Indians the team he'd sign with as a free agent for the 2001 season.

"They had told me that they had seen Christopher quite a bit on television. That was a big part of it [why he chose the Indians]. Of course, I like the family atmosphere that they have here, and I like the fact that they appreciated the hard work that I do. And, of course, I appreciated any club that allowed my son or a family member of mine to be at this ballpark, because a lot of clubs don't allow that. You know what? I thought San Francisco was the only one [allowing it], because I've been around quite some time and I've never seen a kid actually in the dugout unless he was old enough perhaps to be the batboy, like my son.

"He's six now [in 2001], but he knows exactly what he has to do as far as giving the umpire the balls, taking equipment on the on-deck circle, taking it off, getting the bats, whatever. It's not just like a little nursery that we're holding down here."

Ellis feels that his son can handle the tasks, as "he's mature, he watches other kids." He added, "When he didn't get an opportunity to be the batboy, he watched the other kids and I told him, 'If you want to be the batboy one day you're going to have to do these things.' Of course, he has fun with the other players on the team, but he knows his job is to go out here and do certain things on the field."

Christopher also began to know fame by 2001. The local papers and television broadcasts had played up the father-son angle so much that Indians fans recognized Christopher when he was in town. As a matter of fact, the young daughter of a season ticket holder requested his autograph. He consented, and in true big-league fashion, signed a bat "Chris 23." The "23" represented the uniform number worn by his dad.

"He started signing autographs last season," Ellis said. "At first he signed them 'Christopher,' but it nearly took up the whole ball. I told him to go with 'Chris,' and he has."

Ellis said being allowed to be around his son is "definitely a plus to me. I knew they have batboys that they hire, but, of course, that was one of the things that I asked—if my son could perhaps be the batboy on occasion. Not every day, but whenever he's in town and wants to come out to the park. 'Yeah,' they said. 'No problem.' And, like I said, it's a controlled issue. It's not like he's out running around all over the place or we're changing diapers."

Ellis said his two main reasons for having Christopher work at the park were to give his son a chance to have a unique experience, one Ellis never had, and the fact that he simply likes having his son around. "Even if I have a bad game, he's still going to be there," Ellis said.

The Giants' manager, Dusty Baker, who had his seventeen-month-old son at the park for home games in 2000, agreed. "They jack me up, the whole team," he said. The kids are the most enthusiastic cheerleaders around. Baker did insist, though, that the children be in uniform, pay attention, and have their fathers hold them accountable. Naturally, he wanted no youngster injured.

Christopher said there was only one drawback to his job: "People curse a lot. I cover my ears." When things get bad and a player throws a temper tantrum, some of the children, such as Barry Bonds's son Nikolai, said they hide out in the bathroom. Nikolai pointed out, "It's the only safe place."

On May 11, 2001, Christopher, who was still going to school in Colorado, got a chance to visit his father, who was now playing as a member of the Indians, for a weekend in Cleveland. He was permitted to serve as the batboy for a three-game set versus the Tampa Bay Devil Rays. In the first contest, he brought his father good luck, as Ellis smacked a three-run homer, a two-run single, and lofted a sacrifice fly good for six runs driven in, just one shy of his all-time personal best. A Cleveland reporter wrote, "Father and son combined to steal the show . . . [Christopher] delighted the rain-soaked crowd of 42,009 by zipping around, picking up bats and helmets. He is not much taller than his dad's bat."

"He told everyone that he was his dad's good-luck charm," Ellis said. "He had quite a winning record [last year as a batboy]. He's all over the bench, but he knows his job. He did it all last year. Management is friendly as long as he knows what he's doing."

The next day a picture of Chris running off the field while carrying his dad's bat appeared on the front page of the Cleveland *Plain Dealer*. Later that day, the luck generated by Ellis's personal batboy continued unabated. Ellis connected for another three-run homer, a double, and four more runs batted in, again leading the Indians to a win. Indians manager Charlie Manuel joked, "Christopher can stick around for a while if he wants. Heck, we might even let him hit."

Ellis also pointed out another plus of having his son working for the team. "You don't want to run a nursery, but it's good for us to have our boys close as long as they help out with the bats and balls in the clubhouse," he said. "It also helps because the guys clean up their language when the kids are around."

Ellis said baseball is great for him as a way to bond with his son and spend extra time with him, too. "My son was born in '94 and I just wanted to stick around long enough so he could watch me play at some point. That's happening, and I'm very proud of that. I'm glad that he has the opportunity to watch me play and he can go and tell his friends, 'You know, my dad plays for the Cleveland Indians.' And maybe that will inspire him to perhaps, not necessarily be a ballplayer but just to be successful in life and to have his kids be able to come to his job and appreciate it."

While many of the sons of players from an earlier era never got to see their fathers perform, Ellis's case is different. First of all, his son is seeing him as an active player. However, even if his memories of his father should fade with time, today's generation can rely on reel after reel and cassette after cassette of footage to capture athletic feats.

Ellis agreed. "With today's technology, he's definitely going to be able to see me play and witness it firsthand," he said. "Video and DVD, that's fine and everything, but to actually be there is awesome for him. He loves it. He really thinks he's a part of the team, which I'm not one to tell him that's he's not. He's a part of it as long as I'm here."

Ellis understands that his son can't fully appreciate everything he sees, though. For instance, if his father drives in 100 runs, Christopher has no grasp that the 100 plateau is considered special in baseball. However, he does realize that a home run is important. Further, as Ellis said, "Every time that he's come, he's always predicted that I hit a homer and it's happened nine out of ten times. I think there's something to it."

There must have been something to it the weekend Ellis went wild with the bat against Tampa Bay. "That was one of those things that happened, Ellis explained. "You know, you're bound to get hot sooner or later and that was my time, and hopefully I'll get hot a few more times this summer."

He said it wasn't a case of getting overly pumped up because his son was in town, since he tries to stay on an even keel throughout the long season. "I know exactly what I have to do each and every day, but, like I say, I'd like to do something well just to see him react and to see what he says to me."

Christopher had a chance to react shortly after his dad uttered those words. If there was any doubt about Christopher's being a good-luck charm, it was dispelled on June 19. Once again Christopher, just five days short of his seventh birthday, served as batboy, and once again Ellis clicked—this time hitting three home runs, a career first for him.

He was greeted at home plate each time with a high five. Ellis told reporters, "He treated it as no big deal. When we got home, though, he ran upstairs to tell his mom [Dori] that I hit three home runs. He was excited."

Ellis concluded, "He knows I go out there and have fun, I love to play and he just comes out to watch me. And he's one of my biggest supporters."

Chapter Nineteen: My Boys and Me

I have so many memories of baseball and my boys, I'm afraid I'll have to ramble as I relate what is, to me of course, the most important chapter of all.

When my boys were young (Sean is now 26 and Scott is nearly 22), we constantly played baseball, often in our 30'-by-60' backyard. That was during the days before their slugging prowess grew to the point where they began pelting a neighbor's aluminum siding with a soft "baseball" that was, however, hard enough to cause a resounding ping every time it struck the house. The ping was soon followed by an irate "What are you kids doing?" I guess I qualified as an overgrown kid; I know I felt like one when the grouchy neighbor reprimanded us.

We always felt that we instantly knew when one of our backyard players had progressed to star status. That moment took place when he was able to launch a towering drive onto—and later gain the superstar strata, over—the roof of our house. That elusive target was the very same roof that loomed above the White Monster in center field. Our "monster" was simply the house's back facade—balls hit off that surface could take crazy hops—Fenway, we felt, had nothing on our ballpark. To us, propelling a ball over the roof, that far and that high, was a sort of "coming of (baseball) age" ritual. And, while the street the ball landed on didn't have a name as romantic as Wrigley's Sheffield and Waveland or Fenway's Lansdowne, a shot onto Tenth Street remained a pretty good poke.

273

As a boy, I loved what I called Spinner Baseball. It was actually Ethan Allen's All-Star baseball game (I think that's the exact title), and it involved placing small paper disks over a stabilizing piece of cardboard. Players would flick a spinner, which would come to rest over a numbered area of the disk. The number that the pointer landed on corresponded with a code: "1" was a home run and "7" was a single, for instance. On, say, Babe Ruth's disk, the numeral "1" was huge, taking up the percentage of the 360 degrees of the disk that matched his home-run percentage.

It was a very authentic game, and I shared my love of it with my sons. As a kid I had even played out a six-team league, 162-game schedule, keeping exhaustive stats. Suspiciously, when the spinner landed near the line that separated, say, the home run from a fly-out, when a player I liked was up, he "got the call" his way.

Times changed, and Scott rolled on through an entire season, playing out the schedule of a team on his handheld video game, Game Gear. When PlayStation came along, it wasn't unusual to see Sean or Scott in the midst of a full 162-game haul.

We even played a computer baseball game that was based on managerial moves rather than on simply hitting the ball that appeared on the screen. Scott said that the opportunity to manage, say, the 1927 Yankees of Babe Ruth versus the 1957 Braves of Hank Aaron actually taught him some baseball strategy.

I would sit there and make comments, such as "We shouldn't steal with our runner already in scoring position," and Scott would soak up this information, quicker and better than I had ever imagined. It wasn't until we discussed this chapter of the book that he told me this story from his childhood.

Baseball had entered the age of technology for Sean and me by the 2000 baseball season. It was then that we joined forces to "operate" a team in a fantasy baseball league over the Internet. We researched players diligently, drafted our team, kept tabs on our progress, and made moves throughout the long season. To be honest, he often made wiser moves than I did.

Baseball continues to strengthen our already strong relationship. Even though he is a grown-up, we still find baseball, in many venues, to be a bonding agent in our lives, as powerful as epoxy. The same holds true, of course, for Scott, but he never got into fantasy baseball.

Still, looking back, once more I think most of my fondest baseball memories of my sons and me come from the endless summer afternoons spent playing the game not on a TV screen but in the yard. My wife and I didn't mind that our summer schedule of backyard games ruined the lawn. Four bare spots marked where the bases were, and they remained visible in our back yard long after our last game of mushball was played many years ago.

That calls for an explanation—for several years we played our entire season using a mushball (a ball about the size of a baseball but with nothing inside but air, making it softer). It wouldn't carry as far as a baseball, which made it more suitable for our games.

Once, we allowed the grass to grow fairly high, then cut a swath to represent the baseline. Scott even took to mowing the grass in patterns, the way major-league groundskeepers do. At other times, when it came to playing Wiffle ball in the front yard, we drew foul lines on the driveway, which was adjacent to the yard, using blackboard chalk. Another time we added a nice touch by laying down two lines of Gold Medal flour for foul lines in the backyard.

Our front yard still has a small patch of dirt (the grass never grew back) for our pitchers' mound, as we still play an occasional game now and then, though my "boys" are now young men. Although I've reached the half-century plateau, my sons and I still enjoy those times when we dig out the good ol' thin, yellow Wiffle-ball bat.

When they were young, I felt it was necessary for me to keep the games competitive. I would either not play my hardest or impose some other sort of restriction on myself, such as batting the opposite of the way I naturally do. Now it's become a poor-old-dad situation. Hand-eye coordination shot, it is I who need the handicap. The boys graciously (well, grudgingly at first) consented to allow me four outs. Even that isn't enough. I usually get pounded by a decidedly lopsided score. On the rare occasion when I win, I tease my sons with a Homer Simpson–like, "In your face."

Being accurate was also very important to us when we played our games in the yard, and we'd rattle off lineups of major-league teams as we came to bat, often turning around and batting the opposite of our natural way of hitting to emulate the real player.

We also played a game that I had played when I was a young boy called stoop ball. It involved taking a rubber ball or a tennis ball and throwing it off our back steps. The fielder had to catch the ball for an out. If he dropped it or the ball evaded him, it was a hit. The amount of bases the hit was worth depended on our elaborate ground rules. A ball that took a fly-ball trajectory into our aboveground swimming pool was, naturally, a home run. That reminded me of Parc Jarry, the first field the Expos played on during my late teens.

Years later, Scott was still playing stoop ball, sometimes on his own, even through his high school years. He said it helped him develop the quick hands he'd need to play the hot corner. To intensify his drill, he would stand about two strides away from the steps, hurling the ball against different levels. It was as if he were playing pepper by himself.

Another game we all loved was one we dubbed Rob-a-Homa. I probably got the idea for the name from the name of the Braves' mascot, Chief Noc-a-Homa. I remember watching him on TV and often passed such lore on to my sons. When Tom Kennedy told me how his son Adam loved to play a game in which he'd dive into a bush after a thrown ball to snatch it for outs, our countless games of Rob-a-Homa came back to me.

In our case, I'd lob high flies toward a six-foot-high wooden fence that separates our property from our neighbor's. I'd mix in some grounders, announce the game, the batters, number of outs, and so on, and my sons would leap high in an effort to steal homers from imaginary opponents. Of course, when they got taller, I'd have to throw the ball progressively higher. Also, I seemed to notice that when Scott's favorite team trailed in our games, he didn't seem to soar so high to rob their homers; somehow, the Braves won more than their share of contests. That, too, was reminiscent of my cheating days as a kid playing Spinner Baseball or, admittedly, even when I had played stoop ball alone.

As boys, both Sean and Scott collected everything from cards to stickers to special pictures of baseball teams' logos. Sean would spend hours with me, ranking which ones we thought were the prettiest. We loved the Braves and the Cardinals the best. When I wasn't home and Sean, as a preschooler, was alone with my wife, Nancy, he'd get her involved, grilling her for hours about which logo she liked better. "Mom, Atlanta or Pittsburgh? The Cubs or the Phillies? Which one, Mom, which one?" While she didn't really care, she endured his barrage of queries as patiently as any non-fan could.

One night Nancy and I left Sean with his grandmother, Pearl Panich, who lived in Monessen, about an hour from Three Rivers Stadium in Pittsburgh. We went to the game and decided to surprise Sean (Scott was then an infant) by buying him a batting helmet of a team he liked. We got home too late to give it to him, so we placed it on the bed beside him. The next morning, as if it were a mini-Christmas, he opened his eyes and was delighted to get his unexpected gift.

When Sean was around 4 years old, he and his mother came to a game I was coaching at Southview High School in Lorain, Ohio. After the game, my players took a liking to my young son, and my catcher helped Sean don his gear. It's an image I can still conjure up with ease. The bottom of the chest protector scraped the ground as Sean waddled, encumbered, too, by the shin guards, which measured at least half his height. Of course, the mask flopped around, but that was fine, because that was just about all Sean could do—flop around (and giggle).

Little did I know, but both sons would wind up playing for the Southview Saints. I regret the fact that by then I had been transferred to Whittier Junior High School, so I never got to coach my boys at the high-school level.

While I've said that we loved playing our games outside our house, there came a time when they were halted with the suddenness and ugliness of big-league players' strikes. There was even the chance the games would end forever. That sad, aborted season took place the year the doctors told me that I had cancer.

Since we had detected a lump early, doctors told me the operation *should* be successful. Still, my wife and I (who, at the time, kept my situation a secret from our young children) knew that things don't always work out the way you want them to; we were quite worried—no, make that terrified.

I still remember playing what could have been my last game of Wiffle ball ever with my boys. Of course, I was thinking that I didn't want to die, but I had more pressing things on my mind. I dwelled on how much I would miss our games, miss seeing my sons grow up, miss being a family with a wonderful wife and two special boys. Needless to say, it was not a happy game I played that day.

Much later, my final routine checkup revealed that my bout with the disease was being declared a split-decision victory. The radiation treatments I had languished through had done their job, so, five years later, I was finally declared the "winner." However, the CAT scan discovered an unrelated anomaly. A biopsy was ordered. Shortly after, the news came. I had cancer again. This time in my left kidney, a much more serious condition than my first case. This time the boys were old enough to be told. And, this time, all four of us went through the nightmare together.

Watching baseball on TV helped me during my five-day stay on the D.L. in the hospital. After that I was put on waivers and sent home. When I had fully recovered, our games and our love of baseball raged back, stronger than ever.

Even our vacations are usually built around baseball; we try to "collect" new ballparks every year. My sons have encouraged me to shoot for a trip to a park during its inaugural year. For some reason, they have decided that it is essential to see a new park in its opening season. We've managed to do this in Cleveland, which was easy, as we live just about forty minutes away from Jacobs

Field, but we also managed to do so in Tampa Bay, Atlanta, Milwaukee, Pitts-burgh, Baltimore, Detroit, and Houston. Bless my wife for her tolerance!

Recently, Scott began his own tradition of getting a souvenir hat at each park we visit. We also often share a tradition of taking a tour around the outside and the inside of the parks we travel to. We loved walking around Fen-way, especially when our long trek took us behind the Green Monster. In addi-tion, I'll often hand a camera to Scott to take pregame pictures of the facility. He takes sweeping panoramic pictures with the stands nearly empty, and I enjoy glancing through our drawer, which is full of such shots.

One year, not long after returning from a trip to see the Cubs play, Scott and I decided to design our own Wrigley Field model. We constructed it using sand for the dirt infield, warning track, and mound. Green felt became the grass, and string was meticulously laid for our foul lines. We had it down pat, complete to such details as the clock on the scoreboard and the numerals on scoreboard slots for each inning. We even had fungo circles cut out of the felt, and we constructed a "brick" (tiny rectangles colored red with markers) outfield wall, tediously drawn on cardboard—staggering the bricks for the real Wrigley look.

Even my sons' middle names have a baseball flavor. Sean's is Wesley, be-cause I always liked the name Wes, as in slick first baseman Wes Parker. Scott's middle name is Ryan. Again, I liked the sound of the name, and the fact that I was a fan of Nolan Ryan was admittedly a factor as well. Before Sean was born and we were kicking around ideas for his first name, I even suggested Aaron in honor of my all-time favorite player. Nancy promptly vetoed *that* idea.

I found it interesting that Ryne Sandberg's father named his two sons after ballplayers, too. Ryne, who became a huge star for the Chicago Cubs, was named after pitcher Ryne Duren, while his older brother, Del, got his name from Del Ennis, a Phillies outfielder. Ryne even had an autographed ball from Duren that read "To Ryne Sandberg from the first Ryne, Ryne Duren."

Over the years, I have coached my sons from time to time. Two of our greatest thrills came when we went to the finals, only to lose, when Sean was my shortstop; the other was the year Scott pitched and played infield as we won it all. On a cognitive level, winning a trophy for a summer league in a small city in Ohio is virtually meaningless. On an emotional level, it *does* mean a lot to me.

When Sean and I got a trophy for being the runners-up, it marked the first time one of our father-son ventures resulted in our taking home some hardware—that made the trophy dear to us. As for the only other trophy that I still display—it, too, was the result of a labor of parental love. Scott and I constantly scoured the scorebook that year, going over our opponents and their tendencies. We worked diligently that year, so I recognized that trophy as being a worthy symbol for our venture, of the time we'd spent together.

Being a nut for statistics, I've kept track of my kids' numbers—all their batting stats since the age of 8 or so and on through high school. I kept all sorts of statistics, such as on-base percentage, which helped measure my sons' ability beyond batting average, especially since for most of their career they hit in the top third of the batting order. Keeping the stats after each game was yet another way that my boys and I would bond. Although, again, unlike some "modern" parents, my goal was simply to have fun with them, not to go through some psychological mumbo jumbo of being in touch with their needs.

Often, after a game, we'd pull into the driveway, head straight to the desk where their stat sheets were, and update all the numbers from runs scored, to caught stealing, to walks drawn, and, yes, even strikeouts (which were rare in my family, I can proudly testify).

Two Little League stories. Sean can still trace the moment he came of age as a shortstop. At the time of our first tale, he wasn't the full-time shortstop on his Aker's Construction team, but he was pressed into action there. A runner was on third, with one out, when a ball was hit to my son deep in the hole. He snared the ball, then alertly looked the runner back. Since he took some time, Sean's coach began yelling, "Don't throw. Hold the ball." Sean promptly, and confidently, ignored him and gunned the runner out at first on a dazzling play. The runner was stunned, frozen at third base. The crowd was shocked at first, then broke into enthusiastic applause. The coach was impressed, and knew a shortstop had been born. By and large, for many of the rest of his playing days, Sean was at short. Even now, in softball, he will play that position from time to time.

It was, I think, the same year Sean made "the play" that his team went on to win the championship. Nancy came up with the idea to douse the team in "champagne," in big-league fashion, after they clinched. We bought half a case of 7-Up, since it resembled the bubbly we had so often seen in World Series winning locker rooms. In the final inning of the game, we passed out the bottles to other parents. After the last out, we all charged the field and soaked our sons in a baptism of celebration.

To be honest, I initially told Nancy that I thought such a display would be "bush," but Sean recently brought the story up as a footnote of his playing days, saying it was a moment that he enjoyed and remembered well.

When my son Scott graduated from high school, I came up with an idea to give him a special gift from the heart. Knowing that I have no skills aside from writing, I realized that a personalized, handmade gift was out of the question. Our old friend Homer Simpson could, for instance, craft a better homemade bat (or spice rack, for that matter) than I could.

Then it hit me with *Field of Dreams* clarity: use my writing skills. If I write it, he will like it. I decided to write a minibook about Scott's spectacular senior season on the diamond.

Gathering the material was no problem, as I had been compiling his stats and newspaper clippings all year long. I put together a fifty-page book as if Scott were the object of a biography. The text ran around ten pages, but I also included a scrapbook's worth of clippings, packed full of his statistics and accounts of his high-school contests, featuring many of Scott's exploits. Our local newspaper also ran a weekly column of high-school baseball players' stats, and Scott was always among the leaders for offensive categories such as hits, average, runs, and runs driven in.

I also included a section about how Scott pulled a Ted Williams act in his senior year's finale. In his last official at bat as a high-school player, his batting average for the season stood at .39726. He needed one hit to reach .400 and it was late in the game, the fifth inning of a seven-inning contest. He had entered the game at .408 and knew that if he took an oh-for-three he'd fall below .400.

I wrote: "Stewart connected for a screaming double to left center, to lift his average to a Ted Williams–like .405, just a microscopic decimal point short of what Willimas hit in 1941." Of course, I was alluding to the season in which Williams refused to sit on his .400 average, insisted on playing both ends of a season-ending doubleheader, and banged out several hits to hoist his mark to .406.

I also threw in some pages I had xeroxed from the Cleveland *Plain Dealer.* He appeared in their pages on several occasions. For example, they picked local high-school players for a regular feature they called the Player of the Week, and Scott won that honor. His *Plain Dealer* piece read: "School—Southview; Sport—Baseball; Class—Senior; Age—18; Ht.—6'2"; Wt.—185; Season—Hitting .474 has 27 hits in 57 at bats with 27 runs batted in and 20 runs scored. Plays third base and pitches; Personal—Fourth-year varsity baseball player who also plays soccer and basketball. Member of math-science program. Likes playing Wiffle ball, stoop ball, going to movies, watching sports on television, and playing video games."

Then came something that made me quite happy. When he was interviewed, Scott made it a point to tell the reporter about my being "a sports author." I was proud that Scott was proud—once more, baseball had brought us closer together.

Scott also had his name in Cleveland's newspaper when he was selected to an All-Star team, made up of the best high-school players in our area. He played the game, the first of this annual event, and got a hit, becoming the first batter to collect a hit in this new "showcase." Best of all, it was played on a big-league diamond, Jacobs Field.

Of course, I knew he was a highly talented player long before his All-Star selection stamped its imprimatur on him. For example, when Scott was, I believe, a sophomore in high school, we went to a local park for him to take some B.P. I toed the rubber and threw him a round of pitches. One of the pitches I fired became *the* very last pitch that I'd ever throw to him other than during one of our Wiffle ball games.

He smacked a wicked comeback that nearly took my head off. "That's it," I said. "Unless we get an L-screen, we'll stick to you taking grounders." Like Ed Spiezio with his son Scott, I knew with instant clarity that I needed protection against my son's lethal hits. Needless to say, Scott cackled mischievously at my discomfort, grabbed his glove, and headed for third base to take some grounders off *my* bat.

One of the great things about baseball is being able to watch a game with a friend who is as knowledgeable as you are. I love to sit there and share insights and analyze games. For years, I passed my knowledge on to my sons. Now, my two best friends for baseball watching are Sean and Scott. They will often share their insights and views with me, instead of the other way around.

In fact, since I rely on my afternoon newspaper for baseball more than I do on television, it's not at all unusual for Sean, who now teaches in the same building as I do, to say, "Dad, did you hear about the trade last night?" I usually reply that I hadn't, and Sean fills me in, serving as my personal news flash. I love teaching with Sean for many reasons, but talking baseball from spring training to summer vacation and then again down the season's stretch run is one of the biggest pluses.

As for Scott, in his freshman year at college, when he was on his school's team, he began to point out technical insights when we'd catch a game on television. "You see how Lopez is setting up on the outside part of the plate for this guy," he might ask rhetorically. In return, I'd nod, proud of his knowledge of the game.

Having a father who covers games as a member of the media has its pluses and its minuses. Just as my dad got Musial's autograph for me, back before the days when writers were told not to request autographs, I was able to obtain the signatures of men like Mike Schmidt for my sons.

Then there was the time I arranged for Dale Murphy to speak to Sean. It began with a trip to Pittsburgh to cover a game between the Pirates and my family's favorite team, the Atlanta Braves. Sean and Nancy got to the park unusually early, and were sitting in the lowest level of seats behind home plate at Three Rivers Stadium.

Here's what I wrote about that day in my column for *Baseball Bulletin*: "Personal Note—Dale Murphy is, as they say, 'a class act.' My son, Sean, is a Murphy fan. I took him to a Braves game; after doing an interview with Murphy (who has a wife named Nancy and a son named Sean), I rather reluctantly, but dutifully as a father, asked him to wave to my son in the stands. He went toward the stands, spoke to my son, and then asked us if we'd like an autograph. Wish more guys were like this superstar."

What I omitted from that blurb was that when Murphy hollered up into the stands, "Hi, Sean," my son rather unglamorously replied, "Huhh?" After Murphy repeated himself a little louder, Sean regrouped, said hello, and got an autograph from his idol.

When I took my sons with me on a trip to Camden Yards, I sat in the press box while the boys sat in the area reserved for families of players and media, just a few rows below me. A writer seated just in front of me retrieved a foul ball that had richocheted around the press box and looked out the window to see whom he could toss the ball to.

Now, at the time I didn't know exactly where my sons were sitting, but as the writer stood, up popped Scott's head like a jack-in-the-box, surprising me. And I was as surprised and happy, though not nearly as happy as Scott was, when the reporter handed the souvenir to him.

On the other hand, there is at least one negative to being the sons of a sportswriter. Because I have to get to the park hours before game time in order to conduct my interviews, my sons soon grew weary of that routine. When we travel to a city other than our home base of Cleveland, they stay behind in the hotel with Nancy and join me later. I generally record my interviews on tape, pop into the press box to collect packets of statistics and news releases, catch an inning or two there, then meet my family for the rest of the game.

However, there were many other times when my family would ride into the park with me. During those instances, they had to kill a whole bunch of time before the gates opened. It got to the point where they dreaded those visits to the park.

When Sean entered eighth grade, it appeared that I would be his teacher. Under normal scheduling procedures he would, as an advanced English student, be placed in my class. The principal asked me if I felt this would cause any difficulty. I said I was sure there would be no problem. After all, I reasoned, I had coached him many times in summer baseball. As it turned out, the school year with Sean remains one of my favorites. To this day, when I am asked who was my favorite student of all time, the answer is obvious, as I never had the chance to teach Scott—in my school classroom, that is.

I was reminded of my having taught Sean when, in 2001, Aaron Boone and his father, Ray, were together as a player and the manager of the Reds. Would Aaron be accused of being a sort of teacher's pet? If he was in a slump, would he get pinch-hit for or benched—and, if so, would he pout?

I felt they would have no problems at all. From the very start of Aaron's first season with his father, he said that he was happy for his dad when he learned that he had accepted the job, because he knew his dad loved to manage. He also said he didn't think that playing under his father was "going to be an issue." He was correct.

In late 2000, I was skimming through the "transactions" section of the *Plain Dealer* when I spotted an item under the heading of the Montreal Expos. If I recall exactly, it read: "Expos sign RHP Scott Stewart." I immediately cut it out and called my son, who had recently returned to college for the start of his sophomore year.

Since Scott was a right-handed pitcher when he took to the hill on occasion, I told him I would mail him the clipping. If he wanted to, he could show off the item, take a deep inhale in the style of Barney Fife, and boast, "Yeah, they saw me in Florida and want me to help them out with my knuckleball." Scott never actually did that, but he did show it to his roommate. Now, for no logical reason—but who needs logic—I've become a fan of the Scott Stewart who really did sign with Montreal. Just for the record, the newspaper was incorrect, as I later found out the Expos' pitcher is a southpaw.

In his freshman year in college, Scott toed the rubber for his last stint ever. He had been a member of the team as a third baseman, but he had, from time to time, still toyed with his knuckleball. In fact, early in the season during a trip his team took to Florida to get in a few early games, Scott made his collegiate mound debut and finale in the same contest. What a thrill it was for him to find himself working off the mound that the Detroit Tigers used in their spring-training site at Lakeland. Someone snapped a picture of him warming up on that mound. It remains one of my favorite photos. Now, though, with Scott's mound career behind him, if I see a box score indicating that Scott Stewart had pitched, I know which one they mean.

It's interesting to look back at my son's development. For instance, I can still picture Scott's tiny fingers as he tried to wrap them around a Nerf ball. His grasp was weak, naturally, and, likewise, his first throws were erratic. He'd hold on to the ball too long and bounce it in front of me, often skipping by me—in baseball parlance, a wild pitch. Or, his lobs might arch like a rainbow—known in baseball as an eephus pitch. At times, the ball might even be released in such a way as to flop behind him—and *that* is simply not known in baseball lingo at all.

By way of contrast, in the spring of 2001 when Scott returned from college, I wanted to catch his knuckleball, to see firsthand how it moved. I felt the way Brian Moehler's father must have felt—a bit apprehensive—to say the very least. I recalled the adage about the survival of the fittest, and I knew that I might not be fit to catch his elusive pitch. I joked that I'd need shin guards or a partition to protect me.

Then, as we began warming up, I came to realize that it was my hand and not merely my shins that needed protection. Even his long, smooth, easy throws would occasionally sting my hand when the ball wasn't caught in the web of my glove. How different from even his finest childhood "fastballs."

Then there's Sean's arm, which I get to see when he's on the softball diamond now, ranging at either shortstop or in the outfield. Two metaphors come to mind when I think of his arm and mine—rifle arm and candy arm. Sean's is clearly the rifle; mine is pure peanut brittle.

I also delight in watching him roam the outfield, which he does gracefully and swiftly. To paraphrase an old baseball line, Sean's glove is where doubles go to die, as he frequently dashes into the gaps to rob frustrated players of hits.

He'll also utilize his speed to stretch a single into a double or otherwise take an extra base hit. Such displays make me remember the time he was in high school and stole third base in a Junior Varsity game—standing up. A combination of his speed and intelligence paid off when he caught the pitcher momentarily napping on the mound. That snooze allowed Sean to streak to third. His daring made me smile proudly.

Now that my sons are adults, Nancy and I have become their biggest softball fans. Normally, I don't have the inclination to watch adults play softball, but I truly enjoy watching my sons out there on the same team. I've seen them turn a double play and seen one of them drive in the other. Brotherly high fives abound, and, when they trot out to their defensive positions at the start of an inning, my wife and I gaze at their broad shoulders and smile at their camaraderie.

So what if my boys will never play major-league baseball? As so many major-league players who have sons invariably said, "I'm proud of my sons no matter what they do."

Clearly, there has never been much of a generational communication gap with my sons, as baseball has definitely kept us close. If love means never having to say you're sorry, then baseball means there's always something to say. "Murphy hit another one," I'd announce as I pored over the box scores. Or, as I prepared some microwave popcorn, one of my sons would shout from the living room, "Hey, Dad, hurry up! Nolan Ryan's beating up Robin Ventura."

Just working on this chapter, exploring the past and my relationship with my sons, has made me realize once again the depth of our baseball bond. I always *knew* baseball was a huge part of our lives, but hearing my sons relive some moments from days gone by (some I had nearly forgotten but was delighted to rediscover, and a scant few I couldn't recall at all until they revived the memory) made it all sink in. To me, baseball and my two boys are an unbeatable and precious combination.

About the Author

Wayne Stewart was born and raised in Donora, Pennsylvania, a town that has produced several big-league baseball players, including Stan Musial and the father-son Griffeys.

Mr. Stewart now lives in Lorain, Ohio, and is married to Nancy (Panich) Stewart. They have two sons, Sean and Scott.

Mr. Stewart has covered the baseball world as a writer for nearly twenty-five years now, beginning in 1978. He has interviewed many Hall of Famers, including Nolan Ryan, Bob Gibson, Robin Yount, Gaylord Perry, Warren Spahn, and Willie Stargell.

He has written three baseball books, *Baseball Oddities, Baseball Bafflers,* and *Baseball Puzzlers* for Sterling Publications; *Indians on the Game* for Gray and Company, Publishers; ten juvenile baseball books featuring the history of ten big-league franchises; and some of his works have also appeared in several baseball anthologies.

In addition, he has written nearly 700 articles for national publications such as *Baseball Digest, USA Today/Baseball Weekly, Boys' Life,* and *Beckett Publications*. He has also written for many major-league official team publications, such as the Braves, Yankees, White Sox, Orioles, Padres, Twins, Phillies, Red Sox, A's, and Dodgers.

He has appeared as a baseball expert/historian on Cleveland's Fox 8 and on an ESPN Classic television show on Bob Feller. He also hosted his own radio shows on a small station in Lorain—a call-in sports talk show; a pregame Indians report; pregame Notre Dame shows; and broadcasts of local baseball contests.

He has taught English in the Lorain city schools for more than twenty-five years and is currently teaching at Whittier Middle School.

Index